SCENES FROM THE PAST

MANCHESTER TO

- PART ONE -

LONDON ROAD
(PICCADILLY)
AND LONGSIGHT
TO WILMSLOW
VIA THE STYAL LINE

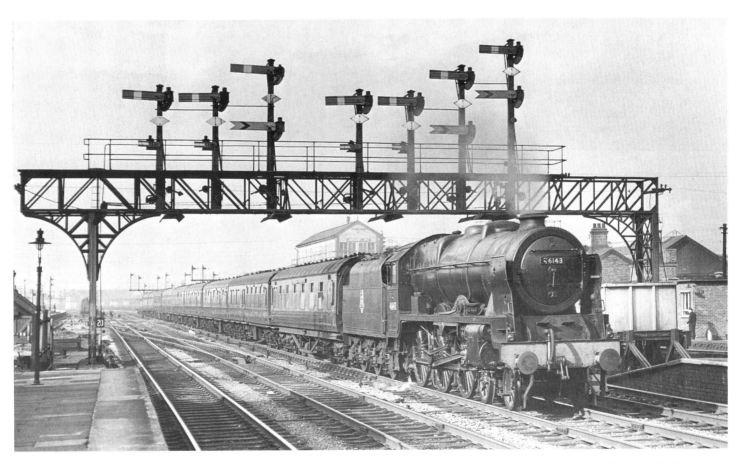

Longsight station, October 20th 1958: A picture that will, for many, typify the Manchester to Crewe railway of their youth. The "Rebuilt Scots" were staple motive power on the London trains for many years, while Longsight, the shed that had served London Road since the very inception of the railway, was the Valhalla of the South Manchester loco sheds. With 'eleven-on' and only a haze at the chimney. "Royal Scot" No **46143** The *South Staffordshire Regiment* is caught at exactly the right moment -"rods down" and just clearing the signal gantry to provide this exhibition photograph of the 2.08 pm express to Euston. The photographer is the late and lamented Tom Lewis. A member of the fabled RCTS portfolio circle, Lewis used only plates, normally Ilford FP3, for his work. Lewis and other superb cameramen of the 1950s, for example A.H.Bryant, Roy Davenport, Brian Green, and William Lees, have endowed us with a rich legacy depicting the wonderful scenes once seen up and down this splendid railway.
Tom Lewis

E M JOHNSON

COPYRIGHT © E M JOHNSON
ISBN 1 870119 87 X
9 781870 119870

ALL RIGHTS RESERVED
PRINTED BY AMADEUS PRESS
CLECKHEATON, WEST YORKSHIRE.
PUBLISHED BY
FOXLINE (PUBLICATIONS) LTD
P O BOX 84 BREDBURY SK6 3YD

DEDICATION I would like to dedicate this book to my lifelong friend, Martin Austwick. With Martin I have shared the pleasure of so many trips to linesides and railway establishments, on foot, by train and by old-fashioned bike. And it was Martin who accompanied me on that historic day - September 12th 1960 - the birthday of the electric railway from Manchester to Crewe.

CONTENTS

Manchester London Road, April 30th 1958: "The Comet" was one of three named trains plying the London Road-Euston route in 1958. Leaving Euston at 9.35 am (weekdays) and arriving in Manchester at 1.20, the 3¾ hour timing of the Down train was the fastest of the day, beating even the prestigious "Mancunian" by 5 minutes in the same direction. Watching "Royal Scot" No **46136** *The Border Regiment* at the head of the train gives the wrong impression; the train is *not* arriving! At this time it was common practice for engines of arriving expresses to assist empty carriage movements by pushing their stock back to Longsight carriage sidings- notice the lifting arm of the Walschaerts gear is in the upward position. It is interesting to compare the practice of almost 50 years ago with that of today. With much tighter stock diagrams, most trains are turned round at the platforms and no longer have lengthy waits in carriage sidings. Between 9 and 17 minutes after arrival was allowed at London Road in the early 1950s before ECS movements back to Longsight. "Patriot" No **45530** *Sir Frank Ree* awaits impending departure at nearby platform 4.

B.K.B.Green

The Comet
Refreshment Car Express
LONDON (Euston) and MANCHESTER (London Road)
WEEKDAYS

		Mons. to Fris.	Sats.				Mons. to Fris. only
		am	am				pm
London (Euston)	.. dep	9 45	9 45	Manchester (London Road)		..dep	5 50
Stoke-on-Trent	.. arr	pm 12 11	pm 12 20	Stockport (Edgeley)	..	..	6 3
Macclesfield (Hibel Road)	.. ,,	12 43	12 52	Crewe	..	..	6 38
Stockport (Edgeley)	.. ,,	1 2	1 12	Watford Junction	..	.. arr	8§55
Manchester (London Road)	.. ,,	1 15	1 25	London (Euston)	..	..	9 20

§—Stops only to set down passengers and on Fridays arrives 8.57 pm

Manchester London Road, March 3rd 1953: Some photographers fought shy of winter picture-taking because of reputedly poor light. Brian Green's superb study of Longsight's "Britannia" Pacific No.**70031** *Byron* gives a lie to this proposition; the engine positively basks in the strong afternoon side-lighting, a winter chill making for high visibility steam effects. The train is the 2.20 pm (SO) departure for Euston via Macclesfield and Stoke-on-Trent; Fairly pedestrian by today's standards, arrival in the Capital was scheduled for at 6.12 pm.after a call at Rugby Midland at approximately twenty minutes to five. Through carriages from Colne were attached at Stockport. Longsight provided 'home' for Britannias *Byron*, *Tennyson* (70032) and *Charles Dickens* (70033) until 1960 when electrification caused their transfer to pastures new, initially to Trafford Park to cover the concentration of services on the Midland line to St Pancras. Other Britannias, namely 70043/44, later Earl's *Kitchener* and *Haig* respectively, served Longsight for a good number of years.

B.K.B.Green

- FOREWORD -

Much has been written, not least by this author, about Manchester's railways and the routes that radiate to and from that great city. What, then, is new? Well, much. After completing my Woodhead trilogy I realised how little, in overall terms, I had said about another electric railway-the Manchester to Crewe line. And having undertaken so much study on Woodhead, its antecedents, infrastructure and traffic, it was nice to get back nearer to home and take a more detailed look at the railway on my doorstep.

From the outset I realised that I was faced with a mammoth task. Research and collection of material for a possible manuscript had been going on for many years, now my biggest problem was not so much as what to include, but deciding what to leave out. I have tried to strike a balance between the old and the new; but the "new" is innately historic as well-can we believe that the first 25kV ac electric locomotives appeared almost half a century ago? So, beginning at Piccadilly, or London Road if you prefer, this book takes the reader as far as Wilmslow via the Styal line. Two themes weave their way through the history of this railway. These are electrification and powered flight. Amazingly, when the

railway was being planned and the alignment surveyed, neither form of power had made much impression. Indeed, in 1899 the Wright Brothers-Orville and Wilbur-had yet to take off from Kitty Hawk. Yet, in half a century, electric traction was on the way to becoming the dominant force for railway motive power. And down the line, close to Heald Green, Manchester's airport was on the eve of a phase of rapid expansion and would eventually be served by the railway.

As with my Woodhead series, this volume does not just concentrate on the locomotive, or indeed, solely on the trains. For the railway, any railway, is more much more than that. People and infrastructure, that word again, all make up the railway and without these there could be no trains, no travel and no excitement. Manchester Piccadilly to Wilmslow maybe only a mere 11½ miles, but there is much to explore en route. A subsequent volume will continue from Slade Lane Junction via Stockport to complete the journey to Crewe. In the meantime, sit back and enjoy your journey!

Eddie Johnson, Burnage, Manchester. July, 2006.

Manchester London Road, September 26th 1953: The end of the island that formed platforms 3&4 was always a popular spot for us 1950s "spotters." From here a good view could be had of most of the goings-on in the station. Sheer delight must have been prevalent with the little gaggle seen here as they witness "Princess Royal" No **46203** *Princess Margaret Rose* (a Crewe North engine) waiting to depart with the afternoon (3.05 pm) West of England 'express' on September 26th 1953. The journey, via Crewe, Shrewsbury, Hereford, Pontypool Road, Bristol (Temple Meads) and Exeter, demanded perseverance by the traveller who undertook the full trip to Plymouth and an expected time of arrival at 12.45am. *Princess Margaret Rose* however continues to grace the British railway system over five decades later in preservation as a result of the efforts of the "Princess Royal Class Locomotive Trust", based at the West Shed of the Midland Railway Centre, Ripley, Derbyshire
W A Brown

Manchester London Road, October 25th 1952: Departing at 10.20 am, "The Pines Express" was the only named train leaving any Manchester station that did not traverse one or other of the routes to the Capital. Through running to Bournemouth from Manchester had origins going back to LNWR days in 1910, though it was left to the LMS-in 1927-to inaugurate "The Pines" title. Here, Longsight's Caprotti "Black 5" No **44687** waits to leave with a Saturday departure. A fairly leisurely affair, "The Pines Express" took just over seven hours to reach Bournemouth in the 1950s. This, of course, was of little concern to the enthusiast as the journey involved travel over the beautiful and much-lamented S&D line through the Mendips from Bath (Green Park); a steeply-graded route involving single-line working. Today, travel from Manchester Piccadilly to Bournemouth can be accomplished in just under five hours-though not, alas, via the S&D route; this having closed as far back as 1966.
R.E.Gee

4

Wilmslow, c.mid-1950s: Bridge No 75A leads from Land Lane to the cricket ground at the back of Wilmslow High School and was a popular spot for photography of southbound trains leaving Wilmslow in steam days. Known as the "iron bridge" to locals, many are the pictures taken at from this point, but the writer was especially pleased to come across this one. On a bright summer day "Britannia" Pacific No **70044** comes off the Styal line and clears Wilmslow station with the Up "Mancunian". At the regulator is Longsight driver Harold Gorton, who the writer was fortunate to know well. Harold provided valuable information about the shed and its workings and the picture is included as a tribute to his memory. 70044 carries the unsightly Westinghouse (air) pumps she entered traffic with in June 1953. Becoming *Earl Haig* in March 1957 (at about the time the air brake was removed), the loco had spent two periods at Longsight, the second ending in December 1958. This fine engine ended her days at Stockport's Edgeley shed (9B) and was withdrawn from there in October 1966. She was cut up at Thomas Ward's scrapyard at Beighton, near Sheffield, in February 1967. *Authors collection*

INTRODUCTION
THE RAILWAY FROM MANCHESTER TO CREWE

Crewe! Could there have been any greater railway attraction for a teenage "spotter" domiciled in Manchester in the mid-1950s? A half fare of around 3/9d was all it took to transport a Mancunian teenage lad to his Nirvana. But 3/9d - that's a mere 19p in decimal money and, surely, you wouldn't bend down to pick that much up off the pavement today, would you?

Alas, it was a different world just under fifty years ago. Why, when my sister and I used to collect bread for our parents, we'd part with some pennies and a farthing! So my 3/9d fare to Crewe was not that easily come by. With the cash carefully stashed away the date was selected - usually a mid-week point in the school holidays - sandwiches would be made - date and banana and potted meat were the favourites, a bottle of 'pop' or lemonade added to boot and then we were ready for the 'off." Crewe beckoned us.

Disembarking from our steam-hauled train with its Stanier suburban coaches and, looking quaint now, those long bench seats from window to window, all haste was made to the north end of the station and to Platform 4. Here we could gaze across the myriad of points and crossings that was Crewe North Junction: left to

Chester and North Wales, ahead to Liverpool and Glasgow and right to where we came in - to Manchester. And from this point it was as if time had been accelerated to just 30 minutes in one hour instead of 60. How could time fly by! Or, put simply: *"doesn't time pass quickly when you're enjoying yourself."*

All the favourite expresses readily spring to mind: London-Blackpool, London - Barrow, *The Irish Mail*, *The Caledonian* (from 1957) and, then the climax of the day: the arrival of the Up *Royal Scot*. This train was somehow special; a "Duchess" guaranteed on the front, the special tartan coach destination boards and that wonderful rear nameboard strapped to the back of the last coach gangway. Added to all this was the fact that the train didn't stop at Crewe. Seeing that feather of steam in the distance and then the shape of the legendary engine gradually homing into view until the number was visible. And as the apparition rolled across the pointwork a great cheer would go up. I always thought the crews sensed they were something of celebrities as they passed Platform 4 and invariably we'd be greeted with a cheery wave from the driver and fireman who frequently seemed to have crossed to his mate's side to view the proceedings.

Came the time for departure and the hallowed notebook, sullied by a day's smutty fingers, was pocketed away; we sank back into those long cushions and headed for home. On arrival it was a question of: "up those stairs and bath!" Yes, the steam-powered junction was a dirty, perhaps filthy place, a term doubtless used by my dear mother, but hadn't we had a good day?! Suitably cleansed with the legendary bar of *Fairy* green soap, it was down the stairs, then tea and lastly to the all-important paperwork-the underlinings in the hallowed Ian Allan ABC.

...As teenage years passed, horizons broadened and modes of transport changed. Now the black roadster bike had given way by turns to my uncle's old Raleigh machine-stolen, to my complete and utter chagrin and then to the ultimate-a "Sun" sports machine with eight gears. Now places like Newton-le-Willows and Winsford could be visited and, never to be forgotten, the little hamlet of Chorlton, south of Crewe where an uninterrupted view of the main line could be had. More importantly was the fact that cycling was free transport-important when the week's income amounted to rather less than 10 shillings (50p). The Raleigh and its "Sun" successor were taken every summer from 1959 onwards on the train to Northampton. Here we stayed with my friend Richard's aunt, Miss Doris Wykes. "Aunty Doris" lived close to the Kettering road and from our base there we cycled out daily,

exploring as much of the county's railways as we could fit in-and there was a lot to see fifty years or so ago. Our favourite spot was Blisworth alongside our beloved LM main line. And, by dint of using the train from Bedford, we journeyed further afield to Sandy to sample the delights of the former GN line.

All the while the west coast main line was in a state of flux. We saw bridges prepared for demolition, travelled down by odd routes, saw lineside masts erected, noted wiring trains and, horror of horrors, had our first ride behind a main line Diesel locomotive. Back home in the summer of 1960 the metamorphosis was complete and all was ready for the big "switch-on" in September.

In the early hours of Monday, September 12th 1960, two teenage boys forsook their beds, snatched an early breakfast and walked through the silent streets of Withington to catch the all night No. 43 bus into "Town". Disembarking in Piccadilly young Martin Austwick and Eddie Johnson arrived at the renamed station in good time to catch the 6.05 am stopping train to Crewe. Determined to be the first fare-paying passengers to travel on our newly-electrified local line, imagine our delight when we were greeted by a reporter from the "Manchester Evening News". And sure enough the evening's paper reported our adventure under the byline "First Passengers". History had been made and weren't we proud!

Crewe Station, c.mid / late1950s: Here they are and this is what they came for! One of the customary gangs of teenage train spotters seen gathered at the north end of Crewe station. It was within this period that officialdom banned spotters from the hallowed precincts - but seemingly to no avail. The writer, who spent many happy days at Crewe within this period, was never asked to leave the station. Conduct, on the whole, was good and vandalism almost unknown. Coming off the Up Manchester line is "Royal Scot" No.**46101** *Royal Scots Grey*. At this time the engine was allocated to Crewe North and is seen at the head of a special working - Reporting Number W456. The driver, leaning out of his cab, looks concerned, as well he might be - for, clearly, some of this little gathering have gone too far. The cable wooden trunking, acting as an impromptu fence, has been breached and a couple of lads are standing within feet of the track! Numbering well over forty, the group all appear to be under-16s, though one adult personage appears near the end of the crowd. Do any modern - day readers recognise themselves? And if so, where, please, is your notebook to tell us what date this was and what else you saw. This, then, is our prelude to Crewe - an hors d'oeuvre for the next part of the story. ***Author's collection***

Footnote: *46101 spent no less than eight separate periods at Crewe North between 1952 and 1955. Within the decade, the locomotive had no less than fifteen changes of engine shed. This was equalled only by one other "Scot"- No. 46165 and beaten only by No. 46166 which changed sheds on no less than nineteen occasions from February 1950 to June 1958.*

The brick structure that would change the face of Stockport for all time, the Manchester & Birmingham Railway's viaduct completing a stage of that company's route as far as Sandbach, Crewe following shortly after. The engraving was produced for Bradshaws Journal c.1890 and the view is from the slopes above the Brinksway area of the town to the west adjacent to Hollywood Park. The large mill nearest the viaduct, Wier Mill, survives to this day although part of it was displaced by the 1890 widening. ***Authors collection***

⌐ A MANCHESTER & BIRMINGHAM PRELUDE ⌐

On Thursday, June 4th 1840, a small group of onlookers were witness to an extraordinary happening. To the east of the centre of Manchester a small railway terminus, founded by two embryo companies, had been established. Travis Street, the thoroughfare connecting London Road and Birmingham Street with Sheffield Street was the home of this joint undertaking. Almost certainly with a degree of trepidation and hesitancy, a little convoy of crude passenger carriages drawn by a six-wheeled, single driver locomotive built by Sharp, Roberts & Company-a Manchester concern-sallied forth over brick-built viaducts on a journey south to the township of Heaton Norris. The Manchester & Birmingham Railway Company was in business.

The company was among the early players in Britain's railway game. The joint terminus was shared with the Sheffield, Ashton-Under-Lyne & Manchester Railway, a concern engaged in a mission somewhat more adventurous than the Manchester & Birmingham fraternity-they had to both cross the Pennines and tunnel through them. But our story eschews their adventure, for the systems split and parted company just down the line at Ardwick.

Latter-day railway historians often overlook the effect felt by early Victorian society imparted by the railways; in particular, the impact made by the system's infrastructure on the townscapes. Here, through the suburbs of one of the biggest, and, it has to be said, at one-time, dirtiest cities in England spread the interloper: spanning genteel Ardwick on a brick viaduct as far as the Hyde Road, entering suburban Longsight and Rushford Park before encountering the boundary with Stockport-then a small cotton spinning and weaving town in Cheshire.

There follows a short extract from a report in the *Stockport Advertiser* on the opening of the Manchester & Birmingham

Railway on that historic summer day-June 4th 1840: *"The Hyde Road was crossed in 5 minutes after starting and immediately afterwards the train passed the timber preparing plant at which point a number of flags waved from a temporary stage. On this we understand, Mr. Thomas Sharp (of the firm Sharp Roberts & Co) as well as several parties of ladies assembled to witness the first transit of a passenger train on the line. The train then passed along the embankment, across the Earl of Ducie's land into Kirkmanshulme and over Gorton Brook at a height of about 30 feet, then a portion of the property of the Warden and Fellows of the Collegiate Church to the Stockport road at which point is to be the Rushford station, the stopping place betwixt Manchester and Stockport. The railway crosses the Stockport road about 100 yards beyond the Rushford bar by a neat cast-iron skew bridge at an angle of 34 degrees, similar to that over Hyde Road. This point was reached in 5^1/2 minutes from starting."*

Most of the section that follows dealing with the formation of the Manchester & Birmingham Railway and its associated undertakings is extracted from a work covering that railway and its locomotives compiled by Mr W G Robinson in 1933. The author acknowledges Mr Robinson's scholarship and does not claim these extracts as his own.

In the early years of the 19th century, at a period when other pioneer undertakings of the British railway systems were bringing the possibilities of steam locomotion to the fore, two ambitious syndicates, the Manchester, Cheshire and Staffordshire and the Manchester and South Union Companies, were seeking Parliamentary powers for their scheme for linking up the city of Manchester with the great industrial centres of the Midlands. The failure of their efforts to materialise resulted in their unification: the result was the Manchester & Birmingham Railway Company.

On presentation of the M&B's Bill, Parliament appointed Major-General Pasley, a military engineer, to examine their scheme. Pasley was obviously happy as the Bill appears to have gone through unhindered, receiving the Royal Assent on June 30th 1837. The Act empowered the M&B to construct a line of railway 45½ miles long from Manchester via Stockport, Alderley, Congleton, Newcastle-under-Lyme and Stone near to the village of Chebsey beyond which place a connection was to be made with the Grand Junction's line south of the present-day Norton Bridge station. Also planned was a 15 mile branch line from Alderley from a point just south of Alderley station to Crewe to connect with the Chester to Crewe line-then under construction, as well as with the line of the Grand Junction Railway.

A further proposal was taken on board when, in 1839, a Bill was presented to Parliament under the title of the Manchester & Birmingham Extension Railway. This sought powers to extend the main line from Crewe, via Macclesfield, Stoke-on-Trent, Lichfield and Tamworth to Rugby; making a connection there with the London & Birmingham Railway. Thus would be provided a direct connection from Manchester to London. However, owing to opposition from the London & Birmingham company, the scheme was defeated. Such a setback, though, did not deter the M&B from making a further determined effort to secure a foothold in the Midlands and, in 1840, a further Bill was laid before Parliament-this time under the title of the Stafford and Rugby Railway. Alas for the M&B, this scheme too was doomed to failure; for though unopposed by the GJR, the London & Birmingham - with the assistance of the Birmingham & Derby company became instrumental in preventing the M&B in obtaining its Act.

In the meantime the original Manchester & Birmingham Act was amended. The result was the abandonment of the Alderley to Congleton and the Potteries route-the proposed branch to Crewe then becoming the main line. Thus the ambitious scheme for a line from Manchester to the Midlands and the south by a direct route-avoiding the circuitous journey via Newton (later Earlestown) Junction and Warrington - resulted in the Manchester & Birmingham merely extending itself no further than Crewe.

The revised plans meant a considerable saving for the M&B, for much costly constructional work would have been necessary. In 1839, on the strength of the first Act, work on the great viaduct over the River Dane at Congleton had already been started. Alas, much to the chagrin of the populace, both here and in other North Staffordshire towns through which the proposed railway was to run, work on the structure was abandoned shortly afterwards.

To return to viaducts: the foundation stone of mighty edifice straddling the Mersey at Stockport was laid on March 19th 1839 and on January 4th 1840 the first 5½ miles of railway, from Manchester to Heaton Norris, on the north side of the river, was opened to traffic. There was just one intermediate station, at Rushford - close to where the railway straddled the Manchester to Buxton Turnpike-the present day A6.

As a proposal for a line from Macclesfield to Derby, via the Churnet Valley, was mooted about thus time, the 11-mile branch from Cheadle Junction (later Cheadle Hulme) was put out to tender on February 25th 1841 with the object or preventing the townspeople of Macclesfield supporting the rival scheme. In the event, the work was not proceeded with until four years later.

The viaduct at Stockport now being completed, the line was opened from Manchester to Stockport; the first passenger train crossing the Mersey on June 30th 1841. Fares were 1/- first class, 9d second class and 6d for the third class. The railway was an instant success; so much so that the Parliamentary Gazeteer of England & Wales volume III, 1842 was able to report: *"Previous to the opening, no road in England had more passengers than the Wellington Road in this vicinity, but it is already becoming overgrown with grass. On 25th February 1841, 458,819 passengers had been conveyed along the line since its opening."*

The line was opened from Stockport to Sandbach, 21 miles, on May 16th 1842, and London Road station, Manchester opened the same day. On August 10th the railway reached Crewe; though the opening of the junction with the GJR was delayed until August 18th 1842, pending negotiations with the latter company reaching a settlement. Full details of the dispute and the terms of the ultimate agreement between the two companies was given in the British Almanac of 1843.

The original service from London Road, Manchester, to Crewe was as follows:

	a.m.	a.m.	a.m.	a.m.	p.m.	p.m.
Dep. London Rd.	4.00	6.45	8.45	11.15	4.45	7.30
			p.m.	p.m.		
Dep.Crewe	4.00	9.00	1.45	5.00	7.30	9.30

The 6.45 am and 4.45 pm trains from London Road and the 9.00 am and 7.30 pm trains from Crewe were mixed trains of first, second and third class coaches, but the remainder were first class only. In the Parliamentary session of 1845 a branch from Heaton Norris to Ashton was authorised and in this way the first steps were made towards the absorption of the Huddersfield and Leeds lines at a later date. In 1854, when stations at Levenshulme and Longsight were opened, Rushford station was closed.

Though the rolling stock of the Manchester & Birmingham Railway was constructed for the standard British gauge of 4ft.8½in., the track was laid to a gauge of 4ft.9in., the object being to provide greater freedom for the wheels to negotiate the curves-a curiosity of early railway construction. The passenger and merchandise stock needs little comment, for it was designed upon the same lines as that of other contemporary railways. The coaches were of sound construction and were well-appointed, being of the stage-coach type and painted in the attractive liveries of the period. Second class carriages were windowless; while third class were roofless and without sides. At a slightly later date the Manchester & Birmingham company made history by applying lamps in their first class carriages. The guards, in their attractive uniforms, rode on the roofs of the first and second class carriages from which they operated the brakes-there being no continuous brakes until many years later. They also blew post-horns after the fashion of the old road coaches. The form of signalling employed was that of coloured discs and uniformed pointsmen with flags.

The chief engineer of the company was Mr.G.W.Buck who was responsible for the design of all the engineering works of the line and the first locomotive superintendent was Mr.John Ramsbottom, with offices at Manchester and, later, at Longsight when the company's locomotive department and works was erected there.

As regards the financial side of the undertaking, the authorised capital of the M&B was £2,800,000 which included £700,000 for the construction of branches. At the first general meeting of the company, on February 2nd.1842, the Chairman gave the following details of expenditure to date:

Cost of Incorporation & preliminary expenses	£157,745 - 7s - 5d
Cost of land and compensation	£513,919 - 2s - 5d
For engineering works and materials	£901,698 - 3s - 2d
Other disbursements	£190,458 -16s - 2d
Making a total of	**£1,762,931 - 9s - 3d**

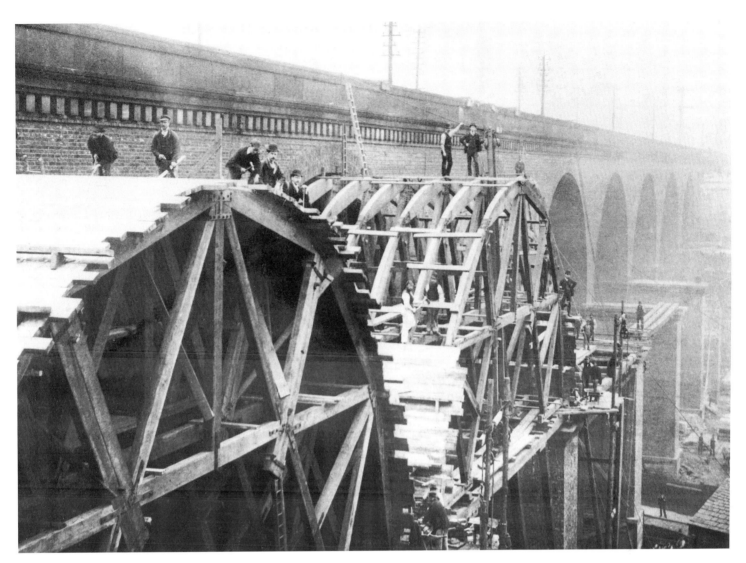

Stockport Viaduct in the course of being widened in 1889 by the London & North Western Railway to allow for increased capacity through Stockport. The massive timber 'centering' on which the coursed 'rings' of brick would be laid are in the stages of erection as work proceeds from the Heaton Norris end. The double line structure forming the background and built by the Manchester & Birmingham Railway will gradually be hidden from view although the eastern - and M&BR elevation - can still be admired and viewed in full from the town centre and users of the M60 Motorway. *Authors collection*

The cost of the principal works were:

Stockport viaduct	£72,700
London Road station	£50,600
Bollin viaduct	£14,360
Dane viaduct	£54,000

Dividends paid by the M&BR during its separate existences were 4% in 1843, 5% in 1844 and 6½% in 1846; whilst the company subscribed £277,780 towards the Trent Valley line and £175,00 towards the Manchester, South Junction and Altrincham line.

The first locomotives constructed for the Manchester & Birmingham Railway comprised six 5ft. 6in. 2-2-2 Singles; four by Sharp, Bros. & Company of Manchester and two by Robert Stephenson & Company of Newcastle-on-Tyne. The engines were to the same general design having cylinders 15in. bore x 20in. stroke with leading and trailing wheels of 3ft. 6in. diameter; the valves were operated by "Gab" motion-an early form of link gear. Details of their original numbers are not known, but Sharps' makers Nos. were 82/83/87&91. Two were delivered to the M&B in January 1840 and the remainder in June and July that year. The first engine of the Sharp four, arbitrarily No.1, suffered a boiler explosion at Longsight shed in 1850; it was rebuilt there with 14in.bore cylinders and was renumbered 401 in August 1857.

Longsight also rebuilt No.3&4 with 14in. cylinders; alas, No.4 blew up in the polygon (roundhouse) shed the first day it was put in steam after rebuilding. The two engines finished their careers a long way from Manchester: at some point between March 1844 and January 1846 they were sold off to the South Eastern Railway.

To return to our chronicle: the friendly relationship that had existed between the Manchester & Birmingham and the London & Birmingham companies, for both had an interest in the Trent Valley line projected in 1845, had its expression in an agreement being reached between the two companies to amalgamate; and, as the Grand Junction system intervened between them a further agreement with the latter company was made for a combination of the three companies. Thus, on August 15th 1846, by Act of Parliament (9&10 Vic.Cap.204), Royal Assent was given for the incorporation of the new Company under the title of the London & North Western Railway Company. The Grand Junction had already absorbed the Liverpool and Manchester Railway, so that from this date the three cities of London, Liverpool and Manchester were joined by direct routes under the command of a single owning company.

The dissolution of the Manchester & Birmingham Railway was not allowed to take place without a farewell celebration by the

This postcard view depicts "The Viaducts, Stockport". The picture is undated but clearly shows London & North Western Railway carriages - many of which retained the company livery until 1926 and others even later - on a train entering Edgeley station. The recipient of the card was informed that *"They (the viaducts) are about one third of a mile in length and consist of 22 semi-circular arches, nearly all of which have 63 feet span. The height from the bed of the river to the battlement is 111 feet. It is computed that the average number of trains passing over the viaducts in 24 hours is over 500."*

Manchester men who had been foremost in the promotion of the undertaking, and in carrying it to a successful issue. By becoming a part of the great London and North-Western Railway it was of course losing its distinctive claim to be regarded as a local undertaking, while the Manchester men who had hitherto controlled its working were to find themselves only a portion of a larger board whose operations extended over a great part of the kingdom. The occasion was made use of by the Manchester shareholders to recognise the value of the past services of their Chairman, Mr.Joshua Proctor Westhead, to whom they presented on the 15th of June, 1847, at a dinner at the Albion Hotel, a dinner service consisting of nearly three thousand ounces of silver, and which had cost £2,000.

From the date of the amalgamation the locomotive control of the new concern was vested in three independent divisions, each under the title of the original company, and each with its own headquarters and locomotive superintendent. The Manchester & Birmingham headquarters were at Longsight, and the locomotive superintendent was Mr. John Ramsbottom who ultimately became Chief Mechanical Engineer to the entire system when its control was centred at Crewe.

It may be mentioned here, though it has no direct connection with our subject, that the Grand Junction Division - though it controlled the former Liverpool & Manchester line-did not renumber that company's locomotives in its own list until 1847 when the new Northern Division list was formed. The Grand Junction Company had exercised running powers over the entire Liverpool and Manchester system from its opening until August 8th 1845 when it absorbed the line. At the same time it took over also the Bolton & Leigh Railway.

Before describing the further new engines added after the formation of the London & North Western Railway it may be well to note that, in 1846, there were still 21 engines on the Manchester & Birmingham list and, with its 96 coaching vehicles and 631 merchandise wagons, the rolling stock of the company was valued at £83,514.

History of the Manchester Railways (1882)
by William Harrison.

Approaching Handforth Sidings, c.1949: Rebuilt "Royal Scot" No **46154** *The Hussar* thunders beneath bridge No 85 - between Cheadle Hulme and Handforth - with a London road to Euston express. This overbridge, taking Stanley Road (B5094) over the railway, is an original M&BR structure and dated from the opening of the line through here in 1842. Just beyond this point was the sidings complex and branch to the RAF depot (61 MU) built in 1943. A series of sidings lay parallel with the main line on the Up side, a separate branch diverging at the south end to the depot itself. The nose of the crossover to the Down line can be glimpsed in the lower left of the picture beneath the quarter mile post. **Tom Lewis**

INTO THE 1960's
PROGRESS FROM CREWE to EUSTON

Come September 1960 and Manchester's inter-city and local passengers had the main line station and the electrified railway they had waited almost four years for. However, there would be no acceleration of main line trains for some time. Piccadilly to Crewe was but a precursor of things to come: the target was full electrification right down to Euston, thence to Liverpool and Glasgow. That was the broad outline: within this framework was to be set electrification via Wolverhampton, Birmingham and Coventry. Very relative to Manchester services was the projected electrification of the so-called "Potteries Loop Line" from Cheadle Hulme via Poynton, Macclesfield and Stoke-on-Trent. At Macclesfield, the station on Hibel Road (formerly LNWR) was closed on November 7th 1960 at the same time the suffix "Central" was dropped from the station that had previously been GC&NSR Joint property and was set now to become the town's main station. Come the winter timetable, from September, there were noticeable differences in the express services to Euston. Recovery times, inserted of necessity whilst electrification took place, now continued. Average journey times over the Euston route stood at 4 hr 25 min down and 4 hr 19 min up. Prestige train schedules, too, suffered, with journey times of *The Mancunian*, and *The Comet* becoming 15 minutes slower than those pertaining in summertime. Indeed, a writer reviewing the 1961-62 BR winter timetables noted with a degree of humour that a quicker journey from London to Manchester could be had by dint of travelling from King's Cross and changing at Sheffield! Even the Midland line, hampered by the Peak route up to St.Pancras accomplished the journey to the Capital in the same 4 hour time slot.

SIX YEARS HARD LABOUR

Working south from Crewe, and through Staffordshire along the Potteries Loop line via Stoke-on-Trent, modernisation of the line to Euston would be accomplished by degrees. As with the Manchester-Crewe scheme, the railway had to function at the same time as it had to modernise. This period, from 1960 to 1966 was a time of great transition on British Railways. For the enthusiast the most noticeable, and for many, regrettable, change was the disappearance of the steam locomotive. By May 1961 all London services south from Crewe were rostered in charge of the EE Type 4 2,000 hp Diesels.

Euston itself was to be in turmoil for the next few years due to extensive rebuilding. A news item in November of that year brought the famed Doric arch into the limelight. Its imminent demise looming, the Victorian Society launched a campaign to save the structure. A fund was set up to raise the £190,000 needed to move the famous stonework nearer to Euston Road. The matter even reached the ear of Harold Macmillan. Alas for posterity, "Mac" would hear none of it and demolition was authorised.

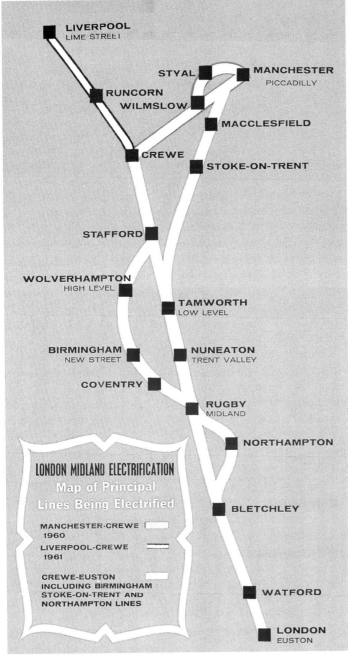

LONDON MIDLAND ELECTRIFICATION
Map of Principal Lines Being Electrified

MANCHESTER-CREWE 1960

LIVERPOOL-CREWE 1961

CREWE-EUSTON INCLUDING BIRMINGHAM STOKE-ON-TRENT AND NORTHAMPTON LINES

Euston, Doric Arch early 1960s: It was certainly imposing, but would Philip Hardwick's masterpiece fit into the new, airport-style Euston? BR's emphatic answer was clearly "No", a view shared, surprisingly given his railway pedigree, by Prime Minister Harold Macmillan. Even in its early days the arch attracted opprobrium: Augustus Pugin, a fervent promoter of Gothic architecture-he had designed the rebuilt Houses of Parliament-termed it *"a piece of Brobdingnagian absurdity"*. In recent years there has been talk of resurrecting the stones and rebuilding the arch. Whatever the outcome, Euston's monument to the early railways will remain only as a memory on the station site.   *J W Sutherland*

Punctuality at this time was reported as being between 10 minutes early and 10 minutes late over 81% of the services. Much debate has raged since as to BR's motive power policies-or lack of them-from the inception of the nationalised system in 1948 through to the disappearance of steam traction in August 1968. Fascinating as all this is, back in the early 1960s things were changing rapidly. As far as London-Manchester services went, the change-over to electric traction at Crewe quickly became an established practice with the Type 4 1-Co-Co-1 Diesels in charge of the workings southwards. By January 1962 the overhead line had extended from Crewe along to Whitmore with steelwork being erected from there towards Stafford. The slog south continued with the sight of wiring in progress from Armitage to Tamworth being reported in March. At the same time foundation work for overhead masts could be seen as far south as Weedon, near to Rugby.

RE-SIGNALLING

Electrification went hand-in-hand with other works of course. Not least of which was re-signalling. The Manchester area will

be dealt with: new power boxes at London Road, Wilmslow and Sandbach while the Stockport area carried on with the four LNWR and one BR box controlling the immediate area. Indeed, these survive today, while (at the time of writing) Wilmslow power box is being demolished and that at the former London Road has long since been supplanted (Q.V.). At Crewe the existing power box at North Junction with miniature lever frames was retained, as was a similar set-up at Liverpool Lime Street. Leaving Crewe, electro-mechanical signalling was the norm with new power cabins and push-button controls being provided at Norton Bridge (another at Stoke, controlled the Potteries Loop from Macclesfield). South from Nuneaton, including Rugby, Bletchley, Watford Junction, Willesden and Euston, power boxes were provided. Some LNW signalboxes hung on for crossing and local duty; examples being at Banbury Lane (near Rugby) and Hademore (for a level crossing south of Lichfield). Larger LNW boxes survived into the 21st century at Tamworth and Lichfield TV. An enlarged system at Rugby now controls the section of newly-quadrupled WCML (Q.V.) as far as Stoke-on-Trent. Control of the line via Birmingham was taken over by power systems operating at Wolverhampton, Birmingham New Street, Walsall and Coventry. At New Street the new box replaced no less than 27 manual ones, though eight were retained for control of shunting operations.

Four-aspect signalling throughout, with continuous track circuiting, train describers and attendant AWS, was set as standard. This gave sufficient braking distance for trains travelling at 90-100 mph (double yellow through to red); while single yellow to red was deemed suitable for traffic travelling at 50-60 mph. A particular requirement inherent with an adjacent 25kV ac traction system was the need to immunise the signalling from stray earth currents. Special measures were needed at Piccadilly where there was a parallel 1500V dc system and between Watford and Euston where the ex-LNWR 630V dc third rail lines ran adjacent and in some cases shared tracks. Contemporary Press attention focused on the fact that a new power box had been built at Euston as recently as 1952 when a system controlled by a 227 miniature lever frame was commissioned.

The total cost of the new signalling and associated telecommunications was set to cost the LMR £37.7M. As a stand-alone figure, the re-signalling cost £56,200 per route mile, while the telecommunications cost £17,000 per route mile. (Manchester to Crewe had cost £17M in total). Offset against this was a reduction in signalmen's positions from 1,231 to 575. A report published by the LMR cited a shortage of signalmen in some areas as a contributory factor in planning the new systems.

ADVENTURES AT HARECASTLE

Back to May 1962: colour light signalling had now been commissioned at Stafford and MAS was now in situ from Liverpool and Warrington down to the county town with coverage to Rugby and Coventry predicted by the end of the year. Midsummer saw the last section of overhead line completed between Crewe and Stafford. Over on the Potteries Loop line bridges between Mow Cop and Cheadle Hulme were in various stages of reconstruction-an essential, yet expensive, feature of electrification schemes. A particularly problematic feature of this stretch of railway were the three Harecastle tunnels between Stoke-on-Trent and Kidsgrove and built in 1846-47. The 1-mile long South tunnel was heavy on maintenance, being prone to water leakage. After much consideration, it was decided to close two of the existing tunnels, open out the North tunnel and from there sweep south in a gentle 2½ mile curve on the west side of the line through Bathpool Park. The nature of the landmass hereabouts-the "Harecastle Ridge"-meant that the deviation could not be entirely tunnel-free and, in consequence, a new tunnel 220 yards long had to be bored through the hard Millstone grit on the north side of the Nelson Pond and Bathpool reservoirs. Fascinatingly, this tunnel had to cross the two Harecastle tunnels of the Trent and Mersey canal on the skew. These, too, were the second tunnels at this site, the first having sunk due to colliery subsidence. One of the biggest civil engineering works of the whole electrification scheme, the cost was estimated at £2M and was scheduled to last around 2½ years. The new alignment opened for traffic on June 27th 1966.

Readers of a certain age may remember that the old tunnels became later immortalised in a BBC play of 1969-*The last train through the Harecastle Tunnel* (sic) in which the character Benjamin Fowler, a London office worker, decides to spend a Bank Holiday weekend by boarding the last train through the soon to be condemned tunnels. During his trip Fowler encounters some very curious characters and stumbles on a dark Staffordshire family secret. Back to 1962: on the Manchester-Crewe-Euston line, schedules remained much the same as the previous year due to the continuation of engineering work south of Crewe. By the autumn, work was proceeding on the track and overhead line between Rugby and Bletchley with E2001, the 25kV ac training loco, arriving at Rugby for further deployment.

FURTHER WORK WITH TUNNELS

Though seen initially as a major problem, the provision of clearances through the various tunnels en route between Manchester and Euston threw up fewer problems than at first thought. Just outside Stockport Edgeley, beneath what was known as "The Armoury", four lengths of tunnel, totalling 216 yards, had to be opened out. After negotiations with Stockport Council, the tunnel complex was replaced by one secondary road bridge-carrying Booth Street between Mercian Way and Shaw Heath, a roundabout at the intersection of the latter two thoroughfares and single footbridge with one central pier.

Youthful observers at Crewe, on seeing smoke and steam from around the avoiding lines that ran beneath the station would shout "Muck Hole!"-the sobriquet bestowed on the freight lines that were tucked away out of sight. These crossed under the main running lines via two single-line and one double-line tunnel. They were of cut-and-cover construction with vertical abutments. Clearances were obtained by lowering the track formation by some 18 inches and driving sheet piling in front of the old foundations with concrete additions.

Further south, at Shugborough in Staffordshire, the 776 yard-long tunnel was found to be slightly adrift in clearance, but this was overcome by realignment of the track. Similarly, returning briefly to the Potteries Loop line: tunnels at Prestbury (267 yards) and Macclesfield Hibel Road (346 yards) were dealt with by a combination of track lowering and realignment. In the twin single-line tunnels at Linslade and Northchurch pockets were cut into the lining for the installation of overhead line structures. By dint of using reinforced concrete block structures major reconstruction was thus avoided.

THE 'ARMOURY' TUNNELS

Edgeley tunnels, Stockport-September 3rd 1959: Among the more drastic civil engineering operations necessary before a 25kV catenary could be erected was this operation just south of Edgeley station, Stockport. The pair of lines seen here, the 'Up' lines, form the original alignment of the 1842 Manchester & Birmingham undertaking. The later tunnel, on the 'Down' side was built to accommodate three lines.Here it was deemed more economic and practical to remove the shallow covering of the tunnels, the simple expedient of "opening out". Whatever today's HSE inspectors would make of this scene is anyone's guess! But, notwithstanding the massive operation, the trains still ran, a thing at odds with today's procedures where "total blockade" is the preferred option. Above the photographer the decking of the new road bridge can be made out; while the eagle-eyed will have spotted the "Crab" waiting in the south bay. *British Railways*

A last major piece of tunnel work was required between Willesden and Euston where the Up empty carriage line was carried through a single-line tunnel 955 yards long. This tunnel was of circular construction and had a cast iron lining. To gain the additional 15 inches of headroom required the side and top segments of the lining were removed and clay was then mined away from the tunnel top. Despite passage beneath various sewers and the Regent's Canal-where a mere 10 feet of cover remained-no water seepage was experienced. After the removal of some 5,000 tons of clay, new cast iron segments were hoisted into position. The new side and top segments turned the profile of the tunnel from a round to an elliptical one. All was completed during the period of the 1961-62 winter timetable. A small aside here is worthy of mention: in January 1967 the 2½ miles of line between Primrose Hill and York Way freight depot in North London were electrified. This was to enable Freightliner traffic to work into the depot directly, avoiding the need for a change-over of traction.

WORK WITH BRIDGES

It is the portals of railway tunnels that turn mere holes through ground and rock into, often, spectacular structures. In overall terms one can quote Box, Woodhead and Severn as three striking examples of the nineteenth century civil engineer's art. Tunnels evoke emotion and mystery. For steam footplate crews they produced nightmare conditions, especially at low speed or when a locomotive was working hard in tight confines. Bridges, by contrast, merely whizzed by, unnoticed in the main by the passenger; mere blinks of the eye and offering only slight interruption between the often continuous passage through open countryside. But not for the civil engineer and his team on the LMR. The total number of bridges on the Manchester-London route was no less than 775, or just a fraction under 2 bridges per route mile of electrified track. Where an increase in headroom was needed, structures could be raised by jacking-up the existing bridge and then providing new bearings at a higher level. 96 girder bridges, along with 80 footbridges were dealt with in this fashion. Where clearances were tight and where road traffic could be either diverted or accommodated on half the bridge width, the bridge was stripped down to the arch ring, and a new saddle arch of reinforced concrete was constructed above the old arch ring. Explosives were then used to remove the original arches-invariably with spectacular results!

These methods, though, were impractical with elliptical arches or where lengthy road possessions could not be had. In such cases the arch was demolished-again, using explosives-to springing level (the point at which the arch rises from its support) and then a new superstructure was provided. Pre-stressed concrete slabs were considered wherever possible and it was noted at the time that uniform quality control could be had, the slabs could be easily manoeuvred and the material possessed the supreme advantage that no waiting time was needed for the setting of concrete cast in situ. ....continued on page 16

Heaton Moor, Stockport. October 20th 1957. 'Thar she blows'. Modernisation takes away much of the remaining infrastructure of the original Manchester & Birmingham as tons of brickwork fly through the air during demolition of the brick arch ring of overbridge No 8 (Warwick Road). Quite literally biting the dust, the picture displays nicely the standard and by now routine technique used for such structures. The existing arch is being blasted away leaving the concrete arch above it. The old arch rings formed the support for the new concrete structure above it and, since the thrust from the one arch is balanced against

the thrust from the neighbouring, it would have been important not to get the loading out of balance. If the centre arch overburden was taken off before that on the neighbouring side arches, there would be an 'out of balance' scenario. This would cause the centre arch to lift and eventually collapse; so the weight would have to taken off all the arches in parallel. Similarly, the rebuilding of the bridge tops would have to be carried out evenly across the whole structure.One or two engineers learned the hard way! However, all looks in order here as, on either side, the other two arches await their turn for destruction. Notice the impromptu staging erected on the 16-ton mineral wagons to enable placement of the explosives. Although spectacular in appearance, little charge would have been needed to dislodge the crown. the man in the foreground is the explosives expert, the wire leading to the charges can be seen along by the lighting tripod. For such operations in the Manchester area, BR used two specialist companies, one being 'Controlled Explosions Ltd', the other being Swinnerton & Miller.
British Railways

Crewe, Independent Lines March 6th 1962: Although Crewe will not be reached until a subsequent volume, this fascinating picture is included to show something of the complexity of the work facing the engineers in their drive south towards Euston after electrification to Manchester was completed. The view is taken from the concrete overbridge that led off from the, then, platform 1 towards the shed. Looking north from Crewe station, here is the back of the fabled Crewe North loco shed (5A) with the yard spread out in front of it. Diving beneath the station is the "muck hole", known as such to the "Spotters" of the 1950s. Crewe North men gave it the equally unglamorous nickname of "the bog hole". Neither term is correct: the railway always used the phrase "Independent Lines" and they date from the early years of the last century. There are six, in three pairs and all carried the suffix "Independent". Running from west to east they are: Down Liverpool, Up Liverpool, Down Manchester, Up Manchester, Down Chester, Up Chester. The Liverpool tunnel opened for traffic on September 24th 1900; the Manchester lines were inaugurated the following year-Down line on March 20th, Up line on April 8th. The three pairs of tracks pass under the Crewe North complex via bridge No.82A, clearly visible here. Obviously, as there was no possibility of raising the bridge, the track had to be lowered to gain the requisite clearance for the overhead line. Just another of the many quasi-Herculean tasks executed in the early 1960s. Once clear of the subterranean gloom beneath Crewe, the Manchester Independent lines join the two surface lines at the erstwhile Sydney Bridge Junction, just past milepost 157 to form a four-track section-two slow and two fast lines as far as Sandbach, the junction for the Middlewich line, but all much altered after the contemporary re-modelling. Much detail can be gleaned from this photograph: in the 1950s, the building on the far left housed the offices of Mr.Bill Body the Crewe North shedmaster and the assistant district motive power superintendent, Mr.Peach. Their offices faced the bike sheds from across the side road. And even such mundane features as these had been standard LMS fittings at one time, being manufactured at the Newton Heath concrete works to a 1944 standard. In this shot, though, the bicycles are outnumbered by scooters and motor bikes! The second building was the shed stores; walking through the left-hand door one encountered the entrance "tunnel" to Crewe North shed. Just visible here is a locoman; having crossed the bridge he is about to pass behind the wooden gates on his way to "book on". Walking down, past the stores window one would be greeted at the far end by the truly magical sight of rows of smokebox door numberplates! Reaching out in front of the stores building is the middle section of the main shed. Within range of the camera a Type 4 Diesel and an Ivatt 2-6-0 can be made out. The steel spans for the overhead, as yet unwired, have arrived in the yard; in front stand one of the floodlight pylons which were erected between March and August 1958. A former Crewe North engineer has related how, on more than one occasion, men had to descend the steps on the far left to attend to suicides. Railway work was never without its touch of pathos.

British Railways

Elton Viaduct, Sandbach, April 1958: Bridge works extraordinaire! Due to brine pumping in the area here adjacent to the River Wheelock, subsidence in the order of 12-14in. had been experienced every year beneath bridge No. 12; The problem had been tackled by removing the original brick viaduct and replacing it by an embankment with the top level maintained by the tipping of ashes and ballast. Severe speed restrictions had been in force over the years. Come electrification and the added complication of overhead line structures meant that something drastic was required to maintain the permanent way in satisfactory condition. The answer came via this novel method of embankment-building. Concrete pipes-5ft.in diameter allowed both the passage of river water and support for the bridge abutments and decking. At the time of electrification it was reckoned that a further layer of pipes would be required every six or seven years. In this picture, engineers have the pipe stack well in hand; what cannot be seen is the reinforced concrete raft below river level supporting the ensemble. In the interim since electrification, brine pumping has stopped and

the traditional permanent way has been replaced by CWR with the now common deep ballast shoulder. But the pipes remain, vindicating this novel engineering technique of over forty years ago.

Martin Welch

continued from page 14.........Mr.A.N.Butland, Chief Engineer (Way and Works) to the BRB at the time, noted that the number of bridge reconstructions for the provision of adequate clearances included 207 arch bridges, 129 girder bridges and 33 footbridges. A critical case study enabled the engineers to do away altogether with 60 bridges over the railway.

CREWE TO STAFFORD GOES LIVE

Come October, the march south of the electrification scheme continued. Colour light signalling had been extended as far south as Lichfield and the sight of semaphores on this railway was gradually becoming rarer. Soon the cries of "clanger on the Down" from the spotters in their famous field at Tamworth, or "peg on the Up" would be no more. Now, the 25kV between Crewe and landmark Stafford had been completed and was due to be energised the following month (actually commissioned 26/11/62) with electric services scheduled to go ahead early in the New Year. This would push the change-over point from Crewe down to Stafford with a corresponding allocation of Type 4s at the latter. It was hoped that Birmingham services from Manchester and Liverpool would be handed over to electric traction then. Beyond Stafford the OHL was due to be completed to Rugby by early 1964. Progress in the shape of the appearance of overhead masts was noted as proceeding from Rugby along to Roade (where the junction with the Northampton line appears) with a target date of December recorded.

THE MIDLAND TAKES OVER

From the week commencing Monday, September 10th 1962, the bulk of Manchester-London trains had been diverted over the Peak route into London St.Pancras to free up Euston whilst rebuilding continued. Taking centre stage since July 4th 1960 had been the

celebrated and short-lived "Midland Pullman", the luxury 6-car DMU whose raison d'être had been to keep the head of the business traffic between the two cities above water pending the huge operation facing the engineers south of Crewe. In the autumn of 1962 "The Pullman" became the fastest train to cover the 190 miles between St.Pancras and Manchester Central by maintaining an average speed of 60 mph. Now eleven expresses daily were put on from Manchester to St.Pancras (including "The Pullman"), with ten in the Down direction. The previous 25-minutes past the hour departures, a hang-over from Midland days, were abolished and an even, on the hour, schedule was substituted.

USE OF THE SMJ

The railway was a very different organisation then and the consideration of parcels traffic was a big one. To handle this traffic away from Euston it was decided to concentrate the West Coast parcels traffic at Blisworth via a temporary sorting centre. A charming wayside spot south of Rugby between Weedon and Roade, Blisworth was the junction for the Stratford-upon-Avon and Midland Junction Railway (SMJ). Blisworth also housed a canal basin on the Grand Junction system and is still, today, a popular spot for canal enthusiasts. A northerly spur connected Blisworth with the cross-country SMJ line from Broom Junction via Stratford-on-Avon in the west over to Ravenstone Wood Junction in the east where it formed a connection with the MR Northampton-Bedford line. A true east-west railway, the SMJ uniquely linked main lines of the GC, GW, LNW and MR.

SLEEPERS VIA THE GC

But parcels traffic was not the only consideration in terms of diversions away from Euston. From January 1963 Sleeper services from Manchester Piccadilly-altered to 11.55pm and 12.30 am-to London were re-routed to Marylebone. Included in this re-scheduling were the 11.45 pm and 1.00 am Down Sleepers from Euston and St.Pancras respectively. All this meant some Longsight men having to learn the former GC road over Woodhead to Sheffield Victoria and then south as far as Nottingham and vice-versa. At weekends, to accommodate engineering work on the main line due to severe colliery subsidence, the Sleepers were routed round via the Chesterfield loop from Staveley rejoining the direct line at Heath Junction; yet another route-learning challenge. To cope with the heavy Sleeping carriages and the taxing route, Diesels in the form of pairs of Sulzer Type 2s later Class 25/1 & 2 (1160 hp) were used for this first leg

A section from one of Harold Gorton's notebooks showing route learning details over the former GC main line north from Nottingham used for the diverted Manchester - London sleeping car trains during the Crewe-Euston electrification from January 1963 to November 1965. Notice the different markings setting out semaphore from colour light signals-all part of the many tribulations endured by footplate crews and indeed others during this difficult period.

of the journey. The locos were fitted with a telephone system between cab and train so the steward could request slower running, extra stops or ask for the train to be moved out of noisy areas. The train engine had to have a working boiler for train heating (not all the class were so equipped) and very often a fitter rode with the train if the boiler was proving temperamental. Another point in the Sulzers' favour was their quiet exhaust. Such consideration! From Nottingham engines were changed, with "Royal Scots", sadly then past their best, being used for the second leg of 127 miles into Marylebone. Another overnight service from Central, though without Sleeping Cars, left at 12.05 am. Manchester Sleeper services returned to Euston from Sunday, November 21st 1965.

MORE OHL AND A DARK NIGHT

Further into 1963 and by May the overhead line was complete

as far south as Nuneaton and services thus far were predicted as starting from September. Further rebuilding was taking place down at Euston where the Euston Hotel, closed in May, was set to suffer the same fate as its companion Doric Arch. One suspects that the average Mancunian had rarely sampled the hotel's delights. Even so, it is worth recording that this had been the world's first railway hotel when it had opened back in London & Birmingham days in 1840. Euston's Station Hotel had been known at first as "The Victoria Hotel and Dormitories".

It was in the summer of 1963 that one of the darkest events in the history of the West Coast Main Line took place. On August 8th the infamous "Great Train Robbery" took place at Sears Crossing, Buckinghamshire. Driver Jack Mills and his mate on D326 at the head of the 6.50 pm Aberdeen-Glasgow-Euston mail train had been tricked by false signals into stopping their train. The two were held captive while the gang uncoupled the high security coaches which were then drawn forward to a point where the remainder of the robbers were waiting. The haul, consisting of £2.5M in used banknotes, was the biggest ever at the time.

Further progress with the OHL was in place when the wire was energised on August 31st from Milford and Brocton (close to milepost 129) to a point two miles south of Lichfield (milepost 114) where Hademore water troughs were sited. At the time of writing (February 2006) Network Rail engineers are engaged here on a project known as "TV4"- the quadrupling of the WCML between Tamworth and Lichfield. On October 21st 1963 Lichfield saw its first electrically-hauled train enter Trent Valley station-this was a press special hauled by E3030. The hope now was for electric traction to be extended to Nuneaton by the end of the year. In the event, the "switch on" took place on January 3rd 1964 and regular services were inaugurated on Monday, January 20th (the first train had actually arrived the previous day). The target date for revenue-earning services to Nuneaton was set for March 2nd and to Rugby by June 5th. Rugby, very much a focal point on the railway south of Crewe, had, in fact, had its catenary in place by the previous October.

AN HISTORICAL INTERLUDE

Birmingham, Capital of the West Midlands, is often overlooked when speaking of Manchester-London services. Ironically, the Manchester & Birmingham Railway only got as far as Crewe! Nevertheless it was from this fine city that the Grand Junction Railway spread itself northwards; from a temporary terminus at Vauxhall (later to Curzon Street station) via Wolverhampton, Stafford and Warrington to connect with the Liverpool & Manchester Railway (via the Warrington & Newton Railway) and opened on July 4th 1837. Thus were enabled the first through trains from Liverpool and Manchester to London. The Trent Valley line, northwards from Rugby via Nuneaton, Tamworth and Lichfield to Trent Valley Junction, south of Stafford, did not open until June 1847.

From the splendid frontage of Curzon Street station it is but a short walk to the monstrous, concrete and half-subterranean edifice that is Birmingham New Street. Now, like its northern and southern counterparts, New Street, too, was to undergo rebuilding. Work commenced there in April 1964 and the £2½M scheme was due for completion by April 1966 when through electric services to Euston were scheduled to begin. Working south through Hertfordshire the celebrated cutting at Tring came into focus in May when the "juice" was due to be switched on from there to Watford. London was in sight!

HIGH-SPEED TRIALS

Early in 1964 BR conducted high-speed tests with E3073, one of the Doncaster-built 3,300 hp Class "A" Bo-Bos (later Class 85). Carried out between Crewe and Stafford, the objective was not so much to ascertain maximum speed, but rather to test the overhead line and equipment, especially beneath overline bridges. Central to the testing was the use of the LMR's "Gondola" coach in which a raised central dome was fitted to aid observation of the overhead line. A Hallade track recorder was installed to monitor track conditions and alignment. The test trains were variously completed with a BSK or a generator coach, the loads being no more than a featherweight 65-85 tons. Testing was carried out on the Up Fast line south of the closed Whitmore station. On a falling gradient of 1-in-398, 80 mph was attained from a standing start with a 65-ton load over a distance of 0.5 to 0.7 mile. 90 mph required 1.05-1.10 miles; 118 mph 4.15 miles and 119 mph needed 4.20 miles. A second series of tests resulted in completing 3.8 miles in 3 min 12 secs with a top speed of 119 mph. The LMR concluded that, in all cases, the overhead line functioned perfectly.

ALL CHANGE AT RUGBY

By September 7th trial working south to Rugby was due to commence and it would be from here that the change-over point from electric to Diesel traction would take place-a move scheduled for November 30th. Alas for lovers of the steam locomotive, it was in the month of September that despair would set in. From the 7th it was decreed that Stanier Pacifics, inter alia, would be barred from working south of Crewe. Now the hated diagonal yellow stripe would appear on cab sides of revered and celebrated engines, the restriction brought about by the reduction of the loading gauge to 13ft.1in. The start of September, also, saw the OHL go live from Tring to Watford.

NORMALITY RESUMES AT EUSTON

Meanwhile in London, the new Euston was taking shape with platforms 3-7 back in use and Nos.8-10 almost ready. Work was well in hand back up north with good progress being reported on the Cheadle Hulme to Colwich line commensurate with the diversion of the new Harecastle route taking shape. South again-at Rugby the biggest change was the commissioning of the new power box which replaced 22 manual signalboxes and controlled 36 miles of line. 1964 went out with a bang in more ways than one when, on Boxing Day (yes, they really did run trains on such days back then!) the pantograph of the loco hauling the 12.23 Crewe to Euston caught a loose overhead wire and brought down some three miles of wiring. All lines were blocked for five hours-a remarkably short time considering the damage and chaos that must have been wrought. Alas for BR's electrical engineers the year's troubles were not quite over yet. At midnight on December 28th/29th E3067 caught fire at Brinklow, about five miles from Rugby. Unsurprisingly, the locomotive was severely damaged in the conflagration.

The process of elimination of steam traction continued early in the New Year-1965. Rugby shed now had an allocation of ten Type 4 Diesels for working trains forward to Euston. From January 5th it was reported that almost all main line steam workings from

Stockport Edgeley, May 28th 1960: From around midsummer 1959, the English Electric Type 4 - 2,000 h.p.Diesels moved in to gradually assume control of main line express working out of London Road. Waiting for departure alongside platform 2 is D214 with a southbound express. Notice the newly-rebuilt platforms with work going on above. Observers of today's Stockport scene will know that the much re-modelled station is now minus its centre roads, popularly known by railway staff of the period as the 'slums'.

Graham Whitehead

Rugby, September 1962: Typifying work required under the Crewe-Euston electrification is this, a BR official photograph showing the completed North flyover at Rugby, around 1¹/₂ miles north of the station near to the former Rugby No.7 junction. The 450 yard concrete structure, carrying a new 1,450 yard single line, was designed specifically to ensure that Up trains from Birmingham to Northampton and Euston would no longer clash with Down train workings from Rugby to the Trent Valley line. Work was authorised in 1958 and building commenced in May 1960. Full operation began on September 17th 1962; the total cost coming out at around £800,000. Under the proposed new electric timetable there would have been some 39 conflictions of express passenger trains alone between the twelve hours from 8.30 am-even more if local and freight workings were brought into the equation. With the flyover in place the number of Down trains through the junction could be increased from 43 to 61 and the number of Up Birmingham trains from 22 to 43 in a twelve-hour period. So pleased were BR with their latest piece of civil engineering that they commissioned a painting which was used, both as a poster and as a jacket illustration on O.S.Nock's book "Britain's New Railway". To enable the artist to produce his

work, several photographs were taken. It is believed that this one has been doctored, albeit cleverly, to produce a better effect. Anyone who has taken pictures of moving trains knows the sheer impossibility of getting two trains together at a precise moment, let alone three! 1A33, on the Up Fast line, is drawn by E3057 and is the 8.42 am Carlisle-Euston, due at Rugby at 2.34 pm. On the Down Fast Trent Valley line, the "Red Rose" appears to be train 1K26, the 12.15pm Euston to Liverpool due here at 1.51 pm-so the two trains would normally not have passed at Rugby. The DMU descending from the new flyover could well be a "stopper" from New Street, due Rugby at 1.32 pm. Maybe the "Red Rose" tailboard was a clever piece of "cut and paste", all long before the days of Photoshop! Behind the flyover is the repositioned Up (Trent Valley) Slow line. Snaking off to the left are the former Down and Up Birmingham lines. The Up track was later removed, leaving the new flyover line as the sole route from Birmingham. *British Railways*

Rugby would be eliminated and included in this edict were the Rugby station pilots. Full electric working from Crewe to Rugby was inaugurated on January 4th. A solitary exception was to be an early morning Parcels train which was worked up from Stafford by a Fowler 2-6-4 tank engine.

SOME PERSONAL NOTES

At this juncture the author recalls two journeys he made from Piccadilly to Euston in the first half of 1965. The first, a trip to see the Model Engineer exhibition at Central Hall, Westminster saw haulage from Manchester to Rugby with E3085 in charge of the 08.00 express. A diary entry records a swift passage down the WCML, the only complaint being the stifling heat in the train. Rugby, as normal, saw the hand-over to a Type 4 Diesel with arrival in Euston noted as being 19 minutes early! Ever the enthusiast, our return was from St.Pancras over the Midland line and, of course, the now long-lamented Peak route through Derbyshire. Arrival back in Didsbury was noted as being at 11.06 pm. A second trip was made on May 12th to accompany my father who had to take some important documents for the Civil Service to an office in The Strand. Again, the 8.00 train was taken, but the loco number was not recorded. Rugby saw the Type 4 attached once more, but the journey from there was noted as being hampered by P-way slacks and a signal failure. Arrival in Euston was two min-

utes down. Our return was via "The Mancunian" at 6.00, the only time I ever travelled on this train. Demolition at Euston was noted as still taking place. After halting at Rugby for the change-over from Diesel to electric haulage we pulled away smartly. Looking out of the train, we passed a waiting Bo-Bo in one of the centre roads, the crew at the loco window. *"Better strap yourselves in!"*, cracked one of them. The diary entry recalls: *"..and he wasn't kidding, either"*. Welded track gave the lie to our speed, but a "thrilling trip" was noted, even if we were three minutes late back into Piccadilly.

ELECTRIC WORKING TO LONDON COMES INTO VIEW

Rugby shed was closed on May 24th, though the turntable was still used. From there north to Coventry overhead wiring was now complete. Unfazed by all the engineering work still proceeding, BR managed to run no less than twenty-five football specials from Liverpool to Euston in connection with the FA Cup final on May 1st. All were worked in what was by then the well-established electric-Diesel format. A target of September was set for Bletchley to be designated as the change-over point from electric to Diesel traction henceforward. Freight traffic, this was still 1965, remember, would, at the same time, become electrically-hauled as far as Willesden. Euston was now equipped with overhead gantries.

Predictions were now being made as to when a full electric

service into Euston might operate. In May 1965 it was announced that the first stage of Manchester-Euston using the Trent Valley route would be ready from January 1st 1966 and that the accelerated service would be inaugurated from March. Electrification from Rugby to Coventry was set for March also; though the second stage-from Coventry to Stafford via Birmingham-would not be completed until the first part of 1967. For the summer timetable of 1965 the standard start to stop time for Rugby-Crewe services (now all electrically-hauled) was to be 63 minutes for the 75 mile journey. Eight minutes was allowed at Rugby for engine-changing and fifteen minutes recovery time was allowed from there to Euston. Now the benefits of electrification were being felt. Compared to the timings extant in 1960/61 this was a huge improvement. Then, something like 1 hour, 46 minutes to 1 hour 58 minutes were typical. Though, as mentioned earlier, substantial recovery margins had been built into those schedules. Further improvements to signalling were made that summer, too. Over the period July 10th-11th, the new power signal box was commissioned at Willesden covering some 11 miles of main line. The Potteries Loop line was still undergoing modernisation at this time with overhead line masts being erected between Kidsgrove and Etruria. Travelling via Northampton, the overhead line from the County town to Queens Park was energised on July 19th with electrically-hauled freights being noted as operating as far south as Northampton itself from July 26th.

Rundown of the GC begins

Its use in the Crewe-Euston programme now coming to an end, it is sad to note at this point the impending demise of the Great Central main line south of Sheffield. The October 1965 issue of the RCTS Railway Observer noted that, from April 17th the following year all passenger services between Sheffield and Aylesbury would be withdrawn. But the GC line would not be the only casualty precipitated by the electrification scheme. Between March 1967 and July 1968 BR would close two vital sections of the former Midland Railway's "Peak" rote through Derbyshire: Peak Forest to Miller's Dale and from the latter to Matlock. Even Dr.Beeching had not recommended this. Thus, by the closure of a mere nineteen miles of track did the nation lose what is a most beautiful and, more importantly, useful piece of railway line. Reverting briefly to the GC. As this piece is being prepared, the magazine *Modern Railways* reports the possible implementation of the Central Railway scheme-a new line taking freight traffic via piggyback style lorries from Northern France through the Channel Tunnel, round London and northwards via some of the former GC route through Rugby to Sheffield, Manchester and Liverpool; all at a cost of mere *billions*.

Euston sees its first electric loco

As forecast, the extension of electrification to Willesden via Northampton took place on September 27th. The same day, steam sheds at Willesden (1A) and Northampton (2E) were closed. Over the period 25th/26th September the new power box at Euston was inaugurated. To enable this to take place smoothly some diversions were put in place to Marylebone and St.Pancras. Then, at last, the wire was energised from Queens Park into the terminal itself on October 25th. Perhaps surprisingly, this did not precipi-

tate some grand arrival into Euston of an electric locomotive. This had happened on September 21st when E3023 was towed in. The great day did dawn of course, and on November 6th 1965, E3110 entered Euston with a pantograph test carriage and BSK. From November 22nd 16 Down and 12 Up trains would be electrically-hauled. The first train out of the newly-electrified terminal was the 08.35 to Liverpool. After almost Herculean labours, Euston had finally gone live. Now, also, began a trend which would continue and grow over the years to come: the introduction of EMU working from Euston to major points north. Such things began on December 13th when EMU working was instituted on the Euston-Bletchley-Rugby-Northampton services.

Elsewhere, up in the Midlands, things were moving ahead also. On November 8th Coventry saw its first electric loco in the shape of E3068 at the head of a wire cleaning train. Into New Year (1966) and from January 3rd four trains daily between Birmingham and Euston were turned over to electric haulage from Coventry. However, full electric working was not due to reach Birmingham until March 1967.

Start of the full electric timetable

Full electric working between Manchester Piccadilly and London Euston was scheduled to begin on April 18th 1966. The culmination of almost six year's work, nearly nine if the first work on the Styal line is counted, was now reached. Between Euston and Manchester there were 14 Up and 13 Down express trains each weekday. Departures from Piccadilly were generally on the hour or around half-past the hour. In the Up direction the fastest timing was the 2hr.36 min.of the 09.00; from Euston to Manchester the fastest schedule was, again 2hr.36 min; this held by the 18.00 "Manchester Pullman." Four such Pullman trains were run each way on each weekday between Euston and Liverpool. These were: Down to Liverpool at 07.45 and 18.10; Down to Manchester at 07.50 and 18.00. Up from Liverpool at 07.55 and 17.40 and from Manchester at 07.50 and 17.35. Pullmans apart, timings were now in the region of 2hrs.40-45 minutes. All-in-all a considerable improvement on the previous timings of around 3hrs.45 min. Twenty-nine new carriages were built for the electrically-hauled Manchester and Liverpool Pullman trains. As well as the First Class fare, a 25/- (£1.25) supplement was charged for Pullman travel. Aside from the electrified route, there were still expresses to the Capital over the Midland line if one preferred, taking in the beautiful Peak District scenery. The 1966 timetable shows 6 Up trains from Central to St.Pancras and a corresponding 5 Down services. How relevant the term "Express" then was is debatable; the Midland schedules stretched to 4hrs.7 min, compared to those of the newly electrified LNW route at well over one hour less.

A fare deal

But, if BR were going to attract passengers to their new railway, then fares would have be a key factor. Back in 1960 the railways were still in a strong position as regards inter-city travel. Little motorway construction had been undertaken, something that kept the express bus competition at bay, as well as the private car. Fast road travel between Manchester and London was not an option until almost the end of 1971 when the last link between the M6 and M1 opened south of Birmingham. Looking first at the initial

Nuneaton Trent Valley, c.1964: It was on January 3rd 1964 when the catenary became live from Stafford to Nuneaton and 25kV working from that point began on March 2nd. BR must have been proud of this as their official photographer was despatched to the station to catch the moment for posterity as E3079 backs down to take a Down express onward over the next leg of its journey. The bridge in the background carries the Midland Railway's line from Leicester along to the town's Abbey Street station. *British Railways*

period of full electrification: Cheap Day Return fares in April 1966 were set at 40% of Ordinary fares and Period Returns could be had at a 20% discount. The new timetable (18/04/66 to 05/03/67) shows an Ordinary Return fare from London to Manchester of £5.00.

Staying with fares for a little longer, back in summer 1960 BR offered Day Excursion tickets to London from both Manchester Central and Victoria (the latter used as part of the diversionary route). These were available on Wednesday mornings; departing from Central at 7.25 or Victoria 8.00; arrival at St.Pancras was 11.20/Euston 1.14; Thursday and Friday nights departures were 11.45/11.36; arrivals-St.Pancras 5.30 am/Euston 4.35 am. Saturday morning departures could be had only from Central-at 7.25 arriving in St.Pancras at 11.45. Departures from London were between 6.00 pm and 1.00 am. Second Class fares were charged at 38/3d or 37/3d if Stockport was used. Tickets at similar prices could be had from a whole host of stations in and around the Manchester area. Unabashed by on-going engineering work south

of Crewe, a year or two later BR still promoted the London day excursion. A leaflet for the winter of 1961/62 shows journeys available for the bargain price of 42/6 (£2.12½p). Though the Midland route to St.Pancras was used, there were nevertheless departures from Piccadilly; one at 8.15 am on Wednesdays; the other at 12.05 on Thursdays. Using Saturday, a departure at the very respectable time of 7.20 could be had from Central, arriving in St.Pancras at 11.25.

INCREASING RETURNS

Come 1979 and an "Economy Return" to Euston could be had for £12.50. Standard Returns had by then jumped to £23.20 and there were also "Awayday Returns", "Weekend Returns" and "Monthly Returns". This was the age of the "Merrymaker Return", a monthly excursion programme to a whole range of destinations at incredibly low prices. For example: Newcastle and back for £3.75, Southampton £4.50, Edinburgh £4.50 and Aberdeen for £6.50. A leaflet dated January-May 1981 and

MERRYMAKER

Bargain offers from the Manchester area

By Special and Selected Trains

January to May 1981

Ideas for days out by train

take advantage, too, by using the much earlier train at 0030! Though some mid-day returns were permitted (at 1150 and 1350), the ordinary tripper had to come back at 1935, 2025 or even at 2350.

LIVE TO BIRMINGHAM VIA THE POTTERIES

On June 15th 1966 the overhead line between Macclesfield and Kidsgrove, where the line from Crewe came in, was energised. On-going work on the new line by-passing the old Harecastle tunnels had delayed the completion of the Potteries Loop programme in the interim. Benjamin Fowler might well have travelled north again, for the opening of the new tunnel on June 27th. George Dow led a party of officials and members of the press in a 2-car DMU for the official opening. With the advent of the new timetable all trains from Birmingham to Manchester and Liverpool were electrically-hauled from Wolverhampton. The first such working was with E3126 which took the 09.05 Birmingham-Manchester. Type 4 Diesels bringing up the rear from New Street. New Street went live on November 16th when E3040 arrived for circuit testing. Electric services in and out Birmingham made their debut on December 6th with the appearance of the 0015 Euston to Crewe newspaper train, a service which had plied that route for many years. From March 1967 it was planned that the "West Coast Postal" train would exchange mail at New Street instead of at Tamworth as hitherto. Tamworth had been a centre for the exchange of mail right back to coaching days-some 2,000 bags of mail per night being exchanged there between the high-level, the former Midland Birmingham-Derby line and the low level, LNW Trent Valley stations. Though hindsight can be expressed as 20/20 vision, it seems a waste of resources that BR had spent large sums of money only as recently as 1962 on a costly rebuilding programme of the two stations at Tamworth, though some work was allied directly to the electrification works. Today, of course, almost all postal traffic has gone from the railway.

END OF THE GREAT CENTRAL

Unconnected with the coverage of the Manchester-Crewe story, but none the less certainly relevant to Manchester-London expresses hitherto, it is sad to record that, from September 5th 1966 passenger services over the former GC main line between Nottingham Victoria and Sheffield were withdrawn. To go as well were those between Aylesbury and Rugby, although a token service between Nottingham and Rugby would continue. Track lifting south of Rugby commenced in February 1967. Nottingham Victoria closed on September 2nd that year. Incredibly, this section of main line had lasted for just 69 years.

THE LAST LINK IN THE CHAIN IS FORGED

Electric services commenced between Macclesfield, Stoke and Stafford on December 5th, but had to be withdrawn two days later due to wiring faults in the new tunnel at Harecastle. What would Mr.Dow have thought one wonders? Working to Stoke-on-Trent finally commenced on January 1st 1967, though only to previous Diesel timings. This event recalls the use of EMUs on Stoke-Manchester services, something long done away with. A small aside recalls that this month saw the connection of Manchester's Mayfield station to the electrified network. Then functioning as a

promoted by Jimmy Saville offered another entire programme of similar bargain fares. Also on offer was an "Awayday Return" from Manchester to London for £18.20, the proviso being that one had to travel after 09.30 on a weekday, though any train could be used on Saturdays, Sundays and Bank Holidays. Weekend returns to a whole range of places could be had then: outward on Friday, Saturday or Sunday, returning on Saturday, Sunday or Monday. Such a ticket to London cost £22.60.

"Capital Fares" were seen in 1980/81 and cost £10.00 Second Class (a mere £12.00 for First Class). Travel was restricted to the 09.34 or 10.12 outward and 18.25 or 19.25 return. This was a period of chronic overcrowding, especially on the evening trains. The author remembers such a journey one January when a relief train was put on at Euston, fulfilling a great need after a long slog of a day. Alas, the train had no heat and no refreshments either! "London Savers" were well promoted in 1985. Prices were set at £14.50 on Saturdays to Thursdays (Railcard holders £12.50) and £19.50 (£17.50) on Fridays. Early risers could certainly benefit, with travel being allowed on the 06.20 service; insomniacs could

MANCHESTER
PICCADILLY

Yesterday's commonplace is today's history. Few enthusiasts would have given this scene a second glance at the time. A Class AL5 standing by the buffer stops with a train of BR Mk II coaches in the blue and pearl grey BR corporate livery. But mention of such a sight today would almost certainly bring waves of enthusiasts armed to the teeth with digital and video cameras. And so we could repeat the process over and over again back to the dawn of picture taking. Its express run over, **E3076** awaits its turn to leave the station resting by the buffers at the end of platform 7. Under the TOPS regime, from October 1973, this locomotive became Class 85 (021) before becoming 85 106 in July 1989.

Built by a joint BR/Doncaster/AEI collaboration, the AL5's, as they were originally designated, were unique inasmuch as they were built in a BR workshop-the first 25kV locomotives to be so constructed. The example seen here was turned out from Doncaster in April 1963. Rheostatic braking was incorporated at the outset; though this had to quickly modified to automatic operation by linking it to the driver's brake valve. A former AEI engineer related that the steam-age practice of relying on the wheel brakes alone was "wearing out brake blocks for fun". As 85 106, the erstwhile E3076 was withdrawn in October 1990.

Authors collection

parcels concentration depot, Mayfield was fed via an overhead bridge from the adjacent Post Office parcels depot in Ancoats on the north-west side of the Piccadilly approach tracks.

MOTIVE POWER DEVELOPMENT POST-1967

After services to St.Pancras were withdrawn in 1967, the former LNW route, now universally known as part of the "WCML", became the monopoly provider of Manchester-London rail traffic. The original 25kV locomotives, the Class AL1-AL6 Bo-Bos, became Classes 81-86. The Class 86 was to prove a ground-breaking and long-lasting design(Q.V). Several of the sub-class, 86/2, were equipped for push-pull working on the Euston-Manchester expresses. Following on from the Class 86 came the Class 87 with a slightly higher top speed (110 mph) introduced in 1973 ready for when full electrification between Euston to Glasgow was operable with the summer timetable of 1974.

Class 89 locomotives first appeared in Manchester on May 1st 1987 when 89 001 appeared at Longsight with a train of Mark IV coaches and two test vehicles.

Between 1987-1990 the British Rail Class 90 electric locomotives were built by BREL at Crewe Works. Distinguishable at once from their predecessors by their sloping front ends, the Class 90 had a top speed of 110 mph. Built primarily to replace their now ageing forebears, the 90s employed a new technology known as a Time Division Multiplexer (TDM). This enabled not only multiple working (i.e.in pairs) but, revolutionary-as far as modern express working was concerned, what was effectively push-pull working via a Driving Van Trailer (DVT). Technically, this was known as a DBSO or Propelling Control Vehicle. This concept was not, of course, a new one; having a history well back into steam days. The chief advantage lay in operating: at terminal stations it was no longer necessary for the locomotive either to uncouple or to run round the train. But there were disadvantages: failure of the control equipment meant reversion to ordinary working; time-consuming as the locomotive had to be uncoupled and placed in front of the DVT.

CLASS 90s APPEAR IN MANCHESTER

Driver training, a necessary precursor to the introduction of new motive power, began in Manchester on August 15th 1988 with 90002 doing two trips daily over the Potteries Loop line; 90008 took over on August 29th. Early the following year, three of the class appeared in Piccadilly: 90002 appeared on the 14.18 to Birmingham International; 90011 took charge of the 12.00 express to Euston, while 90019 headed the 15.30 to Euston. Push-pull, using the DVT system, commenced operation on Monday, November 27th 1989; the Manchester Pullman sets being the first trains to be so-operated. The dedicated Class 90s really were just that, remaining attached to their trains overnight, something that forced maintenance to be done in Longsight carriage sheds.

But whatever the various operating headaches, from late 1989 onwards, the Class 90s and their DVTs became the norm on the Manchester-London route, though the faithful Class 86s were still to be seen up to September 2003. In the wake of the hotly-debated Rail Privatisation the Virgin flag was hoisted and loco-hauled trains would soon be a thing of the past. Their replacements, from 2002, were the 9-car Class 390 Pendolino tilting trains, ushering in a completely new concept in inter-city rail travel. Pendolino, though, is the present and the future and this is the point where our Manchester-London story must end.

ELECTRIFICATION AT 25kV AC -- WHY ?

(Right) The first British Railways built Class AL5 locomotive, No **3057**, to be completed and tested at Doncaster Works (3056 had been despatched as a mock up to the Battersea Power Station Exhibition in 1961). In the cab is AEI Traction Project Engineer, Peter Bosomworth whilst Joe Brown stands in the doorway. The loco would be finish painted after testing.

The history of electric traction on British railways is both long and complex. Now, in the 21st century, even the most ardent disciples of the steam locomotive must look back and realise that steam locomotion-applied via a coal-fired boiler and fed to the rails by coupled motion-was not the most effective means of using coal. Far more efficient use can be made of fossil fuels when they are burnt under controlled conditions in a power station. The resultant power force is, however, still steam, a point lost on many technically inept journalists who, to this day, use phrases such as …*this old-fashioned steam power*. To George Stephenson, true pioneer of rail steam locomotion, is alluded the quote: *"I have the credit of being the inventor of the locomotive and it is true I have done something to improve the action of steam for that purpose. But I tell you, young man, that the day will come when electricity will be the great motive power of the world"*.

That remark was made in 1847. In his book-*Woodhead, the Electric Railway*-(Foxline 2001)-the author, under the heading *Electrification Develops*, set out a summary of British progress in this field and it is not the intention to re-gurgitate it here. The emphasis in the Woodhead book was geared towards the MSW (Manchester-Sheffield-Wath) 1500v dc scheme. Hatched by the LNER in 1936, an electrified railway was seen as the most efficient way of transporting huge volumes of coal from the South Yorkshire coalfield over the Pennines to Manchester and Merseyside.

Sadly, the MSW scheme came and went. Interrupted by the Second War, it was never completed to its original full format-something that might, just, have ensured its survival. Geared, overall, to freight traffic it suffered the misfortune of succumbing to the downfall of the British coal industry. More importantly, it was eclipsed by a system of electrification that had developed post-War across the Channel. That system was 25kV ac. The use of electricity, described at what is technically termed "industrial single-phase current" for main line use had been trialled in 1950 when a 20,000V single-phase, 50-cycle locomotive (CC 6051) was tested on the newly electrified line from Aix-les-Bains to Annecy. CC 6051 was a dual voltage machine capable of working on either 1500V dc, or 20,000V 50-cycle ac. It would perhaps be pertinent here to mention that, as far back as 1913, the French government, alarmed at the fact that the country's steam locomotives were consuming in excess of 10% of France's entire national coal output, set up a committee to travel world-wide and to report back on the feasibility of a wholesale railway electrification programme. Though initially 1500v dc had, in the main, been used-it was the country's post-Second war applications that are of primary interest here.

Buoyed by the success of this first dual-voltage machine, French National Railways (SNCF) went on in 1953 to use high tension current at 50-cycles for electrification of the line from Valenciennes, near Lille to Thionville, in Eastern Lorraine. Speaking at the time to the Society of French Civil Engineers, M.Louis Armand, SNCF Director-General, reported that some 6,200 miles of main line would be electrified in France during the next ten years. Following on from the completion of the Valenciennes-Thionville scheme, the 25kV would be extended to cover the Paris to Strasbourg line. Significantly, M.Armand reported that Russia had plans to equip no less than 11,600 miles of railway on the 50-cycle system.

This is not to say that such a system was entirely a Gallic innovation. In 1906 the Midland Railway had electrified the Lancaster-Morecambe-Heysham lines following experiments between Morecambe and Heysham earlier that year. A single-phase system was used with 6,600 volts at 25 cycles. Interestingly, power to the system was supplied originally by a gas engine generator set at Heysham Dock. By way of a precursor to use of the more modern 50-cycles system at home, the Lancaster-Morecambe-Heysham scheme was adapted to use this frequency from August 1953 following experiments at the end of the previous year. Other railways had used AC systems, but these had been at low-frequency and at much lower voltages than what was proposed in the early 1950s.

But it had not been without some hesitation that British Railways adopted high voltage ac. Soon after Nationalisation, in September1948, the BTC commissioned a report into railway electrification. A remit consisting of six propositions was put forward for consideration. The committee took their time: the report was not published until March 1951. Four systems of electrification were considered by the BTC committee: 750V dc; 1,500V dc; 3,000V dc and 20,000V ac. Comparative costings were set out for a four-track main line. Overall, 3,000V dc faired the best, 1,500V dc, was second, 750V dc third and the dearest was 20,000V ac. A summary appendage noted.. *"It is considered that the possibility of using 50-cycle ac for traction is a development that may prove of considerable importance, and the various systems now being tested are reviewed."* Feeling that ac systems were still of an experi-

East Didsbury, November 1959: History in the making. The first of the initial 23 production Class AL1 25kV ac Bo-Bos, No.**E3001**, stands ready for trials outside the East Didsbury sidings. The locomotive will have just been delivered from the Birmingham Railway Carriage & Wagon Co's works at Smethwick, Birmingham. BRC&W supplied the body and mechanical parts, BTH (then as part of AEI) supplied the motors. Apart from being the first production 25kV locomotives, the AL1s comprised many new features: Alsthom rubber cone pivot body suspension, Stone-Faiveley pantographs, double-skin glass fibre mouldings for the main and cab roofs, integral electrical de-misting and de-icing for the windscreens, mercury-arc rectifiers and the ability to work at dual voltage-25kV and 6.25kV. E3001 is seen with its right-hand side facing the camera. No.1 end is on the right, No.2 is at the rear. The locomotives, weighing 80 tons, turned out 3,300 (continuous) h.p. and had a top speed of 100 mph. E3001's actual delivery date to BR was Friday, November 27th.

Collection of *J Brown*

mental nature, coupled with the technical drawbacks and the increased cost of locomotives-all caused the committee to hold back on ac. That much said, they did-as previously indicated-authorise the up-dating of the high voltage Lancaster-Morecambe-Heysham ac scheme. There were also expressed further technical reservations: would a large single-phase load have an unbalancing effect on the national three-phase supply system? Would high-voltage ac affect railway telecommunications? And, this quite prophetic postulation: what of inter-regional running between a possible new standard system of electrification and the existing 750V dc system on ex-SR lines?

So, with all this in mind and especially considering the commitment in hand to the MSW scheme, the findings favoured continuation of the 1500v dc system, the same as had been recommended in the Pringle report of 1927. (A previous committee, under Sir Alexander Kennedy, had come up with the same system back in October 1920). What has largely gone unreported is the consideration by the 1951 committee of the use of 3,000V dc for secondary lines where traffic was light. And for the first time, an awareness of the use of Diesel traction as an alternative to electrification was put into the frame.

Moving on to 1954 and the publication in December of the BTC's report-*"Modernisation of British Railways"*. A separate dossier was published entitled: *"The System of Electrification for British Railways"*. Though reports tend to be presented by committees, one name stands out above all others in respect of the decision to apply 25kV ac as the new system of electrification. Mr.S.B.Warder had been appointed Chief Officer for electrical engineering on the BTC in 1953. Later, when the BRB was formed in January 1963, Warder became the board's Chief Electrical Engineer. Warder's ideas and principles were summarised in a paper entitled "Railway Electrification in the Twentieth Century. This formed part of a comprehensive package presented at a technical conference in London in October 1966 under the heading "Euston Main Line Electrification".

Back to the mid-1950s and much was happening. Firstly, progress had been made with mercury-arc rectifiers and trials had been made with on-board germanium rectifiers; such devices having been successfully used on an EMU on the Lancaster-Morecambe line. The committee was proud to note that this was a world "first" for Britain. Secondly, following the successful completion of the electrification of the Valenciennes-Thionville line

Dukinfield Works, May 12th 1955: It would be easy to write off the Western Region's essay in gas-turbine propulsion as a failure. But this is not so; the two locomotives acquitted themselves well in terms of power output and successful haulage over the steep gradients of the West of England main line. That some problems were encountered is no surprise; this was a revolutionary form of traction, at least in the UK, little time had been given for crew training and only a small number of men were familiar with this new form of motive power. Nevertheless, sadly, the brave experiment-which had been planned by the GWR-was abandoned. No.18100, in the meantime, was to become a pioneer of a different sort. Full details of this are given elsewhere, but before moving on, here is a fascinating photograph. At this date the locomotive was some way off

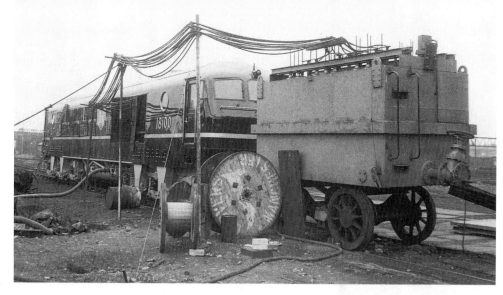

withdrawal and her future re-incarnation had not been mooted. So it can be safely assumed that some further trials of this most fascinating locomotive are in progress. Seen outside the works, 18100 has her three generators connected for some kind of possible load testing experiments. The box-shaped apparatus at the front is, maybe a resistance bank or a transformer in which oil-cooling is in evidence. Notice the cable drums marked "Glovers-Manchester". Cable-makers to the world, Glovers were co-habitees of Trafford Park where 18100's makers-Metro-Vicks-were domiciled. It would be interesting to know the provenance of the locomotive bogie! *Graham Whitehead*

the previous year, SNCF held a conference at Lille in May 1955. Here they presented complete results of their experiences. Suffice it to say that the French engineers' faith in their new system had been vindicated: locomotives were cheaper to produce; overhead line structures, along with the contact wire itself, could be lighter and feeder stations could be spaced much further apart. A subtle point raised in the home report was the interests of international standardisation-helping world trade and British exports-how the world has changed since then!

Prefacing the 1955 report was a map showing routes deemed suitable for electrification. Taking centre stage was the Manchester/Liverpool-Crewe-Trent Valley/Birmingham-Euston lines. Added to these was the Glasgow suburban network, extension of the existing ex-GER electrified line from Chelmsford as far out as Ipswich, Felixstowe and Harwich and extension of the former Southern Railway 750V dc lines to the coastal resorts of Ramsgate, Dover and Folkestone. The East Coast route-King's Cross to Newcastle was shown as being considered for electrification only as far as Leeds and (possibly)York respectively. The grand ECML scheme that came to fruition in the early 1980s-taking the wire as far north as Newcastle, then on to Berwick-on-Tweed and Edinburgh was, as yet, a mere twinkle in the eye.

The crunch, as ever, was cost. Section 67 of the report said it all: the total estimated capital cost of the supply of power for the Euston-Manchester-Liverpool scheme was set at an estimated £29.3M for 25kV ac; costs for a 1,500V dc system were estimated at £38.6M. A further £1M per annum (this was in 1955, remember) could also be saved in maintenance and depreciation of fixed equipment, signalling and motive power. Included in this were savings in the cost of electricity and compound interest on capital. Upon the subject of motive power, the report opined that there would little difference in the total cost of locomotive units between ac and dc systems. In considering the numbers of locomotives required to operate the Western lines services, the committee were way over-optimistic. No less than 660 ac locomotives were deemed to be necessary. Of these, 510 would be of the mixed-traffic type. Should dc power turn out to be favourite, then 720 units would be needed. In the event, the system ran with a mere 225 locomotives (1979 stockbook figures).

One final problem in the application of a 25kV ac system had yet to be resolved. The committee had noted that on the main line from King's Cross to York the average number of bridges per mile was less than 50% of that on the Euston-Manchester-Liverpool lines. Overbridges meant clearance problems in maintaining a safe distance between the contact wire and the underside of the bridge to minimise the risk of flashover-especially in damp conditions. Clearance could be increased either by lowering the track, as was done in the early years of the 25kV scheme on some parts of the Styal line, raising the bridge decking-of which there were numerous examples, or-in the case of tunnels, by opening them out, for example on the south side of Stockport's Edgeley station. More simply the voltage could be reduced to 6.6kV and this was actively considered in the report. 6.6kV was indeed used on some of the ex-GER lines and was considered for use on the LMR south of Kenton. In the event, the use of the lower voltage was abandoned after experience had been gained with better insulation techniques.

Regarding the Manchester area it is worth mentioning that the report saw no justification in up-grading the Manchester-Bury line to 25kV-due largely to the number of bridges and a tunnel, though 6.6kV ac was being considered. Neither did it consider that the MSJ&A line should be converted in the immediate future as the line used a separate platform at London Road. However, it was noted that when equipment needed renewal the conversion could be executed.

No extensions to the existing 1,500v dc MSW system were envisaged back in 1955. Moreover, the rider was added... *"but when it is desired to make them (extensions), and so bring the line into working contact with the London Midland and Eastern Region main lines, it will be necessary to face conversion to obtain full inter-running"*. With full electric working now from both Wath and from Sheffield Victoria to Manchester those words seem prophetic for their time. Little did anyone think then that the MSW scheme was doomed to last for so little time.

That story, though, has been told. and following a brief diversion to look at the introduction of the AM4 EMU's and construction of the locomotives at Doncaster, it will be time to march again along the line from Manchester to Crewe, initially taking the 'Styal Line' to Wilmslow.

Between Heald Green and Styal, c.April 1960: An official record shot taken just past bridge No.13 by the AEI official photographer to record an AM4 EMU on the newly-electrified railway. Thirty-five four-car trains were built by BR at Wolverton, electrical equipment being supplied by BTH (then a part of AEI's traction division). Classified "AM4", the first fifteen sets were ordered for the Manchester-Crewe services; a further twenty were to come onstream in January 1962 for Crewe-Liverpool services. Nine more sets appeared in early 1962 for Crewe-Stafford services. The Manchester trains were made up as follows: driving trailer open second, motor brake second, trailer composite and driving trailer open brake second-the reverse order of the set depicted which has yet to receive its running number. (The front vehicle is numbered M 75645. Total seating was 19 first class and 318 second class. On the Liverpool sets the motor second brake (MSB) was an open saloon. On the Manchester trains compartments were used in the MSB, the other three vehicles having seating in the open saloon pattern (except in the first class section). Liverpool sets had seating capacity for 19 first class and 294 second class passengers. The difference in seats being due to the provision of a large luggage section in the MSBs of the latter. In each case the first class seats were set in compartment style with a side corridor. Toilets were provided in the driving trailer open second and in the composite-each class had its own lavatory! In the Manchester sets a "Ladies Only" compartment was provided in the motor second brake immediately behind the guard's area. As a social aside it is worth noting that only four compartments (in the MSB) were non-smoking. No through access was provided from one coach to another.

Body construction followed conventional practice, being of welded steel construction to 16g. Double skins were used for the body sides, on the Manchester sets these were filled with fibreglass wool; the Liverpool sets, curiously, used sprayed asbestos. A light alloy was used for the doors, these being of the conventional hinged type. The three non-powered coaches ran on 8ft. 6in. Gresley-pattern bogies, a tribute to the design; but perhaps most enthusiasts have forgotten that the great man was designing coaching stock before locomotives! The motor car weighed 53 tons 12 cwt., some 18 tons heavier than the driving trailer and a whole 22 tons more than the other two vehicles. The overall length of the train was 264 ft.6½in. Service speed was a maximum of 75 mph.

The four traction motors, connected in parallel, were six-pole, nose-suspended, self-ventilating machines. They had a power output each of 190/207 bhp (weak field/full field (continuous rating) or 212/220 bhp (1hr.rating). A single Stone-Faiveley pantograph was sited above the motor second brake on a recessed roof section with the air-blast circuit breaker alongside. All the main electrical equipment-transformer, rectifier, oil-cooling gear and contactor cubicle were housed underneath between the two bogies. Air brakes were provided throughout, compressed air being supplied by a Westinghouse CM38 compressor.

Appearing in the (then) BR standard colour of dark green with a single yellow stripe, liveries altered over the years to BR overall blue, then to blue and white-arguably the most attractive of the liveries worn by these trains. Perhaps the worst, though the writer accepts that such things are subjective, was the GMPTE tangerine and brown. The "AM4" designation gave way to Class 304 under the TOPS scheme. As Class 304, the 1960 EMUs served their masters well and were the mainstay of the local electric services for many years. In later years the trailer composite coaches were taken from the sets, leaving 3 cars each only. After 1970 when through running from Altrincham via Manchester Piccadilly to Crewe became the norm, Styal line services had a regular half-hour interval service of stopping trains and locals remember well the clockwork-like precision of the timetable. Before closure of the Altrincham line to BR traffic in December 1992, ...*concluded on page 28*

..........in readiness for the arrival of Metrolink, the 304s were becoming life-expired and were being withdrawn. From the beginning of 1992 their place was taken by the 305 EMUs-units dating from 1960 and introduced for ER services. A dozen of the Class 303 Glasgow units, inter alia, had augmented services in the interim years. Towards the end of 1994 only one of the 304s-No.019-was active in the Manchester area. All had gone by the end of 1996.

Collection of *J.Brown*

(Right) Wilmslow, c.1962. The half minute allowed at Wilmslow is being used to good effect by the guard during this brief call on the journey between Manchester Oxford Road and Alderley Edge via the Styal line. This AM4 four car set, No **045**, was the last of the 'Class' to be built for the Crewe to Manchester/Liverpool/Stafford stopping services, from a design introduced in 1960. The small yellow warning panel is a recent addition, in fact it may well have been applied when the unit was built, given the lateness of its construction. Set 045 was designated Class 304/3 under the TOPS scheme, one of nine units so identified. The four digit route indicator shows 2H51, the number 2 indicating a class B stopping passenger train, the letter H denoting its Manchester South District origins and the number 51 referring to the particular route, Alderley Edge and Manchester (Oxford Road) via Styal. The service was half-hourly throughout the day with extra trains at peak times, scheduled to take 30 minutes end to end either way.

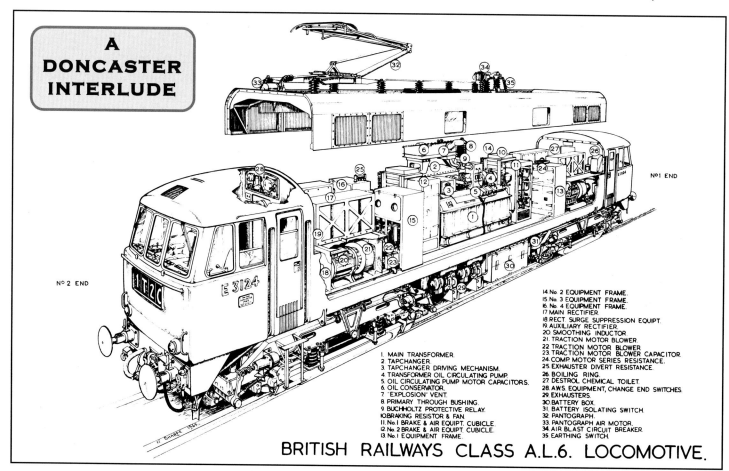

A DONCASTER INTERLUDE

NO1 END

NO 2 END

E 3124

1. MAIN TRANSFORMER.
2. TAPCHANGER.
3. TAPCHANGER DRIVING MECHANISM.
4. TRANSFORMER OIL CIRCULATING PUMP.
5. OIL CIRCULATING PUMP MOTOR CAPACITORS.
6. OIL CONSERVATOR.
7. "EXPLOSION" VENT.
8. PRIMARY THROUGH BUSHING.
9. BUCHHOLTZ PROTECTIVE RELAY.
10. BRAKING RESISTOR & FAN.
11. No.1 BRAKE & AIR EQUIPT. CUBICLE.
12. No.2 BRAKE & AIR EQUIPT. CUBICLE.
13. No.1 EQUIPMENT FRAME.

14. No.2 EQUIPMENT FRAME.
15. No.3 EQUIPMENT FRAME.
16. No.4 EQUIPMENT FRAME.
17. MAIN RECTIFIER.
18. RECT. SURGE SUPPRESSION EQUIPT.
19. AUXILIARY RECTIFIER.
20. SMOOTHING INDUCTOR.
21. TRACTION MOTOR BLOWER.
22. TRACTION MOTOR BLOWER.
23. TRACTION MOTOR BLOWER CAPACITOR.
24. COMP MOTOR SERIES RESISTANCE.
25. EXHAUSTER DIVERT RESISTANCE.
26. BOILING RING.
27. DESTROL CHEMICAL TOILET.
28. A.W.S. EQUIPMENT, CHANGE END SWITCHES.
29. EXHAUSTERS.
30. BATTERY BOX.
31. BATTERY ISOLATING SWITCH.
32. PANTOGRAPH.
33. PANTOGRAPH AIR MOTOR.
34. AIR BLAST CIRCUIT BREAKER.
35. EARTHING SWITCH.

BRITISH RAILWAYS CLASS A.L.6. LOCOMOTIVE.

Class AL6, how does it work? For publicity purposes Doncaster Works produced this excellent schematic drawing showing the main components of an AL6. The roof section of the locomotives was in actual fact a separate entity as one of the workshop photographs reveals. Such drawings were a child of their time. Readers may well remember a contemporary illustration by L.Ashwell-Wood in the celebrated "Eagle" weekly, one could hardly term it a mere "comic". Technically accurate and beautifully-executed, the electric locomotive appeared in a sort of sickly-looking green!

British Railways

Doncaster Works, 1965: Class 86 underframes are the subject of this view and five sets in various stages of construction appear in this photograph. Looking like some gigantic piece of fretwork, the assemblies, some 53ft. long, were essentially fabrications. Works of art in aluminium and steel they were of cellular-like construction-a technique giving both great strength and saving weight in the process. The set over to the left has the underside of the locomotive facing upwards, No.1 end is on the left-hand side. Notice the transverse beams for the bogies appearing as raised cross sections with a circular aperture in the centre. On the AL6 the loco body was supported on the bogie by a pivot consisting of a rubber cone which could flex according to body movement. This was later modified and use of the "Flexicoil" bogie evolved (Q.V.) Angled upwards and forming a deep section at the front, these are for the drawhooks and buffing gear. Once this welded assembly is complete it will be turned over, joined together and a second cell set welded to it to form the locomotive's floor pan-making a very rigid box structure. On this can then be mounted all the necessary control gear, bulkheads, transformers and ancillary equipment. In the right foreground progress is being made with a further locomotive as side panels and a cab roof section are welded into place. *British Railways*

CONSTRUCTION OF THE AL6 (CLASS 86) LOCOMOTIVES AT DONCASTER

Well-remembered by the author is a visit to Doncaster locomotive works in March 1961 with the Manchester Locomotive Society. Two sights stand out from that memorable Sunday afternoon trip: one was the appearance of the A4 Pacific, *Walter K.Whigham* standing in the erecting shop, half-dressed and with just a chalked number, **60028** on the front of its streamlined casing for identification of this East Coast celebrity. Further along the shop, a cluster of bauxite-coloured steel boxes caught the eye. These were the first of the Class AL5 Bo-Bos, later Class 85, forty

of which were turned out from the famous "Plant" between June 1961 and December 1964. Hereafter, the British Railways Board, guided by their Chief Electrical Engineer, S.B.Warder, used experience gained from the first five production series of 25kv Bo-Bo (AL1-5). And so a second generation of locomotive was outlined on the drawing board. This was to be the popular and successful AL6 (Class 86).

No less than one hundred AL6s were turned out. Doncaster built the first forty and these were outshopped from June 1965 to March 1966; production, clearly, having been maintained from the previous AL5 series. Reflecting on this series of locomotives, it is interesting to see just how much of a "joint venture" the design

Doncaster Works,1965. With underframes completed it was time to begin the assembly of the body proper. Here is E3139 (later 86 043) taking shape-chalked on the cab bulkhead can be seen "39 loco 1 end." Various other instructions, all using the time-honoured workshop chalk, appear scribbled around the body-e.g. "drill so" etc. Inside the cab a welder, his face protected by the vital helmet with glare shield, busies himself with his electric arc-welding bit. On the raised platform, a second welder uses a pneumatic angle grinder to dress and face off completed welded joints. Up front, buffers are bolted in place and the draw hook has been fitted. On the underside the exhausters are in place, a third worker having moved during the long exposure, notice the "ghosted" hands. A fourth man, a fitter, is seen assembling equipment in the cab console area. 86 043 was withdrawn in November 2002. *British Railways*

and execution was. English Electric had sub-contracted the motor design to AEI and this company produced the traction motor designated AEI 282BZ. The four machines between them were capable of producing 4,040 h.p.and were used in Doncaster-built AL6s. The remaining 60 of the class were built at English Electric's (EE) Vulcan Foundry at Newton-le-Willows in Lancashire. These, appearing from August 1965 to October 1966, were equipped with slightly less powerful motors. This pattern, categorised as AEI282AZ, turning out a combined 3,600 h.p. EE provided control gear, transformers and rectifiers, these now consisting of the silicon semi-conductor type. AEI had taken charge of motor design, along with a key feature of the new locos-an automatic rheostatic braking system. Originally developed in America, regenerative and the later rheostatic braking had been used on the 1,500V dc MSW electrics and was continued through into the AL1-5 series with 25kV. But, as one former AEI engineer related to the author, "we were going through brake blocks as if they were going out of fashion". This, he continued, was due to the drivers applying former steam locomotive practice. With the new system built in, the electrical back emf took the brunt of the braking away from the wheel treads.

Several other points marked the design out from earlier generations of 25kV locos. Principal amongst these was the abandonment of the flexible drive system with a return to the conventional axle-hung nose-suspended traction motors, the lack of voltage changeover equipment and the use of a single pantograph of the Stone-Faiveley design, though ten of the class were fitted with AEI's own "crossarm" pantographs as opposed to the Stone-Faiveley pattern used on the others. As the class entered traffic and began revenue-earning service, various further modifications were put in place; indeed, the history of this long-lived and successful class is a most complex one. In 1972, 61 of the 86s were rebuilt with higher-powered motors: three (86 101-103) were equipped with 5,000 h.p.traction (via four motors) and 58 (86 204-86 261) could produce 4,040 h.p, again, via four motors. A final difference with is mid-1960s design was the use of individual "power packs" for each motor. The first series of 25kV Bo-Bos had used rectifiers of the mercury arc type. These fed the smoothed (dc) current to the motors from a single point. Now, a silicon rectifier, along with a smoothing choke and a blower unit was fitted to each motor. Each of the so-called "power packs" was fed from its own individual secondary winding on the main transformer.

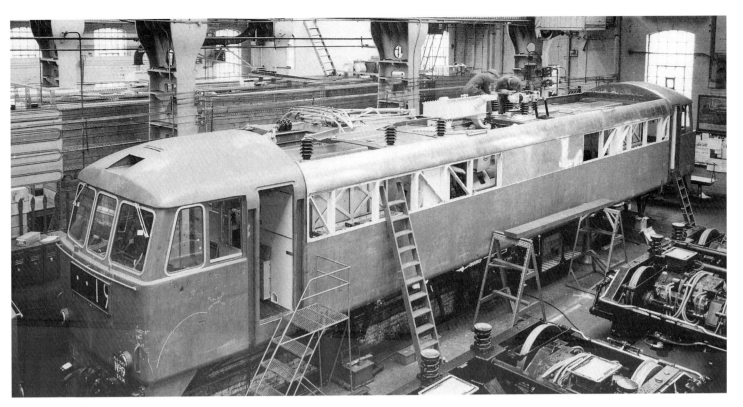

Doncaster Works, 1965: With the superstructure finished and the electrical gear bolted down inside, the whole entity was beginning to resemble a locomotive. Here is one such. Identifiable only as "No.9", this locomotive looks all but ready for lifting off the brick supporting piers and onto its bogies. Extensive use had been made of aluminium and fibreglass for weight saving. Sound insulation had been considered too, though cab floors remained in wood. Provision had been made in all the "AL" series for at least some crew comfort. Padded seats were provided and even toilet and cooking facilities (not a good mix!) were catered for. Around the loco's top centre, notice the oil-cooling unit with the tank and breather on top close to atmosphere and adjacent cooling system. Two engineers are working on the roof; they appear to be engaged with the air-blast circuit breaker and earthing switch situated hereabouts. On the shop floor to one side, the bogies with their motors and wiring harness in place are ready to receive the weight of the locomotive; some 82 tons in all. A last note concerns a sundry, yet vital, fitting-the locomotive's windscreen wipers. On the AL1-6 series the wipers had been mounted at the top of the screen. Over the years this had led to complaints from crews of the whole assemble being blown away from the screen's surface whilst at speed, with consequent serious vision problems. For some time the matter had gone unresolved until one of AEI's bright young engineers came up with a solution: mount the wipers beneath the screen just as in a motor car. Thus positioned, the assembly would be pressed firmly against the glass by air pressure. The suggestion was adopted for subsequent classes, although the Class 92 electrics have reverted to a top-hung assembly once more.　　　　　　　　　　*British Railways*

Birmingham RC&W, 1958: Not quite Doncaster but a rare chance to peep inside a 25kV ac AL1 Bo-Bo electric locomotive while under construction. Anyone who has seen the interior of such a power unit will have been amazed as to how much technical wizardry exists between the point of current collection-the pantograph- and the traction motors. Looking down on a scene of, incredibly, almost 50 years ago now, some of the "guts" of this remarkable machine can be made out. At the top right-hand side the No.1 end traction motor blower is housed. There were four motors, one to each axle; of 6-pole construction these were permanently connected in parallel. Moving down, the device with the transverse bus bars is the camshaft control unit actuated by the driver's master controller and providing 37 accelerating notches and 2 field-weakening notches. The "spaghetti" of cabling is the arrangement for the tapping connections and lead from the main transformer below. To the right here-the rectangular devices with grids on top and pipe connections-are the two Serck radiators for the transformer oil cooling. At deck level an electrically-driven pump circulated oil at 300 gallons per minute through the radiators. Completing the main ensemble in the centre of the lower part of the chamber are the three mercury-arc rectifiers. Here the transformer output current was converted from ac to dc before being fed to the traction motors. Each rectifier had its own automatic temperature control: air was drawn in through the body side and was fed to the base of the unit. The air was then discharged up to the roof chamber and was vented to atmosphere. Temperature was maintained via thermostats and body-side shutters. On the right-hand side can be seen the three cooling and circulating shutters. The corridor is on the left-hand side. Behind the cab roof the pantograph operating cylinders can be glimpsed.

Collection of *J.Brown*

Doncaster Works, 1965: The modernisation of British Railways had presented the UK's electrical engineers with tough new challenges. Dc traction, fed from third rail or overhead line, although well-established, was rapidly becoming "old hat". Much research and development would be needed before the new order would be perfected. Here, then, is the product of such "R&D": a joint production of the English Electric Co. and AEI-a complete unit comprising the essential electrical guts of the Class 86 loco. Whatever one's thoughts about modern traction, surely none could fail to be impressed by the sight of this beautifully-finished piece of British electrical engineering. On the ground, an engineer works away with an air-operated tool as the 45 ton crane dangles the finished product ready for insertion into the locomotive. Underneath is the main transformer, on top to the left is the tap-changer-a device that variously altered the voltage and hence the speed of the motors. The box on the left marked "AEI" is the tap-changer driving mechanism. On top and to the right, the oil-cooler is visible with tank and venting system on top and circulating pump to the right. These pumps worked hard for a living, delivering typically 200 gallons per minute of transformer cooling oil Automatic protection against failure of either pump or low oil-level was provided. Notice the bogies assembled and ready for rolling beneath the completed units. Prominent above the side frames are the coil springs to dampen and stabilise body movement from above.　　*British Railways*

(Below) **Doncaster Works, 1965:** The pantograph of an electric locomotive or multiple unit is the one, vital, link with the electricity supply and without which the unit cannot function. As with all components allied with traction units, pantograph design had progressed over the years. This resulted in the application of pantographs to the Stone-Faiveley design. Supplied by J.Stone & Co.of Deptford, they were used for all the initial series of 25kV (AL1-5) locomotives and EMUs. Similarly, this same type of current collector was used for the AL6 (86), although ten locomotives carried AEI's own "crossarm" design. This bore some resemblance to the "full diamond" type carried by all the electric locos that worked over the 1,500V dc MSW system. Here, in a clearly posed picture, one engineer is tightening a bolt securing a copper bonding strap between the pantograph and its frame; the other man is steadying the unit. The top of the pantograph consisted of two separate current collection bars bolted to the cross-pieces; these were made from carbon sections some 20mm wide. The actual grade of carbon used was crucial: too soft meant rapid wear with burn-out and flash-over problems; too hard could cause premature wear of the overhead contact wire. It needs little imagination to realise which was easiest and cheapest to replace! Upon contact with the overhead line the entire unit became live, so some fairly hefty insulation was needed. The five ribbed porcelain insulators are clearly identifiable and are bolted to the loco's roof. Between each group of moving parts can be seen the bonding straps. Made from braided copper for flexibility, these ensure a constant voltage throughout the whole unit. Failure to meet this criterion would mean creation of a potential difference with subsequent arcing problems. Notice the stabilising bar on the left carries its own insulator. Under normal conditions the pantograph was raised and lowered pneumatically-the twin air cylinders can be observed either side of the cantilevered lifting arm. A reserve air compressor, battery-operated, was available should the main air supply be unavailable. When the pantograph was raised and traction system live, an interlocking system ensured that the doors leading from the cabs at both ends into the high tension compartment remained locked. Only when the pantograph was lowered could these doors be opened　　*British Railways*

Doncaster Works, 1965: Whatever parameters the engineers had used in their designs and however well the locomotive had been built, it was the drivers who were at the sharp end. It was they who would have to handle the machine and endeavour to give it "their best shot". At this point it is pertinent to remember that all the men who had to be trained to operate the new technology were, almost without exception, dyed-in-the-wool steam men. Many of the senior drivers active in the 1959-66 era would have started work in the last days of the LNWR or the early days of the LMS. Working a lifetime of long and awkward hours, they suffered the privations of wartime, with poor pay and low, or almost non-existing pension provision looming on retirement at age 65. To say the least, these chaps had a hard time of it. We enthusiasts revel in the "glorious days of steam" scenario, but it was not us who had to leave our beds on a cold, or pouring wet morning, walk to an engine shed in the small hours to "oil up" a "Scot", a "Jubilee", or a "Black 5" and then endure a rattling, banging, shaking footplate for hours on end behind an engine that may not have been at its best on that

particular day. True, there were steam crews who disliked modern traction and, maybe, some of the cabs of the new medium left much to be desired. But, overall, surely this was a better way forward? In this, the last of our Class AL6 views, we take a look inside a cab. As mentioned, the two ends of the locomotive were differently numbered, though unfortunately it has not been possible to identify here either the end number or the loco in question. To the left of the driver's padded seat-adjustable for height, but not rake-is the AWS indicator; beneath, on the desk, is the brake operating gear with gauges in front to record pressure in the system. The handle for the main controller projects from the centre of the desk towards the front windscreen. The handle has six positions: "OFF" shows at present and in this position current is denied to the traction motors; "RUN DOWN", the nest position, puts the tap changer in its lowest position. This device, mechanically-operated, had 38 positions on an AL6 delivering 0-1,000 volts to the motors. Then comes "NOTCH DOWN", "HOLD", "NOTCH UP", and "RUN UP". "HOLD" is just discernible in the raised lettering on the centre of the console. Broadly, the locomotive's speed was regulated by the driver moving the handle over the various positions. Acceleration was controlled by alternating the handle between "NOTCH UP" and "HOLD". All the while the crucial ammeter readings-seen at the front of the desk beneath the windows-had to be watched. 200 amps or over and the controller had to be moved back. Only when the current had fallen could the controller be "notched up" again. In "RUN UP" the tap changer would automatically increase the voltage from the transformer's windings.to the motors: the higher the voltage, the higher the speed. If pressure was released from the handle, then a spring-loading brought the controller back to "NOTCH UP". "RUN UP" was a useful facility for increasing speed after, for example, when power had to be shut off for a speed restriction or after encountering a neutral section. Below and to the left is the reversing switch-marked "FOR" and "REV". Completing the picture to the right are the line, fault and train heat indicators. Over on the far side of the yard are two items from the railway of yesteryear: a "Deltic" locomotive and a Shell tank wagon. *British Railways*

Levenshulme, May 29th 1974: A once-typical everyday scene, now part of history. Class **86 002**, an English Electric (Vulcan Foundry) product of June 1965, entering service as E3170 , whisks the 16.05 Birmingham New Street train towards Manchester Piccadilly through Levenshulme on the Down Fast line on the last stage of its journey. Though many enthusiasts regarded the end of steam with dismay, the thoughts of an 8-coach train on such a service would be regarded as a luxury in today's climate of overcrowded "Voyager" trains. Still less than ten years old, 86 002 had been re-numbered as part of the TOPS system, and subsequently as 86 402 and 86 602. Withdrawal took place in May 2004, the thirty-nine years in service being testament to the design.

Raymond Keeley

Manchester Piccadilly, pre-WWI: Ten-past one on a sunny afternoon in the Manchester of almost a century ago. So much mention has been made in this book of "London Road" and "Piccadilly" that the chance to include this wonderful scene showing Piccadilly itself with London Road beyond could not be passed up. Piccadilly, arguably Manchester's most famous thoroughfare, was so-named in 1812. It is reputed to have received its title from Piccadilly in London. Piccadilly did, after all, face the London Road and both it and its southern counterpart had a coaching inn named "The White Bear". But before the modern name was applied, the area here had been known as the "Daub Hole"- name coming about due to the excavation of clay and formation of a small lake. Taken by the advertising section of the Lancashire & Yorkshire Railway-perhaps the scene appeared in a one-time brochure or advertising leaflet for the company. This is the junction of Piccadilly with Market Street and Mosley Street. Lowry-like, the figures are dotted over the townscape: strolling, walking, talking, dawdling, hurrying, pausing, travelling, working or gazing-all seem differently engaged. Notice that all wear hats and caps of one kind or another. A policeman wear-ing a contemporary short tunic keeps order at the road junction. Look at the lady to the immediate right of the lamp post in the foreground; with her long dress and stylish hat, how typically Edwardian she looks! All manner of merchandise is being moved across the scene by horse and cart, no cars are seen anywhere. In the centre, two tramcars-the only mechanised transport to be seen-stop to pick up their passengers: a No.42, an open-topped car bound for the Exchange and a No.49 heading out to Sale; a second closed car looms ahead of the No.42. By the pavement the horse-drawn cabs await their fares; flanking them, along the wide pavement, statues survey the scene. Newly installed is Queen Victoria (1901), she is flanked by the Duke of Wellington (1856), James Watt (1857) and Sir Robert Peel (1853). Off to the right, half-timbered buildings have replaced the city's Infirmary which stood here for many years, before moving to the present-day site on Oxford Road in 1906. Looking along on the left-hand side we encounter Lyons Popular Café, the building topped by Moorish-style scrollwork and distinctly eastern-looking "onion domes" atop the building. Moving down the block can be seen Style & Manile Costumiers, Lipton's Market, Singers Sewing Machines, Lloyds and the Mosley Hotel. Meesons-Sweets & Chocolates set alongside Saqui & Lawrence, Jewellers complete the line-up of shops. All part of another world, now gone for ever.

Author's collection

ONE OF FIVE

At one time, Manchester could boast that it was the only city out-side London that possessed five main line railway stations-though Glasgow could have said the same, so we will, perforce, use the qualification "in England." With no less than 17 platforms the city's Victoria station was the biggest and the busiest, especially when the conjoined Manchester Exchange was taken into account-though purists might argue that that station was actually situated in the City of Salford!

INDIVIDUALITY

Victoria, Exchange, Central and Oxford Road all had their own little quirks and nuances. At Victoria it was the art deco refresh-ment rooms and the splendid wall map showing the tentacles of the Lancashire and Yorkshire Railway spread out like some gigan-tic spider. At the same station, a poignant reminder of the follies of war can still be seen in the shape of the L&Y's memorial to the men sacrificed in WWI. Exchange was remembered and was noto-rious for being on the receiving end of the longest railway plat-form in the world-2,235 feet, something every schoolboy knew

once upon a time. The station had been on the receiving end of a devastating incendiary attack in December 1940 and had never regained its previous form entirely. Even in the 1950s a large wooden board proclaimed: OVER THE BRIDGE FOR TRAINS ON THE NORTH EASTERN RAILWAY, a source of wonder-ment to a thirteen year-old trainspotter. At Central an overarching roof-210 feet wide was certainly impressive; less so were the dingy wooden booking offices that were sited in front of what the Americans call a "train shed." Intended only to be "temporary", they remained until the station's closure in May 1969. Round the corner from the Midland Hotel, St.Peter's Square led down to Oxford Road, to reveal certainly the smallest station, yet a build-ing packed with atmosphere. Here the green electric sets-dating from LMS days back in 1931-sped off with clockwork-like preci-sion along to Knott Mill and Deansgate before curving away alongside the Bridgewater Canal to reach Old Trafford and then the suburbs on the fringe of Cheshire: Sale, Brooklands, and Altrincham where the electrics terminated and the tracks of the former CLC continued on towards Chester.

(Left) Five-to-two in the afternoon at Manchester London Road. Horse-drawn cabs outnumber motorised vehicles by three to one in this pre-Grouping scene. Over on the left, the Great Central railway advertise services to *"Marylebone and King's Cross, Oxford, South and west of England"* Not to be outdone, the London & North Western Railway boast *"London (Euston), Birmingham, Bristol, Bath, Bournemouth, South Wales, Leamington, Oxford, Derby and Nottingham."* The Victorian facade looks rather grim and austere and is smoke blackened-something to be expected in Edwardian industrial Manchester. Company names apart, this was the London Road known by generations of Mancunians and would remain in this form until the onset of modernisation in 1958.
National Railway Museum

MANCHESTER PICCADILLY (LONDON ROAD)

relatives, natives of Barnet, often came up from London by rail from Euston. To my delight this involved meeting them off the train at London Road, a precursor to my spotting days which began there in earnest around 1956. Again, the gloom, grime and darkness of a forecourt with none of today's open plan airiness and a plethora of shops. Shops! On a railway station, heavens no! Such things were unknown-well, there was always W.H.Smith, but that wasn't really a shop-not to a 13-year old schoolboy anyway. Shops meant Lewis's, Wiles, Rolfe's-Ye Gods!-they even sold air rifles and guns; Hobbies, Henry's, Bassett Lowke and, if your Mum was really flush, Kendals.

WARRING FACTIONS

Right up to modern times London Road was really two stations in one. Warlike feuds between the Manchester, Sheffield & Lincolnshire Railway and the London & North Western Railway back in the late 1850s led to the station.......*continued on page 42*

ALONG LONDON ROAD

And so, we come to London Road; now there was a station! Dubbed "Manchester's Premier Station" there has been a railway terminus on this site since 1840 and from the very small beer of almost 166 years ago the place has grown and changed out of all recognition. As we will see, the Manchester & Birmingham Railway reached Crewe en route to their goal-the capital city of The Black Country; but got no further. Crewe it was that remained very much a major staging post for services to the Midlands, the Metropolis and the South-West of England.

CHILDHOOD MEMORIES

Early visits to the station are well remembered. My Grandmother's brother-"Uncle Freddie" to us children-and his son were passionate brass band enthusiasts. In those days annual brass contests were held in the King's Hall at Belle Vue and our

Truly, the London Road of yesteryear. This is the entrance to the former LMS booking offices, a photograph taken in 1956. In later years an intensive cleaning programme was undertaken on the stone exteriors of many of Manchester's public buildings. Alas, this never happened at London Road-though it is interesting to speculate what a clean frontage might have looked like instead of the grimy blackness so visible here. Easter came early in 1956; Good Friday, March 23rd, saw special excursions to Hellifield, and Llandudno was on offer all weekend, but neither excursion left from here! Don't miss the spelling mistake on the next poster.
Kemsley Studios

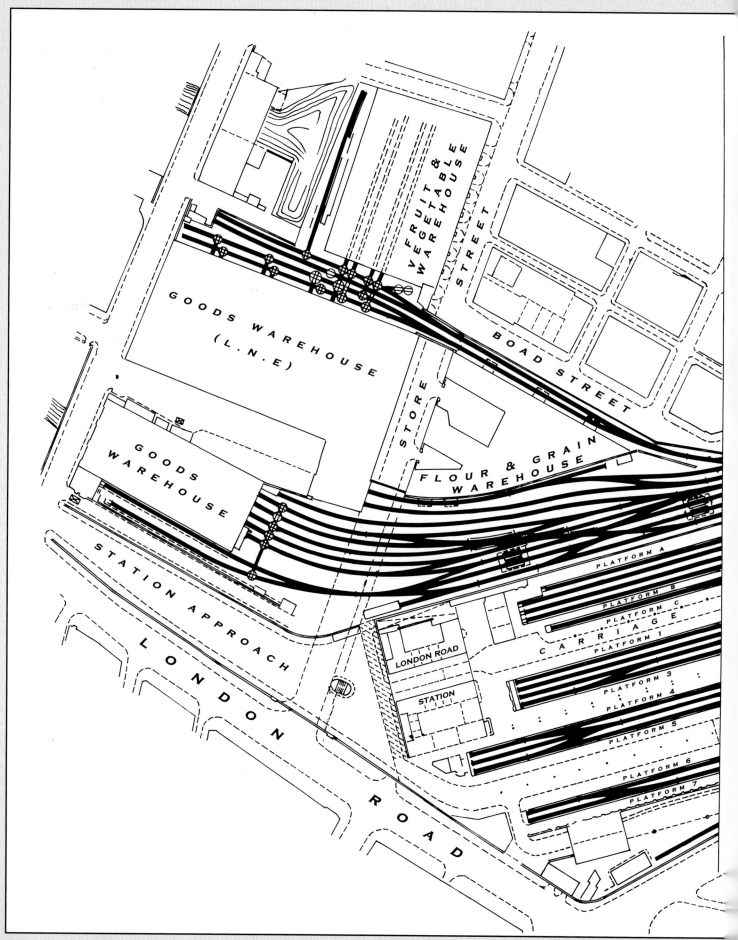

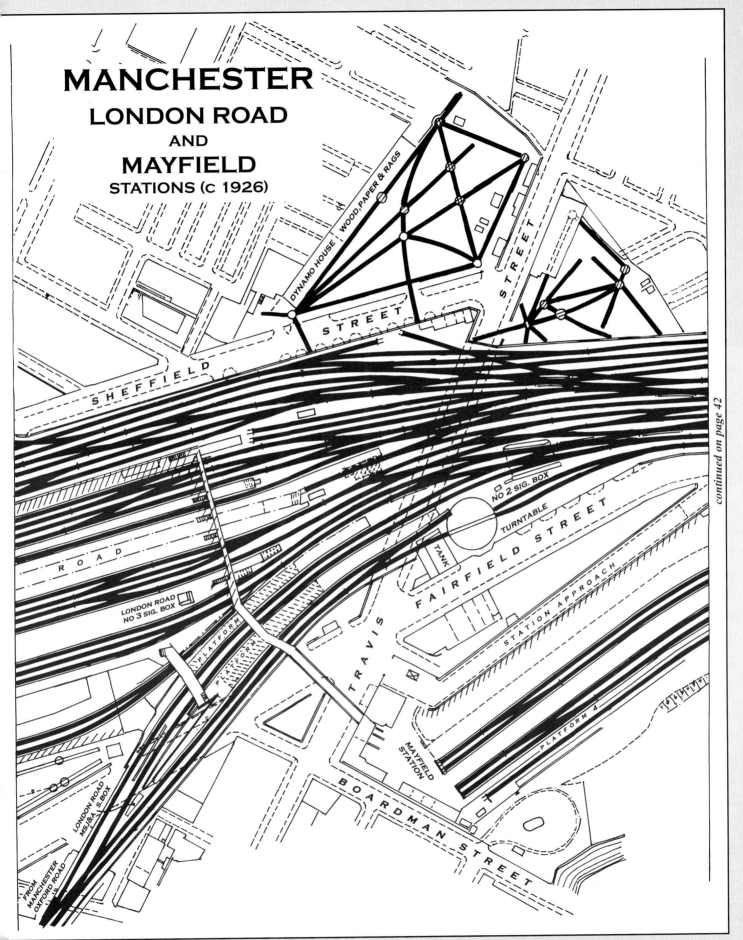

MANCHESTER
LONDON ROAD
AND
MAYFIELD
STATIONS (c 1926)

DYNAMO HOUSE WOOD, PAPER & RAGS

STREET

STREET

SHEFFIELD

ROAD

continued on page 42

NO 2 SIG. BOX

TURNTABLE

TANK

FAIRFIELD STREET

STATION APPROACH

LONDON ROAD
NO 3 SIG. BOX

PLATFORM

PLATFORM

PLATFORM

TRAVIS

MAYFIELD
STATION

PLATFORM 4

LONDON ROAD
MS.18A. S.BOX

FROM
MANCHESTER
OXFORD ROAD

BOARDMAN STREET

Manchester London Road, April 9th 1954: Few photographers got such a privileged viewpoint as this one. Taken from the station's No.2 signalbox a panoramic picture is obtained, encapsulating a scene packed with interest. At platform 4 and taking centre stage is "Royal Scot" No **46120** *Royal Iniskilling Fusilier* departing with the 2.05 pm express to Euston. Over to the right, at platform 1, B1 No **61092** waits to leave, also for London, but travelling via the former GCR main line via Woodhead and Sheffield Victoria, departing at 2.18 its journey time will be just five hours. On the left, at one of the MSJ&A platforms-No.10-a Stanier 2-6-4 tank simmers

away. The train of two non-corridor coaches and three horseboxes is possibly the 12.05 pm service from Liverpool Lime Street which has travelled via Ditton Junction, Warrington Bank Quay (low-level), Lymm and Broadheath Junction to joint the MSJ&A at Timperley Junction. Making no less than twenty two stops on its thirty seven mile journey, the train was due in London Road at 1.59. At platform 5 a "Jubilee" waits with a further, unidentified, train. The 2.05 departure for Euston is of particular interest as this was the service which was joined at Stockport with through connecting coaches from the East Lancashire towns of Colne, Blackburn and Bolton.

Today is a Friday and in later years this day saw an increase from eleven coaches to twelve and double-heading became necessary. Even so, when the East Lancashire portion is added, today's train will consist of no less than thirteen or fourteen coaches-a big load. Leaving Colne at 11.55, the connecting train called at Burnley (12.04), Blackburn (12.41), Bolton (1.11), Manchester Victoria (1.35) and Stockport (2.20). Arrival in Euston was booked for 6.05. Taking an overview, then, this was Manchester's premier station as it will never be seen again. From the wagons in the MSJ&A bay and the schoolboy spotter with his cap and short trousers across to the

distant view of the GCR's grain warehouse with the "London" building towering over all in the background, all has changed utterly. Today's rail traveller no longer has the benefit of through coaches, such things having long since been swept away under that all-covering blanket of "uneconomic". The London service from Colne disappeared in 1962, in the last few years of operation the three daily departures had been reduced to mere connecting services to Stockport. 21st century passengers are now directed to travel to London via Preston, a journey taking around four and half hours. Such is progress.

B K B Green

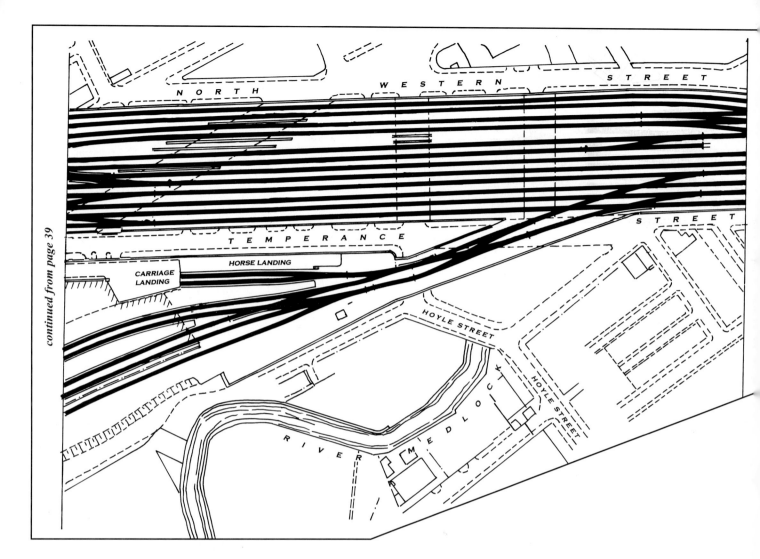

continued from page 39

continued from page 37..........being partitioned under an Act of July 1859 which provided for the partition of London Road station…*"and for the better Management of certain Portions of the said Station, and for improving the Access thereto."*

Hereafter, each side of the station would have its own Station Master, booking offices, clerks, porters and general staff and a committee of management was to be appointed. Prior to the passing of the Act the M&SL paid the LNW £3,490 in annual rent; the LNW paid the MS&L £78 1s 10d! Any additional sums, it was deemed under the Act, would be decided by the "Arbitrators and Umpire." A curious business indeed. Iron railings separated the platforms of the protagonists until the commencement of rebuilding and associated electrification work in the later 1950s. When, in 1882, electric lighting was introduced by the MS&L to their side of the station Sir Edward Watkin, the company's Chairman ordered shades to be fitted lest any light be shed onto the LNW's platform 1 alongside!

ENLARGEMENT AND MODERNISATION

From a shanty-like terminus, first in Travis Street, then in Store Street, London Road-known at one point as "Bank Top"-came by degrees to the size and state remembered by those of us who were mere "spotters" in the 1950s. The station was rebuilt between 1865 and 1866 and further enlarged by the LNWR between 1880-1881; the MS&L opened an additional platform on their side of

the station in 1882. In 1910 the addition of Mayfield Station, a 3-platform affair on the opposite side of Fairfield Street, gave the station yet more capacity. For passengers, alas, this was anything but a boon as a considerable walk was faced by those unfortunate enough to have to use it.

It was the Modernisation Plan, published on January 25th 1955, that catalysed the London Road that we have grown up with over the last 33 years or so. It was that grand scheme, the brainchild of the long-defunct BTC, that pushed electrification to the forefront of the north-west's railways. Manchester to Crewe was but to be the start; Crewe to London and Liverpool would follow, though Glasgow was a long way off; while operation "under the wire" on the East Coast route was still a pipedream.

DAWN OF THE ELECTRIC ERA

Preliminary work on the electrification to Crewe began as far back as May 1956. In March of that year provisional orders had been given for the electrification of two "pilot" schemes at 25 kV single phase, 50 cycles AC: i.e. the Colchester-Clacton-Walton lines in the Eastern Region and, here in Manchester on the Styal line-a convenient loop from Slade Lane Junction to Wilmslow. Initial work on the line consisted of track and point-work alterations at Mauldeth Road enabling trains to run into the former goods yard there directly from the Up line. It was between here and East Didsbury ....*continued on page 44*

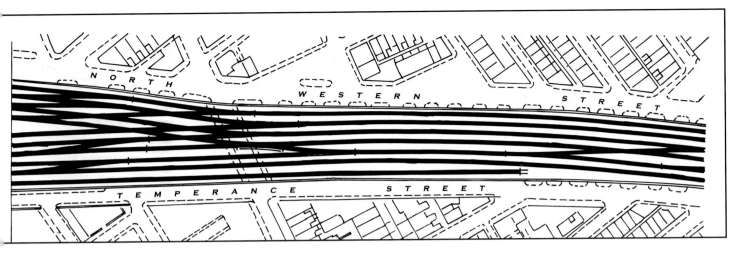

Manchester London Road, May 13th 1958: Taken from the landing of the No.2 signalbox this picture shows well the complexity of the approach tracks and the magnitude of the task facing the engineers as the onset of modernisation approached. Down to the right can be seen Temperance Street and the wall flanking Mayfield station. Through the haze can be seen the early high-rise council flats that fringed the railway approaches and nearby Ardwick Green. Straddling the tracks here is the London Road No.1 signalbox popularly known as "Chapelfield". In the middle distance, through the haze, is the Openshaw district where, still, the famous Gorton Works was sited cheek-by-jowl with Gorton Loco shed, all in an age, soon to be ended, when Manchester was still a hive of heavy industry. Twelve tracks run across the picture, from right to left these are: shunting neck (this continued for some distance and crossed the approach lines into Mayfield), down slow, down fast, up fast, up slow, down eastern, shunting neck (from station), up eastern, down LM goods, up LM goods, down ER goods, up ER goods. Straddling the centre of the view are the signals, nine sets of arms of two distinctive patterns-GCR to the left and LNWR on the right. These date from the re-signalling carried out here in the first decade of the twentieth century following the second widening of the approach tracks from Ardwick Junction. Because the works had been carried out at the LNWR's behest, the company had to pay for the new GC system. The LNW had chosen their own power system, the all-electric one patented by F.W.Webb and A.M.Thompson in May 1897. The GC, under the dynamic A.F.Bound, chose a pneumatically-operated system, something that Webb eschewed. The GC's system, executed by the British Power Railway Signalling Company and brought into operation on October 1909, cost the LNW £5878; the LNW electric system was introduced in two parts: at No.1 box in 1908 and No.2 a year later.

British Railways

.........that much of the training was done with the pioneer 25kV ac traction units. That same year, on October 8th, Diesel units made their debut on this stretch of railway, operating as far as Wilmslow. From that date, too, local services from London Road to Macclesfield and Buxton were taken over by DMUs. The following March work commenced on the erection of over head masts on the Styal line prompting one callow schoolboy to ask a lineside workman (on March 12th actually): *"what voltage will these new trains use, mister?"* *"Twenty-five thousand, son"* came the reply. Information was hard to come by in those days.

Work began in earnest in the Spring of 1957 on the erection of overhead masts along the Styal line with a number of posts in place by the beginning of April and, by August 10th support masts had been installed further south between Sandbach and Goostrey. Back on the Styal line, work was in hand on replacing the 50 year-old standard LNWR station buildings at Burnage, East Didsbury and Heald Green. Mauldeth Road and Gatley retained their LNW buildings, but at all six stations the LNW wooden platforms disappeared to make way for concrete replacements of seemingly inordinate length: 8-car provision being installed as standard, an over-optimistic gesture. By March 1958 the overhead line was complete from Slade Lane Junction to Styal and the march onwards to Wilmslow was well in hand. Here, a new junction with the Stockport line was made further south than hitherto. Causing much upset amongst the local populace was the new signalbox, a large 3-storey affair at the south end of the station and set between the Stockport and the Styal lines. Early in 1958, Mr.David Blee, the LMR General Manager, reported confidently that work on the Manchester-Crewe electrification scheme was ahead of schedule and that tests runs between Wilmslow and Mauldeth Road would begin by mid-1958. Modernisation was on the way.

But it was in London Road itself that the biggest upheaval was felt. Here, a large 13-platform terminal station (two of which carried through traffic) and a quite substantial annexe together with approach tracks, bridges and a signalling system, all little changed from the immediate post-Victorian era, had to be transformed to something more in keeping with a modern railway. It was to prove a mammoth task.

MODERNISATION DESCRIBED

In just over two years, at a cost of £1.5 million, British Railways would accomplish their programme: this comprised a new track layout, new platforms, re-glazing of the roof, re-signalling and demolition of the old LNW/GC booking hall and offices. Ridding the station of its Victorian frontage with provision of a new footbridge, ticket offices and accompanying tower block might have been matters for concern in a later, more heritage-friendly environment, but not then. All was taken in hand at what, today, seems like lightning speed. The station had also to accommodate full electrification to the new 25kV ac standard. Not that London Road was any stranger to electric working: the catenary had appeared at the station's MSJ&A side in 1931 and over the former LNER lines in 1954. The Altrincham line as far as Oxford Road was to be converted to the 25kV ac system, but on the Eastern side the two systems had to run in parallel until 1980-causing a few problems in the meantime. Officially, work had begun on rebuilding London

Road station on September 15th 1958. At this point a bus service took over the running of MSJ&A services between Oxford Road and London Road. A comprehensive booklet issued to passengers for the (extended) weekend of 14th-17th November 1958 announced that, for this short period platforms 4-9 would be closed. Main line trains were scheduled to use the city's other stations; Stockport line trains were terminated at Heaton Norris; those over the Styal line arrived and departed from Mauldeth Road (the first Styal line station.) The booklet explained the situation thus: "During this period a gigantic effort will be made by 2,00 men, working in relays throughout the day and night, to transpose the running tracks outside the station. This will ensure the smooth running of the new electric services between Manchester and Crewe planned to commence in September 1960........Nearly 600 main line and suburban trains use London Road station daily…"

INTERESTING DIVERSIONS

On an on-going basis, the trains still had to run of course. Fortunately for London Midland (the ubiquitous "BR" was not quite so prevalent then) a network of alternative routes and stations was available to them and diversions away from the traditional lines were accomplished with relative ease. One such re-working of the London trains is of particular interest. This involved the re-routing south of Stoke-on-Trent of selected expresses which then wended their way to the Midland main line to arrive in St.Pancras. Initially the trains concerned were the Sunday 1.18 pm, 5.15 pm and 11.35 pm departures of summer 1959. These were extended into the winter (November-June)1959/60 timetable to include the both the 12.00 noon and 11.55 pm weekdays and Saturday expresses; the 11.55 pm differed slightly from the other trains in that it was worked up from Stenson Junction to run via Derby. Longsight men worked both "Royal Scots" and "Britannias" over what was an amazing route of almost 200 miles. Journey times varied from 4½ to 5hrs.35 min. The crews from 9A were joined at Stoke by a pilotman from Derby. The engines were worked back to Willesden and then Camden from St.Pancras by Willesden men.

One of the biggest tasks in the modernisation of London Road centred around the layout on the former MSJ&A side where the platforms stood on a bridge straddling Fairfield Street. Here a massive new single-span concrete bridge had to be installed as well as an accompanying altered track layout. This had required removal of the existing turntable and siding road. By itself this would have been an awesome feat; but this was but one of a myriad of tasks facing the London Midland engineers.

The rebuilt London Road would have 14 platforms, something achieved by removal of storage roads to create extra space. To cope with the new works MSJ&A services ended at Oxford Road from September 15th 1958, special bus service taking over the truncated MSJ&A electric section for the time being. At the front of the station, booking offices on the former GC/LNE side were used while those of the LNW/LMS were demolished. After this, a temporary wooden booking office was erected just outside the former Eastern side frontage. From January 3rd to April 23rd 1960 the former Eastern side lines at London Road were closed to all traffic. Local services were terminated at Ashburys, while main line trains from Sheffield were diverted to either Manchester

Manchester Piccadilly, c.1961: A view typifying the contrast between the old and the new stations. Today's tower block has replaced the grim-looking façade of Messrs.Mills and Murgatroyd, a building designed back in the 1860s. Finishing touches are being applied to the station frontage here and there and, certainly, the 'WAY IN' sign has a very impromptu look about it! A curiosity was the cabman's shelter; the charming little cast iron cupola had overtones of those carried atop the roofs of stations on the GCR's 'Fallowfield Line.' And who remembers Silvana of Ancoats? A Morris Minor 1000 trundles towards the photographer; registration number VVR 751 it was clearly a Manchester vehicle-a survivor perhaps? *Manchester City Engineer's Archive*

Central, Victoria or Mayfield. At Mayfield operations were helped by the addition of an extra platform-No.5-and an independent, though temporary, signalbox. To reach Victoria the eastern-side trains were electrically-hauled over the line from Ashburys West Junction as far as Midland Junction. From there they were taken to Victoria by a Newton Heath or Agecroft 2-6-4 tank via Phillips Park and Miles Platting.Electric services from Glossop and Hadfield, along with other Eastern side local services, were terminated at Ashburys. And on January 22nd 1960, a then youthful observer gazed in amazement on what looked like a bombed-out station concourse whilst waiting for his party from the Domestic & Trades College to travel to London's Hotelympia event.

ONE LAST HEAVE

The final push began on April 25th 1960 when, with just over three months to go before the commissioning of the new station, wholesale diversion of London Midland main line trains took place. All bar five expresses (one West of England, two London expresses, one Cardiff train and one Crewe train) were diverted to the other four Manchester main line stations: Exchange, Victoria, Central and Mayfield. London Road's premier named train "The Mancunian" was diverted to start from Exchange station (leaving earlier-at 9.22); the Stockport route was accessed by running through adjacent Victoria station then via Philips Park, Ashton

Moss, Denton and Heaton Norris. A note in the September 1960 "Railway Observer"-the journal of the Railway Correspondence & Travel Society-recalled the sight of the Up "Mancunian" with a "Royal Scot" at its head hauling the 12-coach train flat out up the 1-in-77 of the bank from Droylsden as being the most memorable of the diversions. But not just London traffic was affected: trains to Birmingham, the West of England and South Wales, all-some-how-had to be accommodated elsewhere. A leaflet advertising diversions from London Road from June 13th 1960 summed up the arrangements neatly. It is interesting to note that, within this brief period, it was possible to reach Crewe from all five of Manchester's main line stations.

In the same period a further fascinating alternative saw Euston expresses leaving the MSJ&A platforms to run through Altrincham and then on towards Northwich. Here the trains swung south onto the single line via Middlewich to Sandbach where the Crewe line was joined and the journey resumed normality. . On reflection, it says a lot for the long-suffering passengers at that time and of the train crews, managers and operating staff, that services survived almost uncut through this, the most traumatic period in London Road's peacetime history.

But some of these diversions were to be a precursor to greater things. For, after the Manchester-Crewe electrification came onstream, attention would be focused on the Crewe-Euston route.

The splendid, but short-lived "Midland Pullman" began running from Manchester Central to St.Pancras on July 4th 1960. In 1962 an altered timetable and lengthened trains up-graded the former Midland services from Manchester so that London Midland's engineers could concentrate their efforts on modernisation and electrification south of Crewe. Type 4 diesels had first made their appearance at London Road in the summer of 1959 and from 1962 they took charge over at Central of the St.Pancras expresses as well.

STEAM GIVES WAY TO DIESEL

The eclipse of steam at London Road was very much a piecemeal process. It began on the MSJ&A side with electrification back in 1931; it continued in 1954 with the 1500V dc system extended over the former GC Woodhead route to Sheffield, taking in the Glossop/Hadfield suburban services in the process. DMUs had arrived in June 1957 to work the London Road-Macclesfield (Central) services via the former GC&NS Joint line via Marple Wharf Junction and Middlewood. Next year, 1958, saw DMUs take over the Stockport, Buxton and Styal lines. On the LM side of the station main line steam was unchallenged until the summer of 1959 when Diesel loco traction arrived. The author clearly remembers the shock of his first sighting of an English Electric Type 4 crossing Slade Lane Junction around mid-July with a Down express. These contractor-built locomotives were turned out concurrently with the rather more powerful "Peak" Diesels (D1-D10) which gradually took charge of contemporary Central-St.Pancras workings. Back on the Western Division EE Type 4s had appeared at Willesden in April; Crewe North in August, while Nos.D227/8 were recorded at Longsight in August also. Diesel traction on the LM main line out of London Road had just over a year to prove itself before the completion of the "big bang" rebuilding of the station saw electrification to Crewe and the arrival of the first 25kV Bo-Bos and the 4-car electric suburban sets.

ELECTRIC SERVICES ARE WHISTLED OFF

The official inauguration of the scheme had been set for September 12th 1960. The great day dawned with a VIP delegation-including the Minister of Transport, Ernest Marples and Sir Brian Robertson, BTC Chairman-descending on Piccadilly station to officially open the "new line". The assembled company was impressive: all the senior members of the BTC, the LMR area board, the senior managers of the LM region, local MPs, Lord Mayors, the Pullman Chairman, executives of the various contractors and one other-a person named H.G.Jenkins of Lewis's Limited. Who, one might well ask, was H.G.Jenkins? Lewis's, so long part of the Piccadilly shopping scene had an exhibition hall and, if memory is correct, this was on the store's fifth floor. How many generations of Manchester schoolboys-the author included-remember the wonderful Gauge 0 model railway that appeared there year after year? And Lewis's were always willing hosts for exhibitions promoting the railway. So, yes, it is very fitting that they should have been represented on that auspicious day.

Marples duly dispatched the 12.15 pm express to the West of England via Shrewsbury with the customary whistle and green flag and as much ceremony as he could muster. The Manchester Evening News carried a picture with accompanying

headline.."Railman Marples short of puff"-the storyline being that the whistle could not be heard down the length of the platform! With typical politician's relish Marples said: *I am especially pleased to be doing this today because my grand father used to work as a porter at Stockport Edgeley station years ago".*

The following day's Daily Mail, in those days never a newspaper to miss an opportunity for a swipe at British Railways, ran the headline: "Super train keeps Marples waiting". Marples and his delegation had arrived at Piccadilly's specially-prepared platform 9 to find it empty. The train, the 3.05 pm to Cardiff did not arrive until 3.23. This was due to the derailment of a steam locomotive at the entry to Longsight carriage sidings. Making use of some more column inches The Mail gleefully reported that this was not the only delay at Piccadilly that day-"The Mancunian", electrically hauled for the first time, had left at 10.10, 30 minutes late. And under the heading "Timetables were late, too" the paper reported the late arrival of the current winter timetable-76,000 copies-delayed at the printers. Hardly the railways' fault, but, no matter, the more opprobrium that could be heaped on BR, surely the better the story.

But, the Mail's asides notwithstanding, electric services to Crewe were now de facto. And, though it would be over five years before through electric travel to London would become possible, the line to Crewe would become the proving ground for British 25kv main line electrification; paving the way for greater things-full electrification fro Euston to Glasgow.

LOCAL SERVICES IMPROVE

As described separately, main line services out of Piccadilly had a long wait before any significant improvements came their way. It was local services that saw the most marked transformation. The arrival of the four-car EMUS-then Class AM10-solidly-built, smooth-running and quick off the mark made even the much-admired DMUs of 1958 seem dated; nothing like this had been seen running over the Styal or Stockport lines before. Of course, on the MSJ&A, on the London Road to Hadfield services and over at Victoria on the Bury line, electric traction had long since been taken for granted. The winter timetable for 1960 gave an hourly service all stations Piccadilly to Crewe via Stockport. Those on the Styal line were paltry by comparison: just four morning all-stations Piccadilly to Wilmslow (only). Things improved drastically the following year's summer timetable when EMU services were intensified. Now the previous hourly service to Crewe via Stockport was retained; but Alderley Edge and Wilmslow were given a 15 minute service to Manchester, running alternately via Stockport and over the Styal line.

The icing on the cake-as far as BR was concerned-was a change of name: from September 12th 1960 the station would henceforward be known as "Manchester Piccadilly." *Not an entirely logical name, the area known as Piccadilly is a good quarter of a mile from the station-but how often railway stations were divorced from places they served! Not that BR got off the hook unscathed. Under the heading "Provincial Piccadilly", this is what The Times had to say about the name change: What has come over Manchester? Can it leave nothing that is well alone?...It was at 12.20, when a four-line announcement arrived that when Manchester's London Road station is rebuilt it will be known as*

Marking a complete contrast with our contemporary steam views is this 1896 picture of an LNWR express making a dramatic departure from London Road, the great train shed roofs and squat LNW semaphores-then manually operated-marking out the location unmistakably. Piloting the express is a Webb Compound 2-2-2 of the "Experiment" class indulging in a furious bout of slipping; the train engine is a Webb Rebuilt "Jumbo" 2-4-0-number and name (of both engines) unknown. All three visible coaches are 6-wheelers-an exhilarating journey to be sure!   *Author's collection*

Piccadilly...Exactly why a new name is needed is not adequately explained...It is not as if London Road were some insignificant terminus. One of the main gates into and out of Manchester, it has stood for nearly 100 years as a solid symbol. Much of Manchester's history has flowed through it. Generations of Lancastrians have known its grimy ugliness with affection. And even though British Railways may now going to put up the handsomest of modern edifices..."Piccadilly" is not likely to catch on very fast.

But, of course, the name did catch on, though some people do still refer to "London Road". It is interesting to reflect that, had the MS&L had their way-back in 1866-London Road station might have finished up in Piccadilly Gardens, for there was a firm proposal to extend the line forward and move the station. The City Council, however, would have none it and the terminus was to stay put.

A bizarre twist concerning the old name for the station lingered until the late 1980s. The new power box had pre-dated the re-naming. Opened in three stages: 1) from Gatley/Heaton Chapel to Longsight on 12th-14th December 1959; 2) 23rd-25th April 1960 and 3) on August 28th 1960 in readiness for the commencement of electric services on September 12th. The box controlled 96 colour light signals, 71 shunt signals and 192 electro-pneumatically operated points. All the signals controlled by it carried the "LR" designation until the re-modelling was completed in September 1988. Thus, "London Road" lasted quite a bit longer than intended! The territory controlled by the new power box extended to Ardwick on the former Eastern side, to Heaton Chapel on the Stockport line and to a point beyond Gatley on the Styal line where control was taken by the late 1950s box at Wilmslow.

These latter-day improvements at Piccadilly included lengthening of Platforms 13 & 14-part of the old MSJ&A section of the station, altered track layout and re-signalling with the new "signalling centre" sited in the tower block of the station, away, incidentally, from any sight of trains. From May 1993 the line to Manchester Airport-a short branch off the Styal line south of Heald Green station-was opened. This brought in its wake a whole new generation of both main line and local traffic to Piccadilly-something undreamt of in earlier years.

INTO THE 21ST CENTURY

Piccadilly station was transformed yet again between 2000-2002. In the summer of 2002 Manchester hosted the XVII Commonwealth Games and no effort was spared to complete the re-modelling of the concourse in time for the opening on July 25th that year. The effects of the exercise were dramatic-the area seems vastly bigger and lighter-something achieved by widening the entrance to the platforms and removing the old bottleneck by the former ticket offices. A two-storey shopping area now overlooks the concourse with its escalator, help desk-and palm trees! Sliding glass doors now form the platform entrances. The old approach road rising up from the junction of Ducie Street and London Road has been closed off to most road traffic and a new frontage at the junction of Fairfield Street and London Road has been created. Here is the taxi rank and drop-off point as well as access to the Metrolink platforms and the main station above. The whole exercise cost £27.9M.

Manchester's premier station has now existed in three separate centuries. From Travis Street, then "Bank Top", London Road has witnessed colossal change in a period of over 160 years of life. Whatever changes are wrought on our railways in the future then the station that stands on London Road should survive to see them.

Manchester london Road, c.1911-1919: The south side of London Road's No 2 signal box was the site of a locomotive watering point and became a focal point for photography in the pre-group era. The cameraman in question was P F Cooke who, without question, took some of the finest pictures of engines ever seen in and around the station. Cataloguing errors have resulted in many of Cooke's pictures being wrongly attributed to W H (Will) Whitworth, a Manchester dentist who, though an experienced and capable photographer, never equalled Cooke for sheer quality of output. In what is arguably one of P F Cooke's finest studies at London road, Webb 4-cylinder compound 'Jubilee' Class No **1939**, *Temeraire*, built in October 1900, has her 2,500gallon tender tank topped up at the water column. The fireman is seen astride the tender top, while the driver, his face blurred by by Cooke's slow shutter speed, observes the back of the tender.

The portly driver of the 'George the Fifth' Class No **1532** *Bloodhound*, keeps a wary eye on the photographer. The picture can be dated to post-May 1911 when the 'George' was built. *Temeraire* was rebuilt as a 2-cylinder simple engine of the 'Renown' Class in August 1919 and was renumbered as LMS 5158 in August 1927 prior to being scrapped in October 1928. ***P F Cooke***

(Centre) London Road, n.d; The LNWR's 'Precursor' 4-4-2 tanks were introduced by George Whale in 1905 for use on the company's suburban trains in London, Birmingham and Manchester. The Manchester engines were used on trains to Crewe and Buxton and could also be seen hauling portions of express workings between London Road and Wilmslow. Two batches of engines were built: the second as portrayed here by No **2223**, had smaller carrying wheels-3ft 3in as opposed to 3ft 9in. standing alongside platform 4, No 2223 displays later features of these big tanks with outside front sandboxes and cab roof ventilator. Curiously, a Midland railway clerestory coach stands in front of the loco.
Authors collection

London Road, July 1924. Express motive power had changed little in the immediate post-Grouping period. Awaiting departure from platform 1 with an express for London Euston are 4-4-0's 'George V' No **2212** *South Africa* and 'Precursor' No **2061** *Eglington*. At the time of writing (December 2005), Virgin Trains have announced a new Manchester-London schedule of 2 hours 15minutes. Eighty or so years ago, express timings over the Euston route were in the order of 4 hours, although the LNWR had tried a 3$\frac{1}{2}$ hour timing back in 1910. Not until 1932 would speeds reach those of pre-First War standards when the LMS accelerated the service to an overall 3$\frac{1}{4}$ hours. ***Frank Dean***

Manchester London Road, c.1923/24: A most interesting photograph typifying the through workings from the South Coast that had been a feature at London Road since the early years of the twentieth century. Entering the station is ex-LNW "Prince of Wales" 4-6-0 No **56**. This was one of four rebuilds of this LNW 4-6-0 class with Walschaerts valve gear carried out in 1923 by Hewitt Beames (a fifth engine was ordered by the LMS in 1924). Reputedly, the rebuilds were known as "Tishies" so called, it is said, because the cross-legged appearance of the valve gear gave rise to the appearance of a contemporary racehorse of the same name. Anyway, "Tishie" or otherwise, No.56 is rolling in to London Road with an express; No.2 signalbox is above and St.Andrew's church, Ancoats, is clearly visible behind.

The first two coaches of the train are made up with LB&SCR "Balloon" stock built from 1905 onwards; the train is the "Sunny South Special". This service originated in 1904 as "The Sunny South Express" and consisted of a through service from Liverpool and Manchester to Brighton and Eastbourne. So successful were these trains that the companies, the LB&SC and LNW, expanded their workings to take in the Kent Coast resorts of Margate and Ramsgate. After the First War, services resumed, but to a modified pattern. It was not until 1922 that "The Sunny South Special" returned to something like its old form. The train, described fascinatingly as a "Restaurant and Tea Car Express", consisted of two distinct portions: the Eastbourne train left at 11.35 and ran to Brighton where it reversed and departed at 12.25 pm.Across on the Kent Coast the second portion left Ramsgate at 11.00 am and called at Margate and Herne Bay (there was also a through coach from Whitstable). Heading towards London the Brighton train travelled via East Croydon (1.29 pm), Kensington (Addison Road) (1.54 pm) to reach Willesden Junction at 2.02 pm. This second portion had to thread its way round South London via Clapham Junction, over a network carrying some of the densest suburban railway traffic in the world. After Willesden (1.55 pm & 2.10 departures) and the home ground of the LNWR main line, the two trains ran northwards to Northampton. Here they were combined into a joint Liverpool and Manchester express which departed for the north to split again at Crewe at 3.28 pm. A separate portion left Northampton for Birmingham New Street at 3.32. Our intrepid recorder, Eric Dalton, noted what he called the "Down Hearne Bay" (sic) on eight occasions in August 1924 at Crossley Road,

Levenshulme and Longsight. The train was drawn by either "Experiment" or "Prince of Wales" 4-6-0s on all occasions. In 1925 Eric noted the "Down Sunny South" train in both April and August, again the engine was an "Experiment". No Up departures are noted, but the corresponding train ran to broadly the reverse format of the northbound expresses. In our own time the nearest we can get to anything quite like the length of the "Sunny South" would be the famous "Pines Express", another service with pre-Group ancestry. But "The Pines" used the fabled S&D route to reach Bournemouth and was quite unlike the amazing services just described.

LOCOMOTIVE WORKING OUT OF LONDON ROAD IN 1924/25

The South Manchester enthusiast, Eric Dalton, has passed down to us detailed records of locomotive and train working in and Manchester for the 1920s. Such records are unique, providing a very rare insight into what is now a lost world. As an overture to Eric's work here is a list showing the principal expresses out of London Road in the winter of 1924/25. These sit splendidly alongside our picture of the double headed express waiting to leave platform 1 in the summer of that year.

8.10 am (SX)	Wilmslow, Crewe and Euston (via the Styal line)
8.15 am	Stockport, Crewe and Aberystwyth
8.30 am	Euston via Stoke-on-Trent (through coaches for Birmingham)
9.25 am	Cardiff and West of England express
9.45 am	Euston (via Styal line)
10.00 am	Bath and Bournemouth (West) via S&DJR
10.10 am	Birmingham (Snow Hill), Oxford, Southampton & Bournemouth (Central)
10.40 am	Brighton and Eastbourne (THE SUNNY SOUTH SPECIAL)
12.00 noon	West of England, Aberystwyth and Swansea (Victoria)
12.05 pm	Euston (via Stoke-on-Trent)

....*continued on page 50*

12.20 pm	Birmingham (via Stoke-on-Trent)
2.10 pm	Euston (via via Stoke-on-Trent)
2.50 pm	West of England and Birmingham
4.10 pm	Stockport, Crewe and Euston
4.30 pm (SX)	Birmingham (via the Styal line)
5.30 pm (SX)	Stockport, Crewe and Birmingham
5.40 pm (SX)	Buxton (non-stop)
5.43 pm (SX)	Wilmslow, Alderley and Crewe (via the Styal line)
6.15 pm	Wilmslow, Crewe and Euston (via the Styal line)
7.10 pm	Birmingham and West of England
11.45 pm	West of England
12.00 pm	Euston (via Stoke-on-Trent)

.Surprisingly, Longsight engines did not work many of the Euston expresses through to the Capital. For example, on Mondays, Wednesdays and Fridays a Longsight "Prince of Wales" took the 8.10am London train as far as Crewe. From here it worked the 9.50 stopping train to Stafford, returning from there with the 11.50 train via Stoke. The celebrated "Precedent" 2-4-0 "Charles Dickens" had achieved immortality through legendary performances with the 8.30 am Euston express. From September 1924 this train was worked by a Longsight "Claughton" on Mondays, Wednesdays and Fridays. Unlike its predecessor, the "Claughton" stayed overnight in London and returned with 8.45 am express on corresponding days as well as the 11.50 morning express on Saturdays.

For the record, Eric Dalton noted the 9.45 express to Euston on the following six occasions in 1925:

Saturday, January 31st	"Prince of Wales" No.354- a Camden engine
Tuesday, February 10th	"Claughton" No.149
Saturday, February 28th	"Prince of Wales" No.354
Tuesday, March 3rd	"Prince of Wales" No. 1679 *Lord Byron*
Saturday, March 14th	"George the Fifth" No.2155 *W.C.Brocklehurst*
Saturday, March 21st	L&YR 2-4-2 tank No.1017 (working to Wilmslow only)

Eric carried on recording well into 1925 noting a mixture of "Compounds", Claughtons", "Precursors", "Prince of Wales" and "Georges" hauling the 12.05pm to Euston via Stoke. With equal diligence, he recorded the motive power on the 6.15 pm express to Euston. This train used the Styal line and stopped at Wilmslow where it picked up through coaches from Colne. A Crewe locomotive was rostered for this train. Given below are Eric's notes for the workings of this service-now over 80 years past.

April 17th	"Claughton" No.2174 *E.C.Trench*
April 24th	"Precursor" No.60 *Dragon*
August 20th	"Renown" No.1940 *Trafalgar*
No date	"Claughton" No.1093 *Guy Calthrop*
August 26th	"Claughton" No.1914 *Patriot*
September 4th	"Claughton" No.1345 *James Bishop*
September 8th	"Compound" No.1166 (LMS engine)
September 10th	"Waterloo" No.814 *Henrietta*
No date	"Precursor" No.1395 *Harbinger*
September 16th	"Precedent" No.919 *Naysmith*
No date	"Renown" No.1946 *Diadem*
September 17th	"Claughton" No.1914 *Patriot*
September 19th	"Claughton" No.5900 *Sir Gilbert Claughton*
September 22nd	"Compound" No.1160 (LMS engine)
September 25th	"Claughton" No.1131 *Lord Faber*
September 28th	"Claughton" No.1161 *Sir Robert Turnbull*
September 29th	"Prince of Wales" No.2152 *Charles Lamb*
No date	"George the Fifth" No.2155 *W.C.Brocklehurst*
September 30th	"Claughton" No.1345 *James Bishop*

All-in-all an amazing record and an example of diligence and accuracy. Just to have handled notebooks from such an age is a privilege and we should be eternally grateful to such people as Eric Dalton for their pains.

London Road, n.d: As the modernisation of the station involved the removal of the turntable it seems appropriate to include a picture of its installation. Two cranes-one from Longsight and another, unknown, grapple with the gargantuan load, a product of Crewe Works and proudly carrying the legend in the centre: "LMSR Crewe Works 1932". As is usual with these operations there is an abundance of observers! Early maps of the station show two 'tables outside the train shed: that on the LNWR side where this, later, larger installation is positioned and a second outside the MS&L's side of the terminus situated above the junction of Sheffield Street and Travis Street, removed when the remodelled track layout was introduced, parallel with the new power signalling of 1908/09. Notice the buildings of Mayfield station in the background; pristine-looking, the form a stark contrast to the bombed-out hulks remembered by most observers in the 1950s and '60s. Collection of *J.Suter*

(Right) London Road, 1935: Former LNWR "George the Fifth" Class 4-4-0 No **5325** *Sir Thomas Brooke* has arrived at platform 1 with an express. Built between 1910-15 these engines were a superheated version of the earlier "Precursors" of the same type. LNW locos had to work hard to earn their keep; double-heading was a rarity and performances of these locomotives were legendary. By now, though, the top link days of both 4-4-0 types were long over and *Sir Thomas Brooke's* trip today was most likely to have been a Down working from Crewe or Stafford. Worthy of note are the twin columns marking out the extension made by the LNWR in the mid-1880s. Platform numbering at London Road was always an odd business; for example there was no platform 2 in those days. These days, however, things are straightforward and the same columns now span platforms 8 and 9.

L.Hobdey/J.M.Bentley **collection**

(Centre) London Road, 1936/37: Inside the train shed in pre-War days: a Crewe North (5A) "Jubilee" No **5587** *Baroda* in gleaming crimson lake waits at platform 1 with an express for Euston. The "two company" status of the station is clearly seen here; notice the iron railings separating the LMS platform 1 from those designated "A-C" and belonging to "the other lot." The picture can be dated as post-15/5/36 when the engine was named (the second-hand Fowler tender [off 6112] was acquired on 11/5/36) and before 11/9/37 when *Baroda* was sent south to Kentish Town. ***Author's collection***

(Right) London Road, mid-late 1930s: In an essentially low-key photograph a "Black 5" approaches with an express from the south. Few were the times when a scene such as this was captured on camera. Yet it is one that must have been replicated umpteen times over: an express runs along the approach tracks to a terminus and slows as it enters the train shed to head alongside its allocated platform. Even rarer is the fact that this picture shows the London Road of pre-World War II. Notice, for example, that the signalbox in the centre-London Road No.2-has no concrete "umbrella" to shield it from bomb damage. All around are features of this terminus of yesteryear: the squat LNW semaphores contrasting with the slender GC types, the water tank, loading gauge and the distinctive signalboxes. Even the peaked-capped figure has now passed into history. ***Author's collection***

"The Mancunian" - To native Mancunians, "dinner" meant a midday meal. In "posh" circles it meant an evening meal. To BR's caterers of the mid-1950s this was the meal served to passengers on this special train –leaving Euston at 6.00 pm and arriving back in London Road at 9.30 after paying the usual call at Wilmslow. Notice the French overtones applied to the various dishes. It was the tradition, right up to modern times, for the language to be used for such purposes-confusing even Frenchmen in the process! The writer, a trained chef, finds the menu to be traditional and very much in keeping with what would be presented in a good class establishment of the time. Notice the lack of any reference to "Vegetarian" dishes-something unthinkable nowadays. But even today, such food, properly cooked and presented, would find a welcome at most tables. Dish names come and go, but good food and wine remains the same whatever the period. Alas, in today's world, with ever-faster schedules, in-train dining has become a luxury and one that now fetches high prices on special Pullman trains that are far removed from BR's 1950s value for money fare. And for those of you who like to "do a bit" in the kitchen at home, spare a thought for the chefs who pre-pared on-train food in those far-off days and try to imagine working in a kitchen just 8 ft. wide, often with an anthracite stove and no microwave cooker. No joke, either!   ***Author's collection***

FAMOUS LMS TRAINS

THE MANCUNIAN
Dinner

16/6

Hors d'Oeuvres Varies
or
Celery Soup

Turbot Dugléré

Grilled Lamb Cutlets, Tomato and Mushrooms
Spinach à la Crème
Duchess and Lyonnaise Potatoes
French Salad

Pineapple Singapore
or
Cheese, Biscuits and Cress

Coffee, 1/-

Cheese and Biscuits, etc., may be served in addition to the Sweet for an extra charge of 1/9

In the general interest, dogs are not allowed in Restaurant Cars

May we draw your attention to the interesting wines now provided at prices as reasonable as any you will find in this country

PLEASE ASK FOR A BILL
BRITISH TRANSPORT HOTELS LIMITED
RAILWAY CATERING SERVICES

"THE MANCUNIAN"
EXPRESS RESTAURANT CAR SERVICE

LONDON (EUSTON)
AND
MANCHESTER

EUSTON dep. 4.10 p.m.   MANCHESTER dep. 9.45 a.m.
MANCHESTER arr. 8.0 p.m.   EUSTON arr. 1.0 p.m.

LONDON MIDLAND AND SCOTTISH RAILWAY

(Above-right) Post WW2 Magazines carried the LMS advertisement of the "The Mancunian" although it was not until the early 1950's that the head-boards appeared on the front of the trains.

Manchester London Road, February 28th 1959: So much has been written about No **46229** *Duchess of Hamilton* since she was withdrawn and so many miles of film have been expended capturing her, that it is inadvertently forgotten that she was once just another "Duchess" in revenue-earning service with the LMS and British Railways. Work in the foreground, the truncated turntable track and rising brickwork-all suggest movement towards change. But the Type 4s have yet to come and steam still has much to do. Steam at 250lb psi roars into the chill winter morning air as this, the mightiest of locomotives pre-pares to roll out of the station. The train is "The Mancunian", the time must be just about 9.34-departure was one minute later with arrival in Euston at 1.20. Running non-stop, this-surely the most celebrated of the London Road to Euston expresses-will take the Styal line at Slade Lane junction. Oh now to stand on Mauldeth Road station to witness the maroon beauty and her matching train: red headboard, coach destination boards painted in the distinctive light blue, tables laid with white linen in the dining car for lunch and running non-stop to boot. What sheer and utter style!   *J W Sutherland*

(Right) London Road, May 21st 1948: Seen alongside platform 4 is 9A's LMS Compound 4-4-0 No **1122**. The photographer has noted the engine as "Station Pilot", though the stopping train headcode would suggest otherwise. Maybe the single coach is waiting to be being marshalled into a local passenger formation. Just visible is the station's No.3 signalbox straddling the platforms. Known as "the lighthouse" it conformed to the usual LNWR practice of numbering multiple signalboxes in ascending order from the London end of the railway. ***W.D.Cooper***

London Road, c.1948: Superb lighting, a low camera angle and a clean engine, all are ingredients in this splendid photograph. Pulling strongly away from either platform 8 or 9 is "Royal Scot" No **46139** *The Welch Regiment* with an express for London Euston. Then allocated to 1B (Camden), 46139 was one of seven of these almost iconic locomotives based at the London shed around the time of this picture. "Scot" buffs will notice the lack of smoke deflectors, a fitting that altered the appearance of these fine engines radically. Noted also is 46139's 2A taper boiler-a process begun in 1943 and not completed until as late as 1954; *The Welch Regiment* receiving hers in November 1946. ***David Wotton***

(Below) The Longsight fireman leans from his cab as "Royal Scot" No **46145** The *Duke of Wellington's Regt (West Riding)* prepares to leave platform 1 (later No 4) with the (Sunday) 10.00 express to Euston on March 26th 1950. Appearing, still, in the 1946 "black and straw" livery with maroon lining. No 46145's tender has yet to catch up with the British Railways era which began about fifteen months previously. The first two coaches of the train look like something fresh from the Hornby-Dublo box and are as yet unsullied by the steam age atmosphere; a few trips to Euston will accomplish the necessary "weathering" no doubt! The "horse" or "carriage landing" between the platforms by the ex-GCR signal box was a popular gathering point for the "spotters" of the day. Attention would often be focused over to the semaphore signals in the foreground which guarded the exit from the MSJ&A platform roads. But, alas, a J39, a "Crab" or a "4F" would be a poor substitute for the 'namer' seen here. ***J D Darby***

A SCHOOLBOYS MEMORIES OF LONDON ROAD

Tony Quirke was a schoolboy at St.Bede's College in Alexandra Park from 1946 to 1951. He passed through London Road station daily en route from his home in Dukinfield before catching a number 80 bus from Portland Street to school. Tony's London Road influences must have worked their magic on him as he became a career railwayman. starting in offices at Gorton works and working his way via various administrative positions, he became eventually Sales & Marketing Manager for Inter City West Coast.

MANCHESTER LONDON ROAD

Date	Year	Number	Shed	Notes
15-Jun	1947	45508	5A	
26-Jul	1947	40107	9A	
23-Aug	1947	45334	27C	ex Crewe Works?
1-Oct	1947	42306	9D	
1-Oct	1947	42356	9C	
1-Oct	1947	42461	9A	
1-Oct	1947	42662	10C	ex Crewe Works?
2-Oct	1947	42305	9C	
2-Oct	1947	42319	9C	
2-Oct	1947	42392	9A	
2-Oct	1947	42402	9A	
2-Oct	1947	45190	84G	
3-Oct	1947	41159	9A	
3-Oct	1947	42669	5D	
3-Oct	1947	45436	5A	
4-Oct	1947	42351	9A	
4-Oct	1947	42577	2A	
4-Oct	1947	44781	26A	ex Crewe Works?
4-Oct	1947	45292	84G	
5-Oct	1947	44838	5A	
6-Oct	1947	42376	5D	
6-Oct	1947	42397	9A	
6-Oct	1947	44969	9A	
7-Oct	1947	42367	9D	
8-Oct	1947	46906	8B	Lymm/Arpley service
8-Oct	1947	67402	39A	
1-Dec	1947	62660	40B	ex Gorton Works
4-Dec	1947	46924	8B	Lymm/Arpley service
22-Jan	1948	45507	5A	
26-Jan	1948	50703	8B	Lymm service
12-Feb	1948	61186	38C	
14-Feb	1948	42369	9C	
14-Feb	1948	42395	9A	
14-Feb	1948	42887	9A	
21-Feb	1948	49285	9A	freight via MSJ&A
1-Mar	1948	42323	9C	
10-Mar	1948	45406	84G	
10-Mar	1948	45638	9A	
13-Mar	1948	44984	14B	ex Crewe Works?
17-Mar	1948	44751	9A	
17-Mar	1948	44752	9A	
18-Mar	1948	42366	9D	
19-Mar	1948	42444	3C	
23-Mar	1948	61063	38E	ex Gorton Works
13-Apr	1948	64918	39A	
17-Apr	1948	40138	9B	
17-Apr	1948	44871	9A	
24-Apr	1948	40002	6G	to/from Derby Works?
24-Apr	1948	61192	38C	ex Gorton Works
26-Apr	1948	42224	33B	ex Crewe Works
7-May	1948	42458	5D	
10-May	1948	43283	8B	Lymm/Arpley service
11-May	1948	42925	9A	
12-May	1948	42372	1A	
12-May	1948	44801	5A	
13-May	1948	61311	39B	
25-May	1948	42344	5D	
25-May	1948	42355	9C	
6-Jun	1948	42391	5C	
7-Jun	1948	40207	8B	Lymm/Arpley service
7-Jun	1948	42322	9A	
7-Jun	1948	42349	9C	
7-Jun	1948	45025	1E	
7-Jun	1948	49322	9A	freight via MSJ&A
7-Jun	1948	45025	1E	
7-Jun	1948	49322	9A	freight via MSJ&A
7-Jun	1948	61074	53A	
9-Jun	1948	45634	8A	
10-Jun	1948	40106	9B	
18-Jun	1948	49514	25A	freight via MSJ&A
21-Jun	1948	42672	5D	
28-Jun	1948	45350	8A	
13-Jul	1948	42430	9A	
11-Aug	1948	40080	8B	Lymm/Arpley service
13-Aug	1948	42935	9A	
28-Aug	1948	42357	9C	
28-Aug	1948	45107	24E	ex Crewe Works?
21-Sep	1948	44763	5A	
22-Sep	1948	42386	9C	
24-Sep	1948	45400	84G	
1-Oct	1948	42775	9A	
2-Oct	1948	45065	12B	
2-Oct	1948	45399	8A	
3-Oct	1948	42889	9A	
3-Oct	1948	43916	17B	freight via MSJ&A
5-Oct	1948	42673	5D	
5-Oct	1948	42675	5D	
6-Oct	1948	42360	5D	
7-Oct	1948	45106	12B	
7-Oct	1948	45143	5B	
8-Oct	1948	45180	84G	
9-Oct	1948	46168	1B	
9-Oct	1948	67445	37A	ex Gorton Works
10-Oct	1948	44764	5A	
12-Oct	1948	44749	9A	
12-Oct	1948	45070	1A	
13-Oct	1948	42463	9B	
13-Oct	1948	42778	9A	
13-Oct	1948	45141	10A	
16-Oct	1948	45281	84G	
16-Oct	1948	45571	24E	ex Crewe Works?
16-Oct	1948	61662	38A	ex Gorton Works
17-Oct	1948	42235	5D	
18-Oct	1948	42923	9A	
18-Oct	1948	42942	9D	
18-Oct	1948	44748	9A	
18-Oct	1948	45139	12B	
19-Oct	1948	42470	3D	
19-Oct	1948	42663	5D	
20-Oct	1948	42667	5D	
20-Oct	1948	42924	9A	
25-Oct	1948	42585	5D	
26-Oct	1948	45129	12B	
30-Oct	1948	40539	9A	
2-Nov	1948	42930	9A	
5-Nov	1948	45316	2B	

LONDON ROAD

Date	Year	Number	Code	Notes
8 Nov	1948	44800	6B	
8-Nov	1948	45347	8A	
16-Nov	1948	45267	14B	
23-Nov	1948	25673	5C	Stafford local
23-Nov	1948	41153	3E	
23-Nov	1948	45422	5A	
24-Nov	1948	45587	20A	
25-Nov	1948	43918	17D	
25-Nov	1948	44709	5A	
26-Nov	1948	40051	9A	
29-Nov	1948	40007	8A	Lymm/Arpley service
10-Dec	1948	42178	5D	new ex Derby Works
4-Jan	1949	61122	38C	
17-Jan	1949	42665	5F	
18-Jan	1949	42666	5D	
18-Jan	1949	47347	9A	
20-Jan	1949	44548	5D	
20-Jan	1949	46420	8D	Lymm/Arpley service
22-Jan	1949	42179	5D	new ex Derby Works
22-Jan	1949	42318	9D	
22-Jan	1949	49661	25D	freight via MSJ&A
8-Feb	1949	49586	27B	freight via MSJ&A
12-Feb	1949	42614	27D	
12-Feb	1949	61343	New	ex Gorton Works
16-Feb	1949	45680	9A	
2-Mar	1949	42343	5D	
2-Mar	1949	42363	9C	
18-Mar	1949	44771	5A	
18-Mar	1949	61344	New	ex Gorton Works
21-Mar	1949	64333	39A	
23-Mar	1949	60051	34E	5 pm Cleethorpes
26-Mar	1949	42364	5D	
26-Mar	1949	42670	5D	
27-Mar	1949	47400	9A	
30-Mar	1949	46663	8B	Lymm/Arpley service
3-Apr	1949	44721	5A	
4-Apr	1949	44738	6G	
1-Jun	1949	45454	68A	
10-Jun	1949	44438	5D	
11-Jul	1949	45195	5B	
18-Jul	1949	45027	1A	
23-Jul	1949	42155	5D	
23-Jul	1949	42543	5D	
23-Jul	1949	42671	5D	
23-Jul	1949	45014	68A	
27-Jul	1949	45530	9A	
30-Jul	1949	44718	8A	
30-Jul	1949	45500	9A	

HEATON NORRIS

Date	Year	Number	Code
26-Jul	1947	42939	5B
14-Feb	1948	49628	25E
22-Jan	1949	42941	2B
27-Jul	1949	44710	2A
27-Jul	1949	45631	9A

WILMSLOW

Date	Year	Number	Code
26-Jul	1947	52466	26A
14-Feb	1948	42398	9A
14-Feb	1948	44970	9A
31-Jul	1948	49093	2B

CHELFORD

Date	Year	Number	Code
10-Jun	1949	48436	8B
23-Apr	1963	42226	5D
29-Apr	1963	43063	9F
2-May	1963	48358	25D

LONDON ROAD

Date	Year	Number	Code	Notes
15-Sep	1949	42119	New	ex Derby Works
16-Sep	1949	42118	New	ex Derby Works
22-Sep	1949	45515	8A	
22-Sep	1949	45501	9A	
22-Sep	1949	45373	10C	
23-Sep	1949	45528	5A	
30-Sep	1949	42234	5D	
4-Oct	1949	62016	39A	
4-Oct	1949	42603	5D	
8-Oct	1949	42121	New	ex Derby Works
10-Oct	1949	42584	5D	
13-Oct	1949	44937	9A	
M4-Oct	1949	42603	5D	
8-Oct	1949	42121	New	ex Derby Works
10-Oct	1949	42584	5D	
13-Oct	1949	44937	9A	
13-Oct	1949	45071	1A	
14-Oct	1949	42569	27D	ex Crewe Works?
18-Oct	1949	46256	5A	ex Crewe Works?
19-Oct	1949	46143	9A	
31-Oct	1949	42772	9A	
31-Oct	1949	42936	9A	
31-Oct	1949	44750	9A	
31-Oct	1949	47528	9A	
7-Jan	1950	44537	22A	ex Horwich Works?
17-Jan	1950	40136	9A	
17-Jan	1950	42353	9B	
21-Jan	1950	44872	3D	
21-Jan	1950	44867	2A	
31-Jan	1950	45510	5A	
7-Feb	1950	45552	12B	
8-Feb	1950	44762	5A	
8-Feb	1950	42788	9A	
8-Feb	1950	45689	5A	
27-Feb	1950	45245	84G	
7 Mar	1950	44780	25B	
10 Mar	1950	46129	9A	
13-Mar	1950	44835	2A	
17-Mar	1950	46252	5A	
22-Mar	1950	46161	6J	
27-Mar	1950	45384	84G	
24-Apr	1950	61181	39B	
24-Apr	1950	42854	9A	
24-Sep	1950	46120	9A	
24-Apr	1950	42594	9A	
24-Apr	1950	42332	9B	
24-Apr	1950	42379	9B	
25-Apr	1950	45740	9A	
26-Apr	1950	45503	5A	
26-Apr	1950	42467	9A	
27-Apr	1950	45512	12B	
28-Apr	1950	42608	9A	
29-Apr	1950	42776	9A	
29-Apr	1950	44938	12B	
2-May	1950	42567	5D	
2-May	1950	42542	9A	
2-May	1950	42427	9A	
3-May	1950	67427	39A	
3-May	1950	45438	10C	
3-May	1950	67422	39A	
3-May	1950	42371	9D	
3-May	1950	41907	9A	
3-May	1950	42362	9C	
3-May	1950	41905	9A	
4-May	1950	41906	9A	

LONDON ROAD

Date	Year	No.	Code	Note
4-May	1950	42381	9C	
4-May	1950	42382	9C	
4-May	1950	42399	9A	
4-May	1950	46250	1B	ex Crewe Works?
5-May	1950	67431	39A	
5-May	1950	45592	5A	ex Crewe Works
5-May	1950	45250	2A	
5-May	1950	42599	9A	
5-May	1950	42575	9A	
8-May	1950	45441	2A	
12-May	1950	42350	9A	
15-May	1950	42664	5D	
17-May	1950	47341	9A	
21-May	1950	46160	9A	
21-May	1950	42478	9A	
21-May	1950	45307	9A	
22-May	1950	42582	5D	
22-May	1950	42446	1E	
24-May	1950	42370	9D	
27-May	1950	45506	5A	
3-Jun	1950	42365	9D	
21-May	1950	46160	9A	
21-May	1950	42478	9A	
21-May	1950	45307	9A	
22-May	1950	42582	5D	
22-May	1950	42446	1E	
24-May	1950	42370	9D	
27-May	1950	45506	5A	
3-Jun	1950	42365	9D	
3-Jun	1950	42607	8B	Lymm/Arpley service
3-Jun	1950	42345	5C	
3-Jun	1950	42354	9B	
3-Jun	1950	42315	9D	
8-Jun	1950	45391	2A	
8-Jun	1950	42468	5F	
13-Jun	1950	44678	New	
28-Jun	1950	61231	36E	
5-Jul	1950	44759	9A	
5-Jul	1950	61633	31B	ex Gorton Works
1-Jul	1950	46458	5A	
21-Jul	1950	42937	9A	
21-Jul	1950	45283	84G	
21-Jul	1950	42609	5D	
23-Jul	1950	42488	3C	
29-Jul	1950	42940	1A	
29-Jul	1950	42445	5D	
3-Sep	1950	42449	5D	
12-Sep	1950	61409	40B	5 pm Cleethorpes
13-Sep	1950	61369	38A	
14-Sep	1950	61406	40B	5 pm Cleethorpes
15-Sep	1950	61408	40B	5 pm Cleethorpes
16-Sep	1950	61407	40B	5 pm Cleethorpes
19-Sep	1950	42233	5D	
22-Sep	1950	46122	9A	
22-Sep	1950	61368	38A	
25-Sep	1950	61366	40B	5 pm Cleethorpes
28-Sep	1950	45685	22A	ex Crewe Works?
30-Sep	1950	46131	9A	
7-Oct	1950	61627	31A	ex Gorton Works
8-Oct	1950	42358	5F	
10-Oct	1950	61658	30A	ex Gorton Works
20-Oct	1950	42605	5D	
11-Nov	1950	42606	8B	Lymm/Arpley service
14-Nov	1950	61367	38A	
15-Dec	1950	46238	12B	ex Crewe Works?
29-Jan	1951	44681	5A	
20-Feb	1951	42256	33A	ex Crewe Works?
21-Feb	1951	70001	New	ex Crewe Works
24-Feb	1951	44831	2A	
2-Mar	1951	67424	39A	
6-Mar	1951	70002	New	ex Crewe Works
12-Mar	1951	70003	New	ex Crewe Works
14-Mar	1951	45000	2A	
19-Mar	1951	42958	3D	
20-Mar	1951	61375	40B	5 pm Cleethorpes
12-Apr	1951	70005	New	ex Crewe Works
18-Apr	1951	46424	8D	Lymm/Arpley service
25-Apr	1951	70006	New	ex Crewe Works
26-Apr	1951	46727	8B	Lymm/Arpley service
27-Apr	1951	70007	New	ex Crewe Works
30-Apr	1951	70008	New	ex Crewe Works
7-May	1951	70010	New	ex Crewe Works
14-May	1951	45418	3E	
14-May	1951	45395	3C	
22-May	1951	70012	New	ex Crewe Works
31-May	1951	70013	New	ex Crewe Works
5-Jun	1951	70014	New	ex Crewe Works
5-Jun	1951	44686	9A	
6-Jun	1951	44687	9A	
9-Jun	1951	45330	84G	
11-Jun	1951	67439	39A	
15-Jun	1951	70015	New	ex Crewe Works
16-Jun	1951	42063	5D	
26-Jun	1951	70016	New	ex Crewe Works
26-Jun	1951	61325	40B	5 pm Cleethorpes
26-Jun	1951	61374	40B	5 pm Cleethorpes
30-Jun	1951	42111	25F	ex Crewe Works?
9-Jul	1951	67450	39A	
9-Jul	1951	67425	39A	
14-Aug	1951	45430	2A	
23-Aug	1951	42683	5D	
16-Mar	1951	62661	40B	ex Gorton Works
15-May	1952	44683	5A	
21-Mar	1953	70031	9A	
29-Feb	1956	70044	9A	
25-Apr	1956	73001	84G	
21-Jun	1957	67782	39A	
28-Jun	1957	67781	39A	
23-May	1961	42110	24B	
5-Jun	1951	44686	9A	
6-Jun	1951	44687	9A	
9-Jun	1951	45330	84G	
11-Jun	1951	67439	39A	
15-Jun	1951	70015	New	ex Crewe Works
16-Jun	1951	42063	5D	
26-Jun	1951	70016	New	ex Crewe Works
26-Jun	1951	61325	40B	5 pm Cleethorpes
26-Jun	1951	61374	40B	5 pm Cleethorpes
30-Jun	1951	42111	25F	ex Crewe Works?
9-Jul	1951	67450	39A	
9-Jul	1951	67425	39A	
14-Aug	1951	45430	2A	
23-Aug	1951	42683	5D	
16-Mar	1951	62661	40B	ex Gorton Works
15-May	1952	44683	5A	
21-Mar	1953	70031	9A	
29-Feb	1956	70044	9A	
25-Apr	1956	73001	84G	
21-Jun	1957	67782	39A	
28-Jun	1957	67781	39A	
23-May	1961	42110	24B	

Manchester London Road, 1957: In the days of the steam railway the period after nightfall wove a special magic. Just look at the scene depicted here: the patchy yellowness wrought by tungsten bulbs provides a world apart from a few hours previous. The train is the 2.50 am Newspaper working from Manchester to Crewe. One can almost hear the gentle roar of steam from the Class 5's safety valves, the dull, throaty rasp of the engine's blower. Carrying "Newspaper Lights", the solitary glow from the oil lamp on the buffer beam looks almost impressionistic. Soon the train will move forward, along platform 8 the 4-6-0 will bark its way east into the sepulchral gloom of night out into "the sticks" and on towards Ardwick Junction on its night time journey south to the Cheshire railway Capital..

W. Johnson

London Road, 1955: A degree of modernisation had come to London Road in 1954 when the Manchester to Sheffield (Victoria) electrification scheme via the Woodhead Tunnel was inaugurated. First mooted by the LNER in 1936, the scheme used power at 1500V dc, the, then, modern standard. The work was all but postponed during the war and, when full-scale resumption came in the 1950s, the pre-war electrification standard was obsolete and was being passed over for the much lighter and cheaper 25kV ac system which had been adopted in France. Leaving platform 1 is Co-Co electric No **27003** at the head of an express probably bound for London Marylebone. 27003 was one of seven of the class designed as something of a mixed-traffic loco-motive-no less than 27 locomotives were proposed originally. Passenger traffic over Woodhead ceased in January 1970 and the line closed for good beyond Hadfield in July 1981. A sad end to a project that had such a prestigious start.

W.Johnson

London Road, MSJ&A, September 13th 1958: Hardly a picture of great composition but, nevertheless, one depicting a scene at a time that would become a turning point in the station's history. Over on the left, at platform 12, one of the green-livered 1500v dc electric units has come to the end of its journey from Altrincham. Motor coach No **M28584M** is at the head of the 3-car train. At platform 10 is the 2-coach motor train drawn by a very grubby-looking Ivatt 2-6-2 tank engine, No **41212**. Today is Saturday and a little timetable research shows that this will be the 8.29 am Warrington Bank Quay (Low Level) due here at 9.26; the electric train was due here at the same time. Across in the main station "The Mancunian", pride of the London Road-Euston expresses, waits for "the off" at 9.35; a little extra time is allowed today-the train, the only non-stop express plying the route, will arrive at Euston at 1.20-fifteen minutes after the weekday arrival time. But how all this would change with modernisation: after completion of the electrification to Crewe in September 1960 the 1500V dc electrics would be banished to Oxford Road never to return. In a similar vein, from Monday services over the Lymm line to Warrington and Liverpool will terminate at Warwick Road for the duration of the winter timetable. After that, they, also, will terminate at Oxford Road. In the early 1960s lovers of named trains must bid farewell to "The Mancunian" and even the porters' barrows will eventually pass into history. Platform 12 had no through running facility, the track ended at a buffer stop at the platform end. A line out of sight to the left of the picture led to the station's water tank and turntable (Q.V.), even a small coaling stage once existed here too.   *Tom Noble*

LONDON ROAD, MSJ&A

Opened in 1849, the Manchester, South Junction & Altrincham Railway was one of Manchester's first truly suburban lines. Leaving the city on a series of viaducts before curving away to parallel the Bridgewater Canal, the 8 mile railway passed first through the urban districts of Cornbrook and Old Trafford. Here was the famed "White City" the home of the Art Treasures exhibition mounted in 1857 and visited by Queen Victoria and Prince Albert. Beyond was the district of Brooklands named after the Manchester banker Samuel Brooks who bought several hundred acres of farmland in neighbouring Timperley with a view to developing sections of the land for housing. Timperley, served by the "Junky", housed a population of a mere thousand or so people when the railway arrived; but this would double over the next twenty years as more houses were built, fuelled by the arrival, from 1865, of another railway-the Stockport, Timperley & Altrincham Junction line-later to become part of the CLC. Timperley remained very much a rural community until after the

First War when estates either side of Park Road-the thoroughfare from the village down to the Chester Road-sprang up. This was more or less the end of Timperley as a market gardening area, the inevitable commercial fact of life being that land commands a much higher price for housing than it does for producing food. And so to neighbouring Altrincham where the line continued through leafy Hale and on to Chester. From here the railway was CLC territory and the "Junky's" remit ended.

Effectively the "Altrincham Line" was in two major parts: that from London Road via Oxford Road down to Ordsall Lane where a junction was made with the LNWR's lines from Liverpool Road (originally the L&M) and Manchester Exchange westwards to Liverpool. Second, at Castlefield Junction where the line swung south-westwards to form the "Altrincham Branch"-as it is known to Manchester railwaymen. Here was very much canal territory, the railway passing close by the Manchester Ship Canal (opened in 1893) and the previously-mentioned Bridgewater Canal-"The Duke's Cut").

MSJ&A, bridge spanning Oxford Road; April 12th 1934: The Manchester City Engineer's photographic department were certainly thorough in their coverage of the city's railway structures and their results provide us with a unique record of structures-images long since consigned to the mists of history. This is an early bridge, sited at the junction of Oxford Road and New Wakefield Street. The structure would have dated from the building of the line back in the 1840s. It was in January 1849 that tragedy struck along this section of railway during construction of the viaduct arches close to Gloucester Street, just west of Oxford Road station. One arch collapsed on withdrawal of timber scaffolding killing two men and injuring several others. The cause was put down to mortar in the brickwork not being properly set, insufficient allowance not having been made for wet weather conditions. No such problems were extant here and the brickwork, sandstone abutments and the six wrought iron girder spans look as sound as they did almost 110 years ago. With the razor-sharp definition obtainable from a glass plate size 12" X 10" it is possible to glean even the smallest details. For example: we can see that cheap return tickets (any day, any train) are available over the MSJ&A from Oxford Road station. Examples seen are: Knott Mill 2d, Old Trafford 3d, Warwick Road 4d, Stretford 5d, Dane Road 7d, Sale 8d, Brooklands 9d, Timperley 10d, Navigation Road and Altrincham were both charged 1/-, all by "fast electric service". Motor fuel in the form of BP Ethyl is stated as "now leading", while "Dangerous Days" is the big film feature at the Deansgate Cinema. And "Savill's perfect pies and sausages" are guaranteed to be made from the same recipe as 1790. Next door is one of Manchester's one-time most famous shops: The Oxford Rubber Company", an emporium selling wares "for the weekend" when such things were only mentioned in whispers. 12 hour opening (10.00 am-10.00 pm) was a rarity in those days and one wonders if the gent in the black coat and Homburg hat is perusing his list before entering to buy, perhaps, one of the store's "Reliable French Specialities"- the mind boggles! *Manchester City Engineer's Archive*

The MSJ&A was run as a joint enterprise right up until Nationalisation. Hitherto, the LMS and LNER had taken over where GC and LNW had left off. The biggest fillip to the railway came in 1931 when the 1500V dc overhead line scheme transformed the line from London Road to Altrincham into one of north-west England first wholly-electrified lines of any length using the newly-prescribed system; though the Victoria-Bury scheme of the L&YR in 1916 must take historical preference as the city's first electric suburban railway.

Traffic passing over the MSJ&A was principally of a suburban nature. The 1931 timetable, instituted upon electrification from May 11th, gave 92 trains each way-increased from 68 up and 67 down-with journey times down from 27 minutes in steam days to 24 and, ultimately, 22 minutes using electric traction. Also using

MSJ&A tracks were the Manchester London Road to Liverpool Lime Street trains via Warrington Bank Quay (Low Level)-some trains ran to Warrington only. These left the system at Timperley Junction and travelled via Lymm, Thelwall and on to Warrington. This service ended on September 8th 1962. Until the opening of Manchester's Exchange station in 1880 the LNWR took advantage of their joint ownership of the line by running a service (albeit sparse) from London Road to Bolton (Great Moor Street) via Ordsall Lane and Eccles. Also working over the branch were the Manchester Central to Chester trains of the former CLC- these joined at Old Trafford Junction, having left the parent line at Cornbrook West Junction. Until around the late 1960s the "Altrincham Trip" was worked by a Trafford Park engine and called with local pick-up freight along the MSJ&A. Another reg-

Manchester London Road, late 1880s; The driver and fireman gaze in earnest at the photographer as their engine waits in the Up MSJ&A platform. Seen here is No.**2004** *Witch*, a former Ramsbottom "Newton" Class 2-4-0 built at Crewe in April 1871. Notice the "oven door" front to the smokebox, complete with chain and the early form of communication cord hanging along the tender-literally that and interesting how the name stuck up to modern times. *Witch* was rebuilt to an "Improved Precedent" or "Jumbo" under Webb in May 1891; she was scrapped in July 1912. Behind the platform wall can be seen one of the earlier LNWR signalboxes that existed here before the power signalling schemes of the early 20th century. Notice the oval and diamond-shaped boards hung on the right-hand framing where the signalman stands. An early form of warning system, these were turned about face to indicate the state of the signals and the telegraph instruments i.e. in working order or not. There were two boxes in front of the train shed in these early years and another, known as "London Road Junction", stood a little way out on the viaduct and controlled movements between the London Road approaches and Ardwick Junction.

Author's collection

ular freight working was the "Evening Ardwick Goods" to Altrincham which was due in the town at 4.00 pm. This train was worked on a five-year cycle, alternating between the LNER using Gorton engines and the LMS who used an engine from Longsight. The former LNW shed at Patricroft worked two freight trips to Altrincham. One was a goods trip which only ran as required and assumed the logical name of "The Patricroft". Secondly was a cattle train on Tuesday evenings from Cross Lane cattle dock in Salford. The "South Junction" section of the MSJ&A has seen Freightliner traffic since the inception of the Trafford Park freight terminal, while the short section of the branch between Deansgate Junction and Altrincham has, inter alia, the daily limestone hopper trains en route to and from Northwich.

Taking an overview, the MSJ&A was a busy railway with a varied pattern of traffic, notwithstanding that, from 1931, its stopping passenger trains had conformed to what might be termed by some as a dull uniformity. Indeed, to cope with the traffic flow, the section from Old Trafford to Sale had been quadrupled under an Act of July 1891.It was the intention to take the four tracks as far as Timperley, but this was reneged upon due to cost limitations. Progress with the quadrupling had gone ahead in fits and starts and by 1897 the widening had only reached Stretford. After the withdrawal of services over the Lymm line in September 1962 the line

was reduced to two track working and remains so to this day. The exception being the two single line stretches (Network Rail and Metrolink) between Deansgate Junction (where the former CLC tracks join) and Altrincham.

Since the 1500V dc electrification was instituted in 1931, the MSJ&A has undergone several major changes. The first came in 1960 when the Manchester-Crewe 25kV ac scheme was inaugurated. This resulted in the "Junky's" electric trains terminating at Oxford Road-something that lasted until May 1971. Through running from Altrincham to Crewe, via either Styal or Stockport, then became possible with the whole of the Altrincham branch being upgraded to 25kV. The service was operated variously by Class 304, 305 and 303 EMUs. 25kV operation lasted until December 24th 1991 when the system was closed awaiting yet another conversion.

ARRIVAL OF METROLINK

For many years there had been talk of both underground and extended suburban rail systems in Manchester. In the mid-1960s an underground system was actively sought for the city centre and many millions of pounds were expended on exploratory and other works. But lack of government finance scuppered the scheme. Then came "LRT" or "Light Rapid Transit" in full. Ostensibly, a

London Road, MSJ&A, c.1914-22: A complete contrast in both locomotive style and rolling stock is presented in this early MSJ&A view. Great Central 0-6-0 class 9D (LNE J10) No.676 (a Kitson product of 1892) blows off at the head of an Up passenger train bearing "express lights". The engine is in the GCR lined black goods livery and the picture can be dated to post-January 1914 when 676 was fitted with a Belpaire boiler-one of the first 18 engines converted, the remainder being so-fitted from new.

P.F.Cooke

completely new concept was being shown to the travelling public. But, of course, it was not new. Based on trams, "Light Rail" was cheaper than its heavy counterpart, but hadn't the city had a tram network-something abandoned in 1947 and seen, even then, as a very old fashioned mode of transport? From the start, there was scepticism: angry letters appeared in The Manchester Evening News-trams had connotations of rough riding, cramped and cold conditions and their renaissance seemed like a bad idea-at least to some older citizens.

So, spawned from the idea of LRT, Metrolink made its debut on the Altrincham line on June 15th 1992-the Royal opening did not arrive until July 17th. Now the MSJ&A had had three separate operating voltages: 1,500 dc, 25 kV ac and now, finally, 750V dc. Much work was needed to separate the line from the BR system at the Manchester end. At Piccadilly station the vehicles run into a new station in the old undercroft behind Store Street. Leaving Piccadilly station trams run along Aytoun Street before threading through Piccadilly alongside the gardens and splitting: one way towards Victoria-where they have taken over the old L&YR line to Bury-and the other along Mosley Street and over St.Peter's Square. From here the Midland Hotel is passed before a raised section takes the system alongside what is now G-MEX (the exhibition centre converted from the former CLC's Central station) and out over the viaduct spanning the Castlefield area. So, 125 years or so after Central station opened, trams are now running over the former approach tracks. Beyond Cornbrook station, where the new branch to Salford

Quays and Eccles deviates, Metrolink takes a steep dive to pass under the re-aligned heavy rail Liverpool line-itself the former Altrincham branch from Castlefield Junction as far as Old Trafford. (Non-Mancunians had better study a map here-the geography is complicated!) One final amendment was made to the track layout between Timperley and Altrincham. From Deansgate Junction through Navigation Road to Altrincham station the running lines are shared between Metrolink and the national network. Metrolink uses the old Up line on the west side while the former Down track is reserved for traffic coming off the old CLC tracks round from Skelton Junction-the path now taken by Manchester-Chester trains, themselves displaced from the former MSJ&A tracks since their take over by Metrolink's trams.

The conversion to Metrolink has not been without its problems. Much criticism has been voiced about overcrowding at peak times. Initially, trams ran in multiple-2x 2-car sets being common, but this now seems to be a rarity. Delays and occasional power failures occur, much to the frustration of the travelling public. Lack of finance to update and extend the system has been sought over the last ten years and a future Metrolink system may eventually extend to the far-flung reaches of Manchester-the airport, Didsbury, Ashton-under-Lyne, Oldham and Rochdale. But this is taking us into ever deeper water and is outside the scope of this work. For the time being, in the 21st century, the railway to Altrincham is as busy as ever. Long may the spirit of the old MSJ&A continue.

Manchester London Road, MSJ&A 1938: Longsight's 2P No **332** casts wisps of steam towards the overhead line after bringing an afternoon train over the Lymm line from either Liverpool Lime Street or Warrington. *R D Pollard*

London Road, April 30th 1958. Straws in the wind alongside platform 10."Crikey, what's that?" one can almost hear something like this emerging from the lips of the three young spotters on the MSJ&A platform as English Electric Type 4 1-Co-Co-1 No **D202** rumbles past. the engine, brand new and fresh from the Vulcan foundry at Newton-le-Willows, Lancashire will be en route to Doncaster for proving trials. From here the engine was allocated to Stratford depot (30A) for express work out of Liverpool street. Whatever the teething troubles of these, BR's first production batch of high powered Diesels, the Type 4's held the reigns of main line motive power for many years surviving into modern times as Classes 40, 44 and 45.
B K B Green

(Below) Mayfield Station, August 25th 1960: Mayfield station seen in its last flush of passenger operation. On the left the DMU, thought to be working the 5.27 pm service to Stockport, occupies the short "platform 5" which was created during the period of the rebuilding of London Road.In the shadow of the station roof a "Black 5" waits with the 5.20 pm train to Stoke-on-Trent. "Crab" 2-6-0 No.**42848** is at the head of the 5.30 pm train to Chelford. Mayfield closed its doors to passengers two days later, on Saturday September 27th.
H.D.Bowtell courtesy MLS.

THE MODERNISATION OF LONDON ROAD STATION

London Road, September 1959: By the middle of 1959 demolition contractors were ripping into the Victorian structure that was the old Manchester London Road. Perhaps if Hitler's Luftwaffe had been better equipped they might have done the job free of charge- and 19 years earlier! Here, workmen from contractors Connell & Finnigan are seen busying themselves amidst a cloud of dust and dirt as wood, masonry, rubble and brickwork fall around them. This well-captured scene shows the remains of the former LMS offices seen in close-up in our earlier picture. Up above, men are variously perched on the remains of demolished ledges awaiting their next task. The Health & Safety at Work Act was still some 15 years off; not a steel helmet, orange jacket or steel-capped boot to be seen anywhere! But cloth caps were de rigeur.

Park Pictures

London Road, summer 1959: Moving slightly to the left-towards the ex-LNER side of the station-Connell & Finnigan move remorselessly onwards. Just look at the man perched high above the second storey-demolishing almost the very brickwork on which he is standing! Unabashed by the work going on above and around them, the passengers and their driver from a Vauxhall Cresta saloon car-registration number 345 FTC-chat blithely away. But it was a different world then and our attitudes to health and safety have changed somewhat in the meantime.

Author's collection

London Road, October 1959: Had the modernisation of the station been contemplated today there can be little doubt that a complete shutdown would have been on the cards. Later in 1959, amidst all the chaos, noise, debris and dirt, two ladies, bags firmly in hand, make their way towards their train. But, doubtless, people from their generation would have been old enough to remember the war and the associated trauma-blitzkrieg and all. This.....was a mere bagatelle. *British Railways*

(Right) London Road, September 1959: With the junction of Whitworth Street and Aytoun Street seen far below, the photographer has moved high up above the ex-LMS offices. Here, two huge lead-covered coping stones have been eased away from their position by a large crowbar. Now the tricky manoeuvre of getting them earthwards begins! This late summer picture shows the appalling risks involved in such tasks; to say nothing of taking the photograph!

British Railways

London Road, c.1959: While London Road's front offices were being rebuilt some form of temporary accommodation was required. Mancunians may well remember this building-the wooden edifice erected at the top of the station approach in front of the former LNER side of the station. By later standards the buildings were quite smart, catering even for 'gentlemens hairdressing.' Notice the 'Sleeper Reservations' sign-a true remnant of a bygone era. *British Railways*

London Road, April 1960. After the demolition of the frontage this was the task facing the builders in April 1960: the rebuilding of the station from the ruins left behind after demolition. Something of London Road's history reveals itself in this view. Notice the twin columns in the centre of the picture; these mark the boundary of the extensions undertaken by the LNWR between February 1880 and January 1883 with extra roofing and platforms being added. Now the concrete supports are in place, the twin columns now stand on the island platform that is today's number 8 and 9.

British Railways

FAIRFIELD STREET

A group of impressive structures spanned Fairfield Street carrying the approach lines to the former London Road station. On the west side two bridges, already described, carried the MSJ&A lines while a short distance further east was this bridge: spanning Fairfield Street at its junction with Temperance Street and dating from Manchester & Birmingham days; numbered 33-opening No.109. A structure, 129 feet wide, the opening consisted of stone abutments with cast iron arched ribs and floor plates; it was later widened with brick abutments, steel main and cross girders and rolled steel beams and floor plates.

Fairfield Street, October 9th 1909: A magnificent study of the bridge looking east along Fairfield Street from its junction with Temperance Street. With its beautifully-laid sandstone abutments-complete with decorative cappings, and the wonderfully-crafted cast iron arches, surely this is a structure qualifying as a work of art. An LNW minute dated November 15th 1905 records.. "acceptance of a tender from Robert Neill, Manchester & Sons (£144,300) for London Road to Ardwick Widening, Manchester." The semaphore signals mark this side out as distinctly LNWR territory. Notice the arms affixed with the 'X'-the re-signalling here was not completed until 1913 when the station's No.2 signalbox opened. Contemporary touches are provided by the poster advertising the Alhambra Theatre; one wonders what sort of entertainment was provided by Bessie Slaughter, Percy Johnson, Kitty Traney and Shaun Glenville-and THE FATAL WEDDING?!
Manchester City Engineers' Archive

Fairfield Street, November 11th 1956: Just under half a century later and this is the bridge viewed from the same spot. Notice now the section spreading out at a tangent from the earlier structure; modernity has given way to 19th century formality. The alteration was doubtless necessary to accommodate an altered track layout. Alas, this was a typical Manchester winter's day; cold, and thoroughly wet. Notice, again, the M&BR coat of arms on the bridge and the two contemporary signs. A glamorous-looking blonde lady tantalizingly advertises "Players Please", while below is seen a long-defunct motor fuel-Mobilgas. Notice that trolleybus wires have replaced those of the earlier trams. Leading off to the right is Temperance Street, the arched brickwork being the boundary wall of Mayfield station.
British Railways

Fairfield Street, late 1958/early 1959: A most interesting view showing bridge 33/109 in the throes of reconstruction. Leonard Fairclough's bridgeworks are well advanced and the SHMD trolleybus is coping well beneath the 16ft.6in. headroom. On the bridge itself Fowler 2-6-4 tank No **42399** moves away during a shunt-possibly in connection with the works. How different reconstruction operations were all those years ago; the emphasis then being to keep the traffic moving wherever possible. In today's climate of "Rolls Royce" health and safety, Fairfield Street would be a "no go" area with total shutdown of the railway being the norm while such work was proceeding.   *Norman Harrop*

Fairfield Street, February 11th 1960: The fourth in our section showing the celebrated bridge 33/109. Now the engineers have gone, their work completed and the rather functional cast concrete arches and decking have replaced the hitherto wrought and cast iron of the Manchester & Birmingham and the LMS. Overhead, the electric line is up and ready for energising later on in the year. The GCR semaphores, visible in the 1958 view, have gone but their LNWR counterparts remain: signalling of the immediate station area was not transferred to the new London Road power box until June 1960.   *British Railways*

Manchester London Road, January 28th 1958: Little had changed here-at the end of the MSJ&A system-since the installation of the 1500V dc electrification in 1931. Clearly visible is the large gantry to support the overhead line: 1500v dc required a lot of support. Apart from the re-numbered locomotive, this photograph could have been taken at almost any time within the last 27 years. The overhead water tank casts a shadow and gives this scene something of a gloomy look; but what a veritable mass of interesting detail is revealed in this broad canvas! 3F 0-6-0 No **43457**-revealed as an old 'dog' from my 1950s Ian Allan combined volume-waits for the road across towards Ardwick with a local freight working. Contrasting styles of signalling can be observed: the LNWR's squat arms were mostly of the Webb electric pattern, though this foreground specimen is wire-worked. In the background is the ex-GCR signalbox: originally installed in 1909 to work the company's side of the station and control the layout as far as Ardwick. Conceived as a pneumatically-operated system, it was converted to electro-pneumatic operation in the early 1930s; notice the large air reservoirs to the left of the box. A last point: what was the purpose of the impromptu coal brazier slung above the centre bearing? The scattered coals suggest this was to prevent freezing; the picture being taken at almost the coldest part of the winter. *British Railways*

(Right) Manchester London Road, July 10th 1958: Prior to re-construction of the Fairfield Street overbridge it was necessary to remove the station turntable in order that the former MSJ&A platforms could be lengthened along with re-modelled trackwork and to provide a site for the station's new power signalbox. Here workmen are busily demolishing the old turntable pit wall with a pneumatic drill; notice the removed timber footboards and the massive centre bearing-Pacifics were turned here once. London Road's No.2 signalbox stands off to the right. The removed turntable is thought to have found a new home at Heaton Mersey shed.

British Railways

Moving east along Fairfield Street to its junction with Travis Street two contrasting views of the turntable site are seen.

(Above) January 28th 1958: Travis Street was the site of the original small terminus built on the London Road site. No evidence of this can be seen today, only the overbridge and the hulk of brickwork supporting the massive overhead water tank by the turntable. A variety of pursuits are advertised to cheer the rather dejected-looking chap in front of the gate. It looks as if he really could do with a break and a *Kit Kat*, though perhaps his pocket lacked the loose change - 5d or 2$\frac{1}{2}$d - required! Failing this he could visit Belle Vue Circus or the performance of "Cinderella" at the Ardwick Hippodrome, nibble a 6d bar of *Néstle's* milk chocolate or down a pint of *Chesters* beer.

(Right) November 8th 1960: The new power box is now in situ, the glass, steel and concrete edifice having taken over the operations of all five of the previous signalboxes in the London Road area some five months previously. Notice the bridge works, too, are now complete with new decking, supports and parapets. Despite the station's change of name to "Piccadilly" in September 1960, signals operated by the power box were labelled "LR" until the new signalling centre came into operation in the 1990s.

British Railways

London Road power box, April 9th 1960: A glimpse inside the new box. Power working was nothing new to the station as both the LNW and the GC had their own systems dating from the early 20th century. But in the new box, for the first time, centralised control of the whole station and the outlying areas was brought under one umbrella for the first time. Seen here is the track diagram sited above the upright panels. These housed signalmans' telephones, the transmitting end of the train describers, overlap keys, control switches for outlying ground frames and emergency telephones. Below can be seen the console holding the route-setting signal switches. One switch sets up a whole route, ensures all the points are detected and allows the signals to come "off." The track diagram shows something of the complexity of the London Road layout: the lines below show the junctions at Ardwick, to the right are those leading to the station platforms-notice the tangent at the top leading to the now long-gone Mayfield station. At the top left appears a row of lights; these are "route lights" showing along the whole length of the section concerned. They will remain lit until a train has passed through and the approach and route-locking released behind it, section by section. Prominent on the diagram are the four-figure indicators: the first figure describes the train-"one" for an express, "two" for a stopping passenger, the second figure gives the train's destination and the last two numbers identify the train itself.

Tom Noble

MANCHESTER LONDON ROAD

Manchester Victoria, June 4th 1960: Whilst the last heave to complete the transformation at London Road was going on, a whole programme of diversions was put in place. Typifying these is this picture showing English Electric Type 4 No **D219** passing along the Up main between platforms 11 and 12 of Manchester's Victoria station. Normally leaving London Road at 9.45, "The Mancunian" today - a Saturday - has left earlier - departing from Exchange station, further along and to the west, at 9.22. After Victoria East junction, D219 will proceed along the Down Slow line* to face the formidable 1-in-59/1-in-47 of Miles Platting bank. Here the line curves round and continues along through Park station on the ex-L&Y's Ashton Branch through Clayton Bridge to Droylsden Junction. From here, "The Mancunian" will be running "over the Snipe", the 1 mile, 29 chain line to Ashton Moss Junction, so called after the famous public house that stood by the bridge taking the railway close to the junction of Droylsden Road and Manchester Road (the continuation of the Ashton New and Old roads respectively). Here, too, was sited Audenshaw station, though this was closed as far back as 1905. From Ashton Moss the train continued via Denton and Heaton Norris to reach Stockport Edgeley again. This diversionary route was a popular one, although the "Snipe" line was closed from July 7th 1969. Re-routing from Stockport to Victoria is still done today, trains now run from Denton via the former LNW line to the site of Crowthorn Junction to take the ex-OA&GB line to Ashton Moss North Junction (ex-L&Y) before proceeding along the Ashton Branch to Clayton Bridge and on as before to Miles Platting.

Tom Lewis

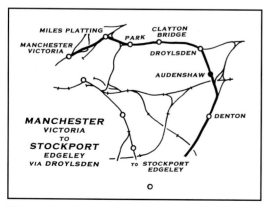

MILES PLATTING — CLAYTON BRIDGE — PARK — MANCHESTER VICTORIA — DROYLSDEN — AUDENSHAW — DENTON — TO STOCKPORT EDGELEY

MANCHESTER VICTORIA TO STOCKPORT EDGELEY VIA DROYLSDEN

Fairfield Street Overbridge August 22nd 1944: This was the massive structure, one of two such bridges, carrying the MSJ&A and associated lines, in and out of the station. Above are carried the two lines that split from the South Junction section to form the turntable road and the adjacent shunting neck. Behind, on the second bridge, are carried the MSJ&A running lines which passed through platforms 11 and 12. In the distance is the third Fairfield Street bridge that fringed onto Temperance Street (Q.V.) This is a wartime photograph: notice the shades over the street light and paucity of road traffic. A solitary lorry-BFM 540-is parked carrying wooden crates and a sack or two. Ahead, a horse-drawn dray carries barrels of beer-hooray, austerity does not quite reign supreme! Doubtless this good cheer has come down from Chester's Brewery in nearby Ardwick. Eventually, the BR Civil Engineer would arrive and ponder: to replace this structure would prove, indeed, to be a daunting task. *Manchester City Engineer & Surveyor's Dept.*

THE NEW BRIDGE OVER FAIRFIELD STREET

Without a doubt one of the biggest problems tackled by the London Midland Region's Civil Engineer in the run up to electrification was the renewal of the two MSJ&A bridges spanning Fairfield Street and described briefly in the adjacent photo caption.

Not only were the existing bridges on a quite severe skew, but they spanned the highway at a junction of three separate streets - Fairfield, Carston and Cotswold. The minimum span on the skew was 168ft and the overall length of the structure was some 388ft with an overall width of the bridge between parapets set at 64ft.

After initial ideas had been floated, it was decided that the new bridge would consist of a single main pre-stressed concrete slab span with two subsidiary parts. The main slab is carried on four staggered "point" supports: two were abutments and two consisted of columns. The new island platform itself formed part of the main slab, this being laid to a depth of 8ft. the tracks were carried on cantilever extensions, both transversely and logitudinally from them in a box-like section part of the slab. the main central part of the slab was of cellular construction, divided by vertical webs into three longitudinal compartments. The maximum width was around 31ft and that of each of the transverse sections was 16ft.

Lessons learned from the renewal of the earlier bridgewere taken on board here, with the hollow concrete slabs being supported on the four staggered "points". At Fairfield Street, massive, heavily reinforced concrete columns were used, each one designed to carry 2,500 tons. Both columns were capped with "point" bearings consisting of Meehanite castings having thick slabs of high quality steel embedded in them as contact surfaces - one flat, the other spherical.The height of the columns was about 19ft. from the underside of the slab to the pavement below.

All concrete was cast in situ and was post-stressed with a total compressive force of 12,000 tons. The bridge was designed for a total load of 5,750 tons. To ensure a satisfactory structure, tests on

71

a model were carried out at the Imperial College of Science & Technology, London. Designed under the supervision of Mr F Turton, Assistant Engineer, Bridges, London Midland Region, the main contractors were Leonard Fairclough who employed Stressed Concrete Design Ltd to prepare the drawings and calculations for the concrete work.

What is remarkable that the entire work, from the time the order was given to design and construct the bridge, was completed by the end of November 1959 - less than just one year from start to finish. Completing the report in *The Railway Gazette* (which was the reference source for the foregoing) the magazine noted that.. *"Such rapid progress is most creditable to all the staff concerned. it has been achieved under the general direction of Mr A N Butland, Chief Civil Engineer, London Midland Region."*

Fairfield Street, looking to London Road, Autumn 1958: Services over the MSJ&A were suspended from September 1958 while the new bridge works got under way. This picture shows well some of the massive amount of preparatory work that was necessary before the new structure could be put in place. Steel trestles are in place along Fairfield Street and, overhead, temporary supports enable the trolleybus wires to be suspended, ensuring continuity of services on the 218 and 219 routes to Ashton-under-Lyne. A sign-"keep left during bridge works"-seems to be the only cautionary note for the unwary. Two contemporary touches beneath the OXO sign are of interest: a lady passing by wearing a headscarf walks past a waiting car-a Ford Prefect-pity a poor motorist parking here now! Overhead, the enclosed footbridge leading across to Mayfield station is still in place, but behind, the bridges taking the MSJ&A tracks have been demolished. Work will quickly proceed now on their replacement. Behind the W.A.Nicholls sign can be seen the remains of the ornate arch that formed the entrance from here up the Altrincham line platforms. To the right is Travis Street, notice the sign for the depot that existed here. This was once the site of the first joint terminus along London Road before the mighty labyrinth evolved all above and around to become Manchester's premier station.
Norman Harrop

(Right) Looking east towards Temperance Street, this was the view on August 8th 1960, some nine months after the new works had been completed. Looking slender by comparison with its predecessor, the new bridge gives an altogether lighter and more modern look to the surroundings. Notice the trolley bus wires have been reinstated. Service No's 218 and 219 ran along Fairfield Street, the former to Stalybridge via Ashton, the latter to Ashton via Guide Bridge. Above the station site, work proceeds on the new footbridge, the previous structure that connected Mayfield with the main station having now been removed. Since the 2002 remodelling, further changes have taken place in the vicinity, the area to the left having now become the main road access point for taxis and passengers arriving at Piccadilly by road. The three shuttle services that connect with the city centre, along with the much vaunted 'rail service replacement' buses, are now the only passenger vehicles allowed up the old station approach in front of the concourse.
Graham Whitehead

Fairfield Street overbridge, MSJ&A lines, n.d: Probably dating from mid-1959 when the new works were in full swing, this was the view looking down towards Oxford Road-the old 1500V dc masts are clearly visible beyond the curve. Dominating the scene are the myriad of steel reinforcing rods for the concrete work. Hard to believe that, by the end of the year, the trains will be running again.

Raymond Keeley

The same scene, 1959: Once the main structure was complete the trains began to run again-unhindered by the plethora of health and safety regulations and allied "safety cases" that rule today's operations. A "Black 5" runs through with an unidentified train while work goes on above on the new footbridge. Notice the train is working "wrong line", although eventually this section would become signalled for bi-directional working. Below, the "Regent" petrol hoarding and two parked lorries add vintage touches.

British Railways

London Midland
British Railways
Region

EWS SPECIAL
(MANCHESTER EDITION)

No. 4   AUGUST, 1960

A MESSAGE TO PARENTS

VIEWPOINT

THE REAL ANSWER RESTS WITH THE PARENTS

ENGINEERS WORK ROUND-THE-CLOCK TO COMPLETE ELECTRIFICATION SCHEME

AHEAD OF SCHEDULE

LONDON ROAD READY FOR AUGUST 28

Final Testing Commences Shortly

SIGNS OF THE TIMES

MINISTER TO OPEN NEW SCHEME?

ELECTRIC SERVICES START NEXT MONTH

EXTRA AND FASTER SUBURBAN SERVICES

FACTS AND FIGURES

BRITISH RAILWAYS MODERNISATION
getting on with the job

Manchester London Road No.2 box, April 25th 1957: Half-past midday inside No.2 signalbox. This overlooked the station throat and was the second former LNW box on the approach tracks after No.1. Three others- the ex-GCR cabin, London Road's No.3 and a box covering the MSJ&A lines shared control of operations in the vicinity. As mentioned, this system was a joint enterprise: the brainchild of F.W.Webb, A.M.Thompson and one, I.A.Timmis, from the latter years of the nineteenth century. Known usually as Webb's "Crewe" electric system, it was but one of many similar contemporary systems. The miniature levers, spaced at 1 3/4in.centres, had three positions: normal-as seen in the first sixteen or so; pulled to midway the lever actuated a set of carbon blocks, thus completing the circuit to the point or signal. Pulled right back, the lever operated any facing point locks and also engaged a series of check locks. Interlocking was accomplished mechanically by a series of sliding tappets. Points were activated by a motor driving a worm and pinion, while signals were solenoid-operated from a 220 volt supply. A bonus for both footplate and lamp men was that the signals were electrically-lit also. As London Road No.2 sat on an elevated gantry, all the electrical switch and interlocking gear had to be housed in the steel-fronted cases below the levers. On the shelf above the lever frame, popularly the "block shelf", sat the various signalling instruments. To the side of the block bell nearest the camera can be seen an antediluvian telephone, next are two power warning lights, then the four circular train describers. Clearly visible is the pin and chain used for setting the routes. Typical indications were: Wilmslow via Styal; Buxton stopping at Stockport; Buxton not stopping at Stockport and stopping train between London Road and Stockport. Adjacent to the describers are two LNW wooden-cased, single-needle block instruments: the first communicates with the ex-GCR box for movements from the "Horse Landing" which sat on the former GC side below the box. Further down, other block instruments are for the Up Slow and Up Fast lines and for Down Slow and Down fast lines. The miniature levers are set in eleven individual banks: four, three and four more. Above the gap between the first and second bank can be seen clearly the large track diagram; showing the platform roads and the tracks into Mayfield station, the various lines are interspersed with red lights, each corresponding to an individual track circuit. A curiosity, a glass-fronted case with apertures beneath, is seen at the far end. This was to indicate movements from the station shunter's cabin and showed any movements between platforms 4-9. Normally, daytime operation of No.2 called for two signalmen and a "booking lad". Well-remembered here was Harold Adams-nicknamed "Bodkin" after the infamous doctor of the mid-1950s. London Road boxes Nos.1-3 closed on April 24th 1960, their duties being assumed by the new power box. *J.W.F. Scrimgeour, Signalling Record Society*

Piccadilly, September 1960. the work is complete and now the trains can run uninterrupted again. A scene showing the new power box above Fairfield Street, the redesigned track layout and the brand-new 25kV ac overhead lines.Prominent in the view is LR168, the multi-aspect colour light signal at the end of platform 11. Notice the recently closed (to passengers) Mayfield station in the background. Some years later, in 1970, Mayfield was connected via a high level overhead conveyor to Ancoats mail distribution centre for the Post Office. Policy changes throughout the postal industry during the 1980's ended this arrangement and consequently the huge overhead structure was finally removed during December 2003. *British Railways*

Manchester London Road, April 9th 1960. From around 1958 onwards, the overhead wiring trains had been a familiar sight on the ex-LNWR lines out of London Road. However, the curious ensemble seen here comprised an assortment of vehicles which warrants a little more attention. On this occasion, the train is in the hands of an 0-6-0 diesel shunter. The two vehicles to the left of the engine however were completed in 1950 as an 'overhead construction vehicle' which consisted of a two-car self-propelled articulated unit comprising a repair van and mess van with driving compartments at each end, specifically for the installation and maintenance of overhead suspension equipment on electrified lines. An independent vehicle (not seen here) for unreeling contact and catenary wire had also been built. When new, the unit was initially deployed on the Manchester South Junction and Altrincham line. To avoid the use of new material, the unit was, wherever possible, constructed from items of equipment which were readily available. For example, the underframe, bogies and two power units driving on the centre bogie with control gear were obtained from the two end units of the experimental three-car articulated diesel unit operated by the LMS from 1938 onwards and since withdrawn, whilst the main portions of the coachwork consisted of reconditioned bodies. The construction vehicle has a continuous flat roof, approximately 5ft. 4in. wide and 11ft. 11in. nominal height from rail level, by approximately 130ft. long. Comparisons with a similar view of just under two years earlier (page 43) show a track layout altered considerably to cope with new platforms and through running from the MSJ&A side of the station. Work is proceeding here on the erstwhile Eastern Region side of London Road. With only five months in hand before commissioning, the engineers have their work cut out to complete the mammoth task. At this date, though, substantial diversion of express services meant much less obstruction. Notice the spans and structures, some of which will carry a 1500V dc catenary. The station retained a dual voltage system until the end of 1980, something which, it must be said, weighed heavily against the survival of the former GC route over Woodhead. *Tom Noble*

Piccadilly, September 27th 1960. A brave new world has dawned: the 25kV electrification scheme is now up and running, to the relief of all concerned. In an early scene, typical of the new era, E3039-one of the pioneer GEC "A" series 3,300hp locomotives which entered service that year-prepares to move the empty stock of the 8.55 morning train from Cardiff off platform 8; the platform clock shows 2.15. Notice the drive-still sporting the customary "grease top"-acknowledging "the tip" from the platform staff. Though seen as a revolution at the time, the sight of a blue and white locomotive hauling a train of maroon carriages would be viewed as almost a vintage train today. *Michael Mensing*

LONDON ROAD GOODS

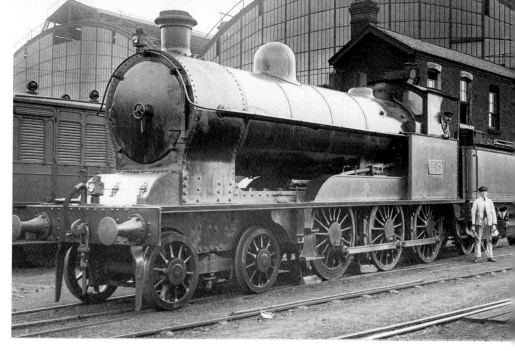

(Right) Manchester London Road, n.d: The driver and his fireman pose obligingly for the photographer as Whale "19in. Goods" No.**1479** waits to back down the LNW goods lines into the yard. With coupled wheels 5ft.2½in.diameter, these engines had appeared in 1906 as a mixed traffic version of the famous "Experiment" passenger class. 1479 is seen in its later life with Bowen-Cooke buffers, windshields to the sand pipes and raised reversing rod. Numbering 170 engines, the "19 in.Goods" (so called because of their cylinder diameter) would have been a common sight at London Road. A typical working for the class in the immediate post-Grouping years was the 8.05 pm MWFO) goods from London Road to Rugby; the engine returning the next day with the 5.35 pm Rugby to Adswood (near Stockport) freight. In the same period, Longsight used these engines on a small number of passenger turns integral with the shed's goods rosters. One such was the 5.40 am from London Road to Stafford which then worked back with a local train to Crewe. A second roster involved the 5.00 pm (SX) train from London Road to Macclesfield, followed by a freight train from Macclesfield to Adswood. Leaving Adswood the loco travelled light engine to Philips Park to work a train from Moston to Heaton Norris. The 11.10 pm train from Stockport to Buxton (WFSO) was another turn on which these small-wheeled 4-6-0s appeared. To complete the picture an ex-MS&L 6-wheeled van is seen in the background. No.1479 was built at Crewe in May 1908, was re-numbered LMS 8809 in June 1927 and was withdrawn in August 1935.

P.F.Cooke

SPANNING THE DECADES

(Centre) London Road, January 30th 1954: To the travelling public, the most visible members of railway staff were seen behind the ticket office window, on the station concourse and in charge of their train. Typically unseen were the many office staff who worked behind the scenes, maintaining vital aspects of the railway system. Examples of such personnel are pictured here: taken in the Eastern Region freight train office are four members of staff-now depicted over half a century later. Standing, left to right, are: B.K.B.Green, B.Jagger, Alec McRae and S.("Sammy") Hancock. Seated in front is R.D.Pollard who was head of the section, a church organist and in his day a notable railway photographer-how sad it is that we are rarely allowed the opportunity to see his work. Brian Green went on, too, to become an outstanding photographer, not just of the Manchester scene, but countrywide. Notice the wicker baskets-one for "typing"-the desk blotter and that telephone!

B.K.B.Green collection

London Road-Station approach 1953. A reminder that much of the commercial activity in Manchester was based around the city stations is clearly evident in this view of "Coronation Year" (1953) posters. Passengers on foot both arriving and departing from London Road station were given scant protection from the elements whilst being reminded that their holidays would be in good hands with an array of destinations reached by train. Freight vehicles in the background are but a memory on a site now occupied by Gateway House, Piccadilly Station Car Park and street level retail outlets which include a bank, cafés, bars, travel agents-extolling the virtues of destinations far beyond New Brighton and Grange (over-Sands), and of course the redoubtable transport treasure that is the Ian Allan Bookshop.

British Railways

(Above-left) **View from station forecourt, May 30th 1961:** By this time the new station was opened and electric traction was in the ascendancy. However, some older features of the station hung on and sat for some years to come. Two small buildings were sited at the top of the approach road: to the left, complete with cast iron cupola atop is a cab man's shelter-a hangover from the days of the horse-drawn carriage. To the right of the shelter, in the centre, is the glazed entrance to the stairway that existed for many years. The stairs led down to Store Street and were probably used more by railway staff than passengers as this street was the site of the LMR Railwaymens' club. Behind are the temporary wooden booking offices referred to elsewhere while standing loftily over all (left to right) are the former LNWR goods warehouse, the GCR's "London" warehouse and the same company's grain warehouse. **(Above-right) View from station tower block, March 27th 1962:** The former GC side offices were among the last parts of the station to be demolished and cleared away. Thus we can obtain a rare glimpse of their now long-gone architecture as well as taking a final peep at the station's goods warehouses. Plenty vans still await attention down below in the former LNW premises, though shortly the Beeching Report would spell doom for such (as it would be deemed) antediluvian practices. *Graham Whitehead*

(Left) London Road, the writing on the wall: Old names die hard on the railway. Almost 42 years after its demise, here is the LNW still being spoken of along with the "London" warehouse. Will "British Railways" survive in like manner?

(Below) Manchester London Road, goods depots: Two goods depots existed at London Road. That of the LNWR can be dated to 1880 when the company accepted a tender of £6,113.9/2d from J.Parnell & Sons of Rugby "for low-level goods station at London Road, Manchester." In like manner to the passenger facilities, the depots sat side by side each going about their business until their demise in the mid-1960s: **(Below)** On August 7th 1965 the photographer stands in the centre of the two sets of descending tracks. To the right can be seen the walls of the former GCR grain warehouse whilst in the middle distance the two gabled fronts of the ex LNWR goods sheds still stand. The occasion was the arrival of Fowler 2-6-4 tank No.**42343** drawing several brake vans as part of an LCGB rail tour. To the left, in front of the arched low roof, can be seen two wagon hoists. These were used to bring the traffic up from the bowels of the goods station which lay beneath the arches supporting the train shed. *H D Bowtell/MLS*

London Road Goods, the remaining approach lines to Ducie Street warehouse, March 11th 1967. Clinging to life, the warehouse still sports a little traffic-notice the continental wagons standing on the bridge with Store Street below. With the LNW warehouses now demolished,work is progressing with the construction of the "Lazy-S" building that would become Gateway House (left). Directly ahead is the ex-GCR "London Warehouse". Still standing today minus verandah, the structure, surrounded by a huge car park, has metamorphosed into a block of luxury apartments known as "The Place". Closure of this, the last goods facility at London Road, took place on 2nd October 1967. *H D Bowtell*, courtesy Manchester Locomotive Society

London Road, from Ducie Street, March 12th 1966: Much had changed the following year: Looking up from Ducie Street the goods warehouses are all but demolished now. Work has begun on the foundations for Gateway House, the curving glass and concrete edifice that wends its way along the station approach. Here today is the Ian Allan Bookshop, the National Blood Transfusion centre, Morgan Computers and Greggs Bakery-a changed world indeed from that of over forty years ago. *H D Bowtell* courtesy Manchester Locomotive Society

Leaving London Road, February 26th 1953: Longsight's "Royal Scot" No.**46160** *Queen Victoria's Rifleman* heads along the Up fast line with the 12.05 pm express for London Euston, the clock of St.Andrew's church in Ancoats bears witness to the hour. Journey time for this Restaurant Car express was 3 hours, 40 minutes with stops at Stockport, Macclesfield and Stoke-on-Trent. A mid-day departure such as this was an almost perfect time to look forward to a leisurely lunch and perhaps a post-prandial nap before reaching the Capital. No queuing at a buffet car counter for a microwaved snack in those days! Whatever would Mr.Kirkham have thought? The acutely-angled tracks off to the left lead into Mayfield station.   *B.K.B.Green*

ONWARDS THROUGH ARDWICK

The district of Ardwick is just three quarters of a mile from London Road. Despite its close proximity to the industries of Manchester its famous "Green" was described by Joseph Aston in The Lancashire Gazette of 1822 as… *"one of the most pleasant villages in the Kingdom and is universally admired for the beauty of its appearance and the neatness of the buildings which surround it."* Aston, of course, was penning his lines some twenty years before the coming of the railway and its supporting viaducts which spread across the district-close, perhaps too much so, to the fashionable Ardwick residences and Ardwick Hall. From the inception of the two railways passing through the place, Ardwick had its own station hard by the junction where the M&B left the SAuL&M to Sheffield. A second junction, nearer to London Road, was made on November 20th 1848 when the L&YR opened their line from here to Philips Park and Miles Platting. Known up until modern times as "The Lanky Branch" it was a sparsely-used connection, though its usefulness was extended from 1888 when the short spur from Ashburys West Junction connected with "The Lanky" at Midland Junction above Ashton Old Road.

Goods facilities were once extensive at Ardwick. Adjacent to their main Sheffield line the MS&L had set out capacious sidings on a former brick croft above Blind Lane. These had humble beginnings: an early map shows just a coal yard, the property of Stanhope & Silkstone Main, with two sidings a wagon turntable.

North of the Ardwick yards, between the Ancoats Branch and the Ancoats Junction line, the Midland Railway had their first Manchester goods depot. This was before the opening of the company's main goods complex at the nearby Ancoats depot in1870. In 1932, on land formerly occupied by the Ashbury Railway Carriage & Iron Co. Ltd., the LNER opened a new modern goods station. Titled "Ardwick East", the 20-acre site was bounded by Pottery Lane, Ashton Old Road and Gorton Road. At the same time the earlier depot was re-titled "Ardwick West". Ardwick East fell into dis-repair in the early 1980s and was subsequently closed.

On the south-east side of the Crewe line, close by Ardwick Junction was a curious series of sidings. These ran back from the Sheffield line via a steeply-graded incline and underneath the Crewe line of the LNWR. One set was known as "Bennetts' Sidings-being the property of one, John Marsland Bennett and H.A.Bennett under an agreement dated May 1st 1865. Bennetts were timber merchants-plans show a timber yard, saw mills and a drying shed. Bennett's sidings were always known as the "Kobo Sidings," though the reason for this odd title is obscure. In modern times they were owned by Messrs.Beatties, coal and coke merchants. Bennetts also possessed an iron foundry nearby; this was sited slightly further along the Sheffield main line, on the Down side.

Bennett's foundry stood next to what was once the Ardwick Football Club's ground-later home to Manchester City FC. Behind

Approaching London Road, June 20th 1953. Westinghouse-fitted "Britannia" No **70044**, then un-named, has cleared London Road's No 1 signal box and is running along the Down Fast line towards the station. Today is Saturday and our train - "The Comet" - has left Euston at 9.30 this morning. If she is anything like on time it should now be around ten-minutes past one; the train is due in London Road at 1.12; Once in the station, 70044 will assist the station pilot engine by pushing the stock out and along to Longsight's carriage sidings. After "booking off", the crew may well make for one of 9A's hostelries for a "pint" or two. Favourite watering holes were "The Junction" - a *Chesters* house, "The White Bear" and "The Wheatsheaf". Walking along and around no less than twelve tracks presented a major hazard for any railwayman and Brian Green recalls that, despite possessing a lineside photographic permit and being a railwayman himself, he was never allowed in this area unless accompanied by an Inspector. Brian's mentor was usually the late Les Walkington, a Signalling Inspector here for many years and, clearly a man who "knew the ropes" when entering such potentially dangerous territory.

B K B Green

the Crewe line and next to Bennett's sidings was a further set of sidings, this time belonging to the LNWR. Laid out fan-shape and consisting of four sets of two siding roads each, the yard was equipped with a travelling crane and goods shed. Its installation must have caused heartache to at least some Ardwick residents. An OS map dated 1849 shows the land on which the LNW sidings were built to be laid out as gardens for two substantial dwellings with trees, wooded groves and a sun dial (!) This little piece of Arcadia backed on to the thoroughfare then known as "Summer Place." It was later re-named Devonshire Street, the section running from Hyde Road towards Ashton Old Road and, from 1838, the site of Ardwick Cemetery, resting place of the eminent scientist, John Dalton. One last feature worth mentioning at Ardwick station was the ticket platform built for the LNWR on the Down side of the Crewe line. Something of an anomaly, it closed as early as October 15th 1902. The location of Ardwick LNW sidings can be identified clearly today as the car park in front of Universal Buildings (later known as The Great Universal Stores "GUS"). In the early months of 2006, further railway development has taken place along the north side of the erstwhile GC main line, site of the former Ardwick west yard. Here Siemens Transportation Systems have built, and are now operating, a major depot handing the maintenance of the new Class 185 DMUs to be used on Trans-Pennine services.

The railway through Ardwick was carried on a viaduct as far as the Hyde Road (A57). Originally consisting of two tracks, the for-

mation was widened to four tracks in the early 1860s (Q.V.) and again, under an Act dated June 17th 1898. The second widening, on the north side of the line, created North Western Street from what was known as Upper Sheffield Street. North Western Street survives today stretching from Fairfield Street to Chancery Lane. To the north of this thoroughfare, named of course after the railway that overlooked it, was a whole series of streets and houses-almost a small village, now long gone. Here was the King's Head hotel (about the only building surviving today), John Street and Ainsworth Street. The latter took its name from one, James Ainsworth, over whose land the railway had been built. Under an agreement dated September 14th 1839, the railway company were required to pay (to A.Bennett) a perpetual yearly rent of £94.3 (sic)-a large sum of money in those days. Ardwick saw some of the earliest domestic high rise buildings in Manchester and bad as some of these may have been, one cannot but wonder what nineteenth century life was like here-in Hewitt Square, Briscoe Street, Meridian Street and Union Place: the life of the hapless residents punctuated by the almost constant noise of the passing trains with all the attendant noise, smoke and filth from the unchecked industrial pollution beyond. Today, a car dealership stands to the side of North Western Street and small commercial developments nestle under the arches over which once Ramsbottom's Problems, Whale's Precursors, Robinson's Sir Sams and Directors, Fowler's Scots and BR's Britannias strutted their stuff on their passage to and from the south and east.

Approaching Ardwick, August 17th 1952: "Royal Scot" No **46160** *Queen Victoria's Rifleman* heads towards Longsight with the twelve coaches of the 10.05 morning express to London Euston. The former L&Y branch to Philips Park and Miles Platting runs off to the right of the picture. ***B K B Green***

(Below) Ardwick-former L&Y branch, May 7th 1950: A rare scene indeed. The photographer leans from the rear of the train, diverted due to track relaying in the Longsight area. St.Silas's church dominates a rather grey Manchester skyline as the 2.30 pm London Road to Birmingham slowly traverses the viaduct from Ardwick along towards Midland Junction. Drawn by a "Black 5" No.44749, the express will have a tedious trip to reach Stockport Edgeley. Over Midland Junction, where the short line from Ashburys West cuts in, the train

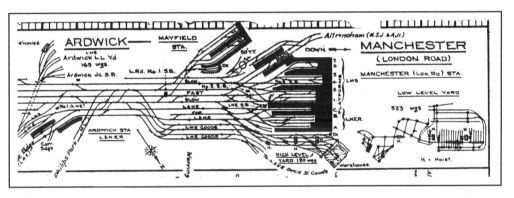

will head towards Philips Park No.2 box; here a right fork will be taken to Park Station Junction. Travelling on the goods lines, the former L&Y main line ("The Ashton Branch") will be joined at Baguley Fold Junction. Going east now through Clayton Bridge, Droylsden Junction is approached where the ex-LNW line is encountered and the train is now turned south over Ashton Moss towards the junction of the same name and then on to Denton Junction to access the Heaton Norris and Guide Bridge line. At last, a little speed will be gained, as the section down through Denton and Reddish was then a busy four-track railway. Finally, at Heaton Norris Junction, the Stockport line will be re-joined with Edgeley station just across the viaduct. All a bit drawn out perhaps; but the trains *ran* in those days: the phrase "bus replacement service" had yet to be coined. ***Harold D Bowtell*/MLS.**

Ardwick Junction, 1958: Fowler 2-6-4 tank No **42381** waits for the road with a short train of four vans, probably en route to Longsight. Ardwick then looked pretty much as it had done for the last six or seven decades or so: terraced houses mixed in with light industry and bisected by the railway. Over on the far left, St.Andrew's church marks the beginning of the Ancoats district whose mills and chimneys yet survive. Behind our little train stands the white form of the King's Head hotel, a solitary beacon in an otherwise grey-black and coal-black landscape. ***J Hilton***

Ardwick station, c.1958. The powerful-looking A5 4-6-2 tanks were a regular sight here in steam days being used on the stopping trains over the GC&NS Joint line from Marple (Rose Hill) to Macclesfield. No.69806 belonging to Gorton (39A) pulls sharply away from the Up platform and round towards Ashburys with a train composed of Gresley stock. The building on the right is the former LNER carriage shed, a reminder that this area was once very much "two company" territory. ***W A Brown***

Ardwick station, May 21st 1971: Multiple aspect signalling, controlled from the Manchester London Road power box (not, note, "Piccadilly") is now in charge here, though Ardwick No.1 box, a typical GC structure over on the right, survives to control the former LNER goods lines and sidings. The picture looks along the Up and Down Fast (Eastern) lines; the Down passenger loop passes behind the far platform. Dipping steeply down in front of the signalbox is the line to Bennett's sidings ("The Kobo") and the former LNW yard along Devonshire Street. Official railway literature describes these as "Bennett's Yard" and "The Ardwick Warehouse Branch." ***M A King***

Ardwick Junction, June 4th 1959: The LNW signalbox controlling Ardwick Junction was a lofty, brick-based affair sited at the London Road end of the LNW yard. The manually-operated box towers over the railway in this scene along Temperance Street forming the site for our photographer as he (she?) points the camera along to capture openings Nos.55-59 in bridge No.33, the viaduct that stretched from here to London Road station itself. With wrought iron and steel girders and jack arches, the structure was strengthened in 1900. The first London Road to Ardwick widening was planned in the early 1860s. For reasons that are obscure, the original contractors, Farrel & Ledger refused to carry out the work. Eventually the contract was awarded to Robert Neill & Sons, but the work was not completed until 1880. Powers for further widening were obtained in 1898 and a contract was awarded to Robert Neill & Sons at a tendered price of £144,300; this was dated November 15th 1905. At Ardwick, this spot forms a confluence of five historic local thoroughfares: Temperance Street runs alongside the viaduct right up to Fairfield Street; to the left, Chancery Lane runs beneath the railway to connect with Higher Sheffield Street; ahead, the curiously-named Blind Lane also burrows, catacomb-like, towards the entrance to Ardwick station and the site of the early coal yard; straight ahead is Devonshire Street, the one-time Summer Place, whilst to the right is Higher Ardwick, leading round towards the famous Ardwick Green. By the junction with Blind Lane the yard entrance, Hollands Pies, from Baxenden in Lancashire, are making a delivery-lunchtime sustenance maybe?

British Railways

Ardwick, Chancellor Lane, June 4th 1959: This is the opposite side of Chancellor Lane, leading up from Ashton Old Road (A635) towards the Hyde Road (A57). The cast iron bridge columns and white glazed tile walls will soon be a thing of the past; this photograph was one of several taken for the attention of the Civil Engineer prior to reconstruction for the impending electrification. Again, the railway bisects the district on the skew. Our surroundings are full of history with street names echoing Ardwick's railway past. By the far left-hand side of the viaduct stands Higher Sheffield Street, but North Western Street, directly opposite, by the Guinness and Player's advertisements, has a later pedigree, being re-named from Upper Sheffield Street, while off to the left, in front of the bus stop, is Midland Street. Two contrasting forms of transport electrification vie for attention: traversing the viaduct is the 1500v dc belonging to the Manchester to Sheffield scheme, soon to be augmented by the up-and-coming Crewe 25kV ac system. At street level the trolleybus wires of Manchester Corporation's 213 route which, incidentally had just been abandoned (on May 31st) in favour of the internal combustion engine-the route becoming numbered 123. More pies are on the way-notice the Hunter's van coming towards the camera. Disappearing through the arch on the left, a policeman is seen on foot patrol, his full-length tunic looking rather anachronistic now; alas, such a sight would be very rare here today!

British Railways

(Above) Ardwick, former LNW sidings - "Bennet's Yard", n.d: The Beeching report urged the movement of freight away from uneconomical single wagonloads towards the "train-load" concept. A forerunner of today's Freightliner was the London Midland Region's "Speedfreight" rail-to-road concept, a fast overnight freight service and something of a precursor to the later "Speedlink" operation introduced in 1972. "Speedfreight" services were shown in working timetables by a Maltese Cross symbol and only vehicles carrying the "XP" coding could be used. Here, the Royce 40-ton overhead crane drops one of the standard 10-ton "Speedfreight" containers onto a waiting Bedford trailer. Enthusiasts of road vehicles may notice the "PRO" registration of the two lorries. "PRO" emanated from Hertfordshire, the chosen county for BR's commercial fleet. Universal Buildings, now long a part of the GUS mail order empire, form a backdrop to the picture. Surviving today, the structures dominate the ground here-space that has long been given over to car-parking.

British Railways

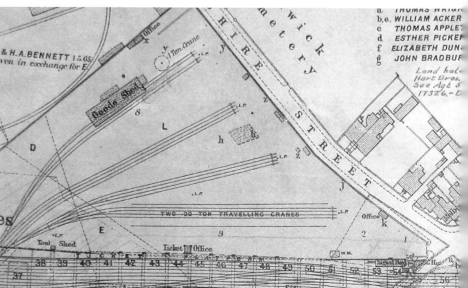

This pre-1900 diagram shows how little "Bennets Yard" Speedfrieghtchanged in the next seven decades until the Speedfreight launch. Also of interest is the ticket platform for (Down) Manchester-bound trains which lasted until the quadrupling between London Road and Ardwick in 1908.

Bridge over Hyde Road (bridge No.30), March 21st 1957: Spring has dawned today in East Manchester and the official photographer is busy-this is the tenth picture he has taken of this structure ready for the Civil Engineer and his team; this is but one of many bridges that will be rebuilt between Manchester and Crewe in the next couple of years or so. To the right New Bank Street runs along towards and alongside Longsight depot, 9A. Confronting us are the massive sandstone piers with their stone cappings and, to quote the bridge register: *"Brick abutments, wrought iron main and cross girders, floor plates. Cast iron columns under inner girders only, dividing them into three spans. Slide plate bearings (overhead wires under bridge)."* Notice how little traffic is present; moving away in the distance is a trolleybus, this was the number 210 service to Hyde (Gee Cross). A schoolboy, complete with cap and long socks glances across at our photographer, his roadster bicycle looking antiquated now. To the left is a secondary bridge, this time a simple brick arch; this was bridge No.31-a structure with a 36ft.span and an occupation bridge-described as "Thornton's Bridge." After this and its almost identical neighbour, No.32, the railway was carried entirely on a series of viaducts all the way into London Road station. *British Railways*

HYDE ROAD

Hyde Road, the A57, began at Ardwick Green where it diverted from the A6, Stockport Road. An old-established thoroughfare, Hyde Road, like its Stockport counterpart, was a turnpike-dating from 1818. At Ardwick Green, the Hyde Road was flanked by Ardwick Hall where the later Hippodrome theatre would be established. To the rear of Ardwick Hall was Hyde Place and then Burgess Terrace, homes of gentry, even after the coming of the railway. An OS map dated 1849 shows few houses after passing these two groups of dwellings; Belle Vue Street (curiously, not connected with the well-known pleasure gardens) led down to the Corn Brook which was straddled by the M&BR's infant line. The Corn Brook was the site of the toll bar and weighing machine owned by the Manchester, Hyde & Mottram Trust who collected

their dues here. Continuing along Hyde Road and passing White Cottage the traveller quickly encountered what would become in later years bridge number 30-119 feet on the skew-spanning the thoroughfare. Bridge No.30 was to achieve a certain notoriety when, on September 18th 1867, it was the scene of an attack by a gang of Fenians (Irish Republicans) on a Police van en route to the jail at nearby Belle Vue. A Police officer, Sergeant Brett, was murdered in the ensuing melée and the miscreants-Larkin, O'Brien and Kelly were later tried and hanged at the New Bailey prison, reputedly the last public executions in this country. For many years an annual memorial service was held under the bridge and this was usually followed by a march to Moston cemetery where the Republicans were buried.

Bridge over Hyde Road (bridge No.30), April 2nd 1957: In many ways the railway scene of our youth presented us with a diorama that was timeless; one we took for granted and, so most of us thought, would always be with us and would never change. It is only when we step aside from the immediate railway-the track, stations and the trains themselves-that we realise we have left our time warp behind. Now the photographer has returned for more pictures and we are left gazing on a little slice of social history-and how things have changed in almost fifty years! Just look at the little café on the corner of Marsland Street and Hyde Road; the street corner café or snack bar once abounded-to be replaced, alas, by more sophisticated things. Who remembers Player's Weights and Craven's cigarettes? "Pop in for a Pepsi" invites the sign by the door-and the lovely little curtains! How those windows must have rattled to the rumble of train after train, no double glazing then! A passing dog vies for the affections of the two ladies-probably the café's owners. And then, as now, street advertising was a powerful medium. "Sunfresh is made

from whole oranges" and Sunblest was "the sign of the good bread" all those years ago. Mancunians (and others) could visit the Daily Mail's Brighter Homes Exhibition, on until April 15th and the same newspaper offering the chance to win 1001 prizes. Not to be outdone, the Daily Mirror were sponsoring "New Champions"- table tennis players by the looks of things. Eric Delaney's band were playing at the Palais-de-Danse Ashton-under-Lyne and *The Gay Tyrolese* were appearing at the Free Trade Hall. Things have changed!

British Railways

Hyde Road, Bridge No.30, March 22nd 1959: Two years and one day after the first picture was taken engineers have moved in to replace the bridge-this was the point of all those pictures! Today is a Sunday and a whole weekend possession will be in force to do the necessary work. Make no mistake about it this is a major piece of civil engineering work. Over 40 men are visible in this view and the collective expertise is massive. All pointwork and signalling has been disconnected and cranes have removed the existing wrought iron parapets; notice the box section, while the new decking sits to one side awaiting rolling into position. The view looks towards Ardwick and Manchester London Road. Visible through the haze, to the left, is the (then) MCTC "Car Works"-aka the bus depot on Hyde Road and Bennett Street. Looking at all the intricacies of a structure such as this should make us realise just how important such work was to the functioning of the railway. Spare a thought for the poor souls whose houses not just "backed on" but almost touched the railway. ***British Railways***

LONGSIGHT
STEAM SHED
AND STATION FOR BELLE VUE

Longsight, Summer 1963: Seen at the end of the North shed with the carriage shed in the background, is this line-up of motive power. With steam up and waiting to go is "Royal Scot" No **46140** *The King's Royal Rifle Corps*. The "Scot" had arrived at Longsight week ending June 22nd; by a very strange coincidence the same summer date had seen the centre engine - "Jubilee" No.**45733** *Novelty* – arrive at 5A (Crewe North), while the third loco – "Black 5" No **44818** had entered service at Newton Heath (26A) from the same date as well. The appearance of the "Black 5", carrying the remains of a special working board – "T6XX" – cannot be explained, but none the less all part of the rich tapestry of locomotive and train working that continues to intrigue and perplex us enthusiasts over forty years later!

Author's collection

Better known for its locomotive shed, surviving today as perhaps the oldest locomotive depot in the world, than for anything else, Longsight is easily dismissed as just that. Yet, research shows a great deal more. For the place originated as the home of the some of the first steam engines working south from Manchester on the embryonic Manchester & Birmingham Railway in 1842. Equally important, Longsight was to be an important manufactory prior to the pre-eminence of Crewe.

A company minute dated July 15th 1841 records that Mr.Buck, the M&B's Engineer, be… *"requested forthwith to prepare Working Drawings and Specifications of the buildings which will be required at the General Depot, Longsight."* A contract was awarded to Bramah, Fox & Co.at an agreed price of £14,000 provided that iron was used for the roof as a substitute for the specified timber. The "General Depot" was built on land owned by the Earl of Ducie and acquired by the M&BR under two separate agreements dated April 11th and December 30th 1840. Longsight Depot opened for business in 1842 complete with workshops and a carriage shed. Thus had arrived on the scene a name still extant on today's railway; though West Coast Train Care seems a bit prosaic to a generation weaned on London Midland Region.

THE SHED AND ITS ENVIRONS

But though thought of historically as a locomotive shed, Longsight had just a bit more to offer. The station, approached via ramp up from Kirkmanshulme Lane-just off the main A6 trunk from Manchester to the south via Stockport-had its own excursion platform. The prime purpose of this was to serve the nearby pleasure gardens at the famous Belle Vue site just down the road. The station's platforms served only the Slow lines between Ardwick and Slade Lane Junction-where the Styal Line left the main line from Manchester to Stockport and Crewe. Serving the main lines were two large LNWR signalboxes-Longsight's No.1 and No.4 boxes. One of the distinguishing features at Longsight in those days were the splendid LNWR semaphores. Long-serving sentinels, one wonderful set was perched high up on a gantry at the north end of the platforms spanning the tracks across towards the engine and carriage shed. Here, long Saturday afternoons could be spent watching the traffic passing to and from London Road; minus, though, the Eastern traffic over Woodhead which had turned off at Ardwick.

THE ENGINE SHED BECKONS

By far the best views of trains passing through Longsight and locos 'on shed' was to be had from the south-west (Down) side of the line. Access to the depot, though, from here was well-nigh impossible as the full width of running lines had to be crossed, all under the beady eye of the "bobby" in Longsight No.1 signalbox. To penetrate the shed it was necessary to go back down the station approach ramp, under the low bridge that took the lines over Kirkmanshulme Lane and then round the back of the station -

individuals dodged and weaved their way past the inevitable loco men and foremen and got in as best they could. One big snag here was that the footbridge leading to the shed came down right outside the foreman's office! Older, bolder souls could manage night time visits in autumn and winter. Here, under dim lighting, one could sneak an entry and avoid the inquisitors by hiding in the shadows. Notebook and torch in hand the eagerly sought-after numbers could be gleaned before escaping unscathed into the dark and, often, murky Manchester night.

HOW TO FIND THE SHED

One, R.S.Grimsley, had published in 1947 his British Locomotive Shed Directory. Subtitled - *"A complete guide to all main line locomotive sheds and works in Great Britain"* - Grimsley set out for the shed basher the most direct route and point of access to the main steam depots. In his Preface the author solemnly warned would-be Gricers that his manual *"......IN NO WAY GIVES AUTHORITY TO ENTER THESE PLACES."* I have to confess that I never came across Grimsley's guide until many years after my last steam shed "bash." In any case, costing 7/6d., such a publication would have been way beyond the means of us financially-challenged schoolboys. Why, for such a sum, one could visit Crewe for a whole day! We will leave mention of the Locomotive Shed Directory with the entry for Longsight: *"City to Longsight. Board a No.35 (Hazel Grove, Stockport), or a No.37 (Levenshulme) tram outside Exchange Station, in Market Street, Piccadilly or London Road, and alight at Kirkmanshulme Lane. Walk up Kirkmanshulme Lane, fork left into The Avenue, (the latter was at the rear of Belle Vue) and turn right into Redgate Lane. A cinder path* (what else?) *leads to the shed from the left hand side of this road. Journey time 25 minutes."*

M&BR MOTIVE POWER, LONGSIGHT EMERGES

The first locomotives to be provided for the Manchester & Birmingham Railway comprised six 5ft. 6in. 2-2-2 Singles; four by Sharp, Bros. & Company of Manchester and two by Robert Stephenson & Company of Newcastle-on-Tyne. The engines had were to the same general design having cylinders 15in. bore x 20in. stroke with leading and trailing wheels of 3ft. 6in. diameter; the valves were operated by "Gab" motion-an early form of link gear. Details of their original numbers are not known, but Sharps' makers Nos. were 82/83/87&91. Two were delivered to the M&B in January 1840 and the remainder in June and July that year. The first engine of the Sharp four, arbitrarily No.1, suffered a boiler explosion at Longsight shed in 1850; it was rebuilt there with 14in.bore cylinders and was renumbered 401 in August 1857. Longsight also rebuilt No.3&4 with 14in. cylinders; alas, No.4 blew up in the polygon (roundhouse) shed the first day it was put in steam after rebuilding. The two engines finished their careers a long way from Manchester: at some point between March 1844 and January 1846 they were sold off to the South Eastern Railway.

EARLY ENGINE ACCOMMODATION

Nothing much seems to be known as to exactly where the first Manchester & Birmingham locomotives were housed.

Duffield's map of Manchester c.1845 shows a "carriage and engine depot" on the site. Consisting merely of two long buildings on the North (Up) side of the line, the structures sit alongside what looks like a small roundhouse. Two lines of rails set at right-angles to the running lines lead into the depot. Access to the facilities was from the south side of the railway. Kirkmanshulme Lane has yet to appear and the Longsight toll bar sits across the Stockport Road, roughly where the present-day junction with the A6 and Plymouth Grove stands.

A year after this, in April 1843, Longsight station would open its doors to passengers-a simple affair at first serving just two tracks.

The Manchester & Birmingham Railway survived until July 16th 1846; now would see an Act of Parliament which forced amalgamation with the Grand Junction, the London & Birmingham (The Liverpool & Manchester Railway had been absorbed by the GJR the previous year). Thus was born the colossus that would stand astride the railway world- The London & North-Western Railway with Longsight becoming part of the company's North-Eastern division.

LOCATION OF LONGSIGHT

An Ordnance Survey map of the Longsight area dated 1848 shows the depot to be sited somewhere south of the later carriage shed. Records show that year the capital expenditure of £35,281 on "the factory at Longsight." The "engine house" is shown as a round shed; some sources quote this as being around 130ft. in diameter complete with a 38ft.turntable. Fairly quickly the premises were enlarged: four roads of an adjacent carriage shed were taken over making room now for about 16 engines in all. As early on as 1847 the closure of Longsight works was contemplated-Captain Mark Huish, General Manager of the LNWR reporting that:.... *"in six months the Locomotive Establishment may be moved to Crewe and that the Longsight Works need only be used for needful local purposes."* Repairs and, certainly, building, was scaled down but the workshops themselves soldiered on until 1897.

EARLY LOCOMOTIVE BUILDING AT LONGSIGHT

John Ramsbottom of later Crewe fame, was engaged as an engineer with the famous Sharp, Roberts & Company locomotive builders. Ramsbottom was born at Todmorden in Lancashire in 1814. His involvement at Sharps was contemporary with the famous Charles Frederick Beyer who, with Richard Peacock, would found the celebrated Beyer, Peacock company in 1854-the famous "Gorton Foundry"-a mere mile or so away from Longsight.

Sharps-the name was changed to Sharp Bros. & Company in 1843 and again to Sharp, Stewart & Co. in 1852-had premises, the famous Atlas Works, on Oxford Street near to Manchester city centre and close to the Bridgewater Canal. Atlas Works survived in Manchester until 1888 before moving to Glasgow, still under the "Atlas" name. Sharp, Stewart & Co. became part, inter alia, of the North British Locomotive Company in that city in 1903.

INFLUENCE OF CHARLES BEYER

Beyer, a German born in 1813, was Sharps' Chief Draughtsman, having joined the company in 1834. Beyer's influence on nineteenth century locomotive outline and development cannot be understated. He certainly influenced Ramsbottom who moved from Sharps to join the Manchester & Birmingham Railway as Locomotive Superintendent in 1842 aged just 28. In 1849 the North Eastern division of the LNWR was formed with Ramsbottom, then aged 35, still at the helm at the Longsight works.

Further Sharp engines had been delivered to the Manchester & Birmingham in 1845/46. These were further 5ft.6in. 2-2-2s with 15in. x 20in. cylinders and "Gab" motion as before. Running numbers were 25-27 (the M&B does not appear to have gone in for naming its engines). They were rebuilt to saddle tanks at Longsight by Ramsbottom in the period 1859-1860. Delivered in 1845 also were the first examples of the "Sharps Common Passenger" type-these being replacements for four of the earlier "Gab" engines. These locomotives differed from the earlier Singles in having a new type of valve gear which would become known as the "Stephenson Link Motion;" it had been designed and patented by William Howe, a fitter employed by Robert Stephenson & Co. The engines were M&B Nos.8/9/10&15; renumbering took place in August 1857 when they became

408/409/410&415. 410 was sold in May 1873 to Allen & Co. of Swansea. Two engines-Nos.408&409-were rebuilt by Ramsbottom at Longsight in 1860 and 1859 respectively. Conversion to saddle tanks took place in 1869; again, all the rebuilding work was done at Longsight.

GOODS TRAFFIC BEGINS

Goods engines arrived at Longsight in 1842 in the shape of four 4-coupled goods engines from Sharp, Roberts & Co. These were 0-4-2s with 4ft. 6in. coupled wheels and with cylinders 14in. bore x 20in. stroke. They carried M&B numbers 21-24 and makers Nos.190/91/93/95. These locomotives must have looked pretty little machines: they were fitted with the classic square-based Sharp domes of the period located close behind the chimney. The cylinders were inclined upwards with all the motion beneath the leading axle. In the dome casing there was a lock-up safety valve with a spring balance valve placed in the brass column on top of the firebox. Renumbered 421-424 in August 1857, No.423 was sold to the St.Helens Railway in August 1857 becoming their No.2 "Trent. It reverted to LNWR stock in July 1864 whereupon it took the number 1368. Mr.Isaac Watt Boulton of Ashton-under-Lyne bought the engine from the railway company in 1864.

Meanwhile, further goods engines had surfaced at Longsight. In 1846 Bury, Curtis & Kennedy of Liverpool supplied two six-coupled goods locomotives with cylinders size 12in. diameter x 18in. stroke. These were acquired for work on the Poynton Colliery branch. This railway left the M&B's Crewe line at Cheadle ("Cheadle Hulme" after 1866) and had opened for traffic on June 9th 1845 with the line reaching the Cheshire silk spinning town of Macclesfield on November 24th that year. Both engines left M&B service in on December 22nd 1858 when they were sold to the St.Helens Railway Company. Longsight, with its sub-shed at Ordsall Lane in Salford, would remain as the dominant LNWR running shed in the area for some years to come-it was not until 1863 that the railway reached Buxton where two sheds existed-one each for the LNWR and the Midland. And a full twenty years would elapse before Stockport (Edgeley) shed (the eventual 9B) opened its doors to locomotives.

AN EARLY OVERVIEW

It is hard to imagine exactly what Longsight and its environs looked like in those primitive years. Sketchy though its early history is we can perhaps close our eyes and see a small line of Sharp and Stephenson 2-2-2s all painted in a rich medium green, their numbers cast in brass on the puny cabsides; polished brass domes shining behind tall, black, copper-capped chimneys and steam hissing gently from slender safety valve columns. "Blackberry Black", the colour so beloved of LNWR locomotives, would not emerge until 1871-over a quarter of a century after the period that we are studying.

Five engines of two distinct types came from Sharp Bros.&Co. in 1846-47, two were constructed at Longsight from parts supplied by Sharps themselves. One was a "Common Passenger" type Single, two were six-coupled goods engines; the last two being outside-cylindered well tanks with inside frames, though they were otherwise exactly similar to the Single driver passenger engine.

All were renumbered in the North-Eastern Division as 430-434 in August 1857; No.434 was again renumbered 1922 in 1874. At a later date Nos.33 and 34 were converted to "Sharps Common Passenger" type and were provided with tenders and worked between Manchester London Road and Macclesfield. No.33 had run 37,243 miles by the end of May 1848. Nos.30 and 32 were long-boilered goods engines with barrels 13ft. 6in. long, 3ft. 6in. diameter containing 175 brass fire tubes; the valves were located beneath the cylinders and the locomotives were fitted with cast iron wheels. Weighing 24 tons each, they were by far the most powerful engines that had appeared on the NED. Trials

DETAILS OF THESE ENGINES ARE:

No.	Makers Number	Type	Dr. Wheel Diameter	Cyls.	Re.No.	Rebuilt as side tank	Scrapped
30	348	0-6-0	5ft. 0in.	18x24	1222 (2/66)	3/58	
31	N/A	2-2-2	5ft. 6in.	15x20	Tra.to S.Div		
32	399	0-6-0	5ft. 0in.	18x24	1228 (6/66) 1141 (1/72)	1858	
33	408	2-2-2T	5ft. 6in.	15x20	??	1857	4/1873
34	409	2-2-2T	5ft. 6in.	15x20	??	1857	4/1873

made with No.30 on August 15th 1846 proved the engine capable of hauling 97 wagons of merchandise weighing 264 tons (gross weight 586 tons) at an average speed of 15-25 miles an hour. On October 3rd 1846 the same engine conveyed a train of 101 wagons, weighing 597 tons, from Longsight to Crewe at an average speed of 13.7 miles an hour. During construction of the Whaley Bridge line (en route to Buxton), No.30 was used for the haulage of ballast trains being the only engine available of sufficient power. It was re-boilered at Longsight and converted to a side tank on March 27th 1858.

LONGSIGHT'S SECOND DECADE

In 1854 there emerged a new series of Sharps "Common Passenger" type engines. These were built at Longsight from parts supplied by Sharp, Stewart & Co. Sharps supplied a considerable quantity of materials required by Longsight from time to time. These 11 Longsight engines are detailed as follows:

No.	Built	Re.No. (8/57)	Rebuilt	Re.No.	Scrapped
2	1854	402	1868	1856 (9/74)	2/79
3	1854	403		1858 (9/73)	4/74
5	1854	405	1868	1834	9/75
6	1854	406	1868	1830 (9/74)	12/78
14	1854	414		1830 (9/73)	6/74
24	1854	424		1895 (9/73)	4/74
68	1855	468	1871	1929 (10/74)	11/77
85	1857	485	1871	1931 (10/74)	3/78
486	1857	----		1933 (10/74)	9/79
487	1857	----		1934 (10/74)	9/78
469	1858	----	1868	1930 (10/74)	7/79

Note: the last three engines were delivered after the combined list was formed and therefore did not carry M&B numbers when built. Locomotives Nos.5 and 6 were rebuilt at Longsight by Ramsbottom as saddle tanks in 1868. Three engines-Nos.402/486 and 487-migrated to the Ordsall Lane shed in Salford where they worked local trains as far as Wigan.

LONGSIGHT AND THE "DX GOODS"

Writers on LNWR matters state that the first DX Goods 0-6-0 tender engine (flat valve, express goods) was completed at Crewe Works on September 3rd 1858. This is not so: the first DX engine was No.214 "Shap", constructed to Mr.Ramsbottom's design at Longsight in 1856 or 1857-just prior to his departure for Crewe. Other sources have rumoured that Ramsbottom based the engine design on a Sharp locomotive; this, too, is incorrect-the confusion arising from the name "Shap"-not "Sharp!" No.214 was rebuilt to a saddle tank in 1863 and the name was removed in 1866 (it had been applied first to an engine of the Lancaster & Carlisle Railway) being borne subsequently by two 2-4-0 tender engines-a Ramsbottom "Samson" and then a Webb "Waterloo" Class No.764.

On August 1st 1857 the North-Eastern Division of the LNWR had a stud of 87 engines, a number of which were replacements of original locomotives. Arrangements were made to replace thirteen more of the older engines: orders being given for one passenger and twelve goods engines. The passenger engine-one of "Sharps Common Passenger" type-was completed at Longsight. Seven of the goods engines were supplied by Sharps themselves; the rest by Beyer, Peacock & Co. The North-Eastern Division retained its independence until 1862 and further engines were supplied by Crewe to suit the requirements of the Running Department which was controlled from Manchester.

LAST REBUILDS FROM LONGSIGHT

A final note on Longsight's early years concerns seventeen engines rebuilt there between 1857 and 1862. These were:

DATE REBUILT	NUMBERS
1857	413, 433, 434
1858	432
1859	409
1860	408, 427, 460, 465
1861	410, 426
1862	444, 445, 446, 471, 472, 475

Engine Nos.413, 433, 434 & 427 were converted to saddle tanks when first rebuilt as above; but numbers 408 and 426 were not converted until 1869 and numbers 444, 445 and 446 were dealt with in 1870. No.410 was presumably never converted, being sold in its original form in May 1873. Six-coupled goods No.432 was converted to a saddle tank in 1858, but engine numbers 460 and 465, first rebuilt in June and November 1860 respectively, were not converted, No.460 being rebuilt later as a side tank engine. Fairburn 0-4-2 goods engines were again rebuilt, No.471 in 1875 and Nos.472 and 475 in 1874.

By November 10th 1859, ten of the "Sharps Common Passenger" type engines had been converted to saddle tanks and 14 had been so altered before the end of 1862, all at Longsight, including Nos.412, 427, 432, 433 and 434.................*continued on page 92*

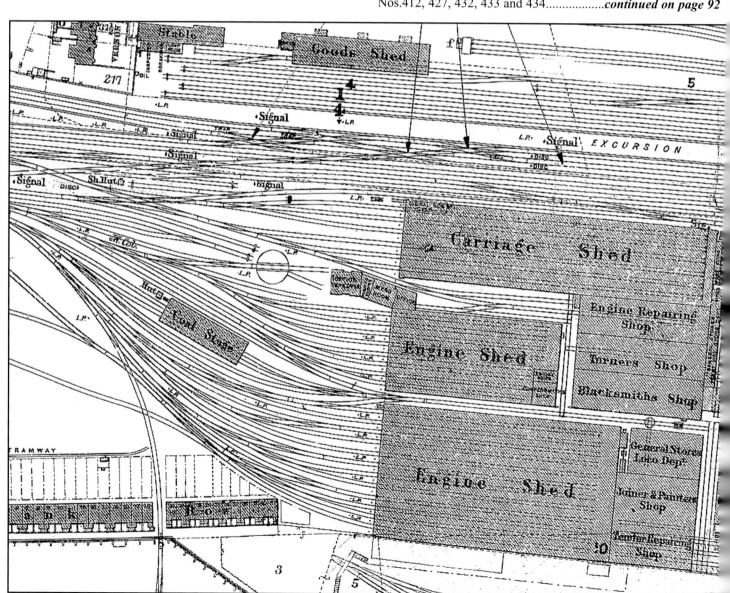

Location unknown, post-1868: A typical suburban train of the 1870s/1880s when places like Cheadle were the outer limits of the suburban passenger services out of London Road. The picture, reputed to be taken at Stockport, shows an aged product of Sharp, Stewart & Co., No.**402** - having been rebuilt in 1868 as a saddle tank. The original locomotive first saw the light of day at Longsight in 1854 as No.2, a 2-2-2 tender engine assembled there from parts supplied by Sharps. The load, six four-wheeled oil-lit coaches, was probably sufficient for the locomotive to manage on level track! Generally, the Cheadle-bound trains worked engine-first out of Manchester, returning bunker or tender-first. Early pictures taken at Heaton Chapel show this practice clearly. All Longsight turns, except the 7.15 am to London, did this trip to Cheadle before taking up main line duties, something which explains the use of all types of Longsight engines on this duty. This utterly charming picture, doubtless especially posed, shows two children with three platelayers and their trolley off to the right. The locomotive carries "express lights" – a rather dubious headcode for this period, as LNW engines were never fitted with spare lamp brackets. It is more than likely that the lamps have been placed so as to keep them upright and out of the way of the crew on this tiny footplate. Of particular interest and on a fashion note, are the different uniforms and just look at those hats! Billycocks, Bowlers, uniform caps and cloth caps – all the characters seem differently attired; notice the fifth character from the left is wearing a "Stovepipe."*Author's collection*

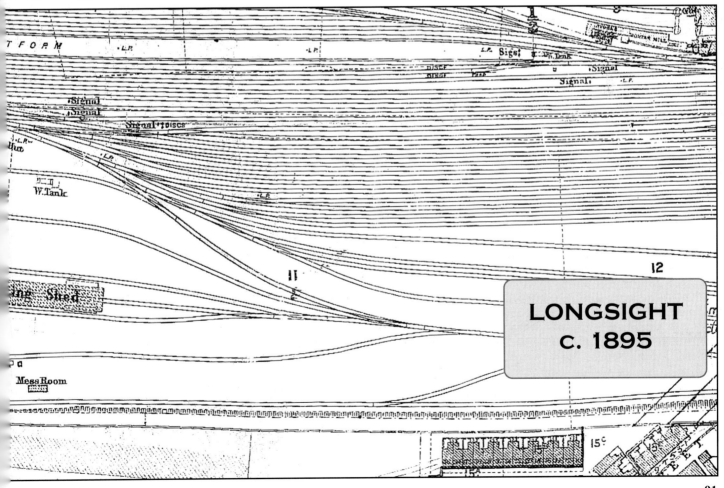

LONGSIGHT
c. 1895

..........Ahrons states that a large number of the Sharp Single tank engines worked local trains between Manchester London Road, Stockport and Alderley Edge-close to Ramsbottom's home and between Manchester and Wigan as well.

RAMSBOTTOM LEAVES LONGSIGHT

Francis Trevithick resigned as Locomotive Superintendent of the LNWR's Northern Division at Crewe in 1857 concurrent with the amalgamation of the North-Eastern and Northern Divisions of the company. As for Ramsbottom, he progressed to higher things from Longsight-being appointed Chief Locomotive Superintendent of the whole line from March 3rd 1862 with Crewe having become the headquarters of the enlarged division from August 1st 1857. John Ramsbottom's career on the LNWR is often overshadowed by his successor, Webb, maybe a more charismatic and somewhat enigmatic figure. Francis William Webb succeeded to the LNWR locomotive throne in 1871and ruled until 1903 before being succeeded by George Whale. Ramsbottom died in 1896. He seems to have been a genial soul, a man possessed of a generous and happy disposition, beloved and respected by all. Though always associated with the invention of water troughs, Ramsbottom designed a patent safety valve-1858-and, just as importantly-the steam injector in the same year. Neither should it be forgotten that, along with Beyer, Mc.Connell and Stephenson, Ramsbottom formed the Institute of Mechanical Engineers in 1847. And if all that does not assure Longsight's place in history, then nothing will.

FORWARD TO THE 1860s

Things remained static at Longsight through to around the decade beginning in 1860. In the period that followed, Manchester's London Road station would be substantially enlarged with a corresponding demand on motive power needs. In 1861 the LNWR accepted a tender of £23,340 to R.Neill & Sons for the widening of the viaduct between Ardwick and London Road. In 1866 the remainder of a carriage shed at Longsight was converted into an 8-road straight shed. On July 15th 1869 a minute records that R.Neill's tender of £11,700 be accepted for ..."engine shed at Longsight." This was a new straight shed purpose-built to house 72 locomotives. The structure was built from brick with three hipped and slated roofs, each covering four roads, i.e.12 roads in all. Measuring 320ft.long and 180 ft.wide, the new shed was flanked by a coaling stage with water tank on top-itself a new provision. All this new building meant the old roundhouse was now redundant. The new structure now stood alongside the old 8-road shed with just a single line passing between them. 1869 would see further changes in the arrangement of running lines at Longsight. That same year work was put out to tender for widening of the lines between here and Ardwick: S.Warburton of Harpurhey, Manchester was awarded the contract for the sum of £52,167. Longsight station, too, would have been affected by the widening, though-apart from the excursion platform-the station only ever served the Slow lines. A minute dated February 14th 1877 records the acceptance of a tender of £2,502 from J.Collins & Sons of Warrington for: "goods warehouse at Longsight." Little by little, Longsight was becoming a bigger and busier place.

ACCOMMODATION IN THE ERA OF F.W.WEBB

In 1876 Webb recommended that the old roundhouse, out of use for a long time, should be demolished. A minute records that..."materials be used for putting the premises into a somewhat similar condition to those at Carlisle; its (the roundhouse) removal would also enable a good job to be made of the sidings and dis-

pense with about 13 (sic) turntables." The proposal was taken on board and the roundhouse, one of the oldest parts of the M&BR buildings, was finally demolished, the adjacent works building being turned into and 8-road shed housing 48 locomotives. A new 6-road carriage shed, sited alongside the main line was built in lieu of the original straight, 8-road shed. The loss of workshop space was compensated by extending the 12-road shed backwards to provide a 3-road repair shop-access to this being by way of the single line running between the 12 and the 8-road shed; this made connection via a traverser with the shop.

It was ever a risk in the days of steam that hot coals and wooden structures do not always go well together. Fire has ravaged many a railway building over the years and Longsight was no exception. The 8-road shed was gutted by fire in 1901 and the loss of this building, coupled with the growth in traffic, meant further building work. Now a new 12-road shed was to be built back-to back on the north side of the 12-road shed of 1870. This new building, completed in 1903, would have the famous "north light" pattern of roof.

TOWARDS THE TWENTIETH CENTURY

The new structures were divided into two convenient parts: at first known as the "old and "new" sheds, they became later known as "north" and "south" sheds. The old M&B locomotive works had survived until 1897-indeed, 2-4-0 tender engines working on the Cromford and High Peak Railway underwent heavy repairs and boiler re-tubing at Longsight almost until the end of their careers-c.1892/94-before facilities were moved south to Crewe. The 1903 works also provided for a new turntable of 50ft. diameter along with a new loco coaler at the north end of the yard, again with a water tank sited on top. A company minute dated April 24th 1903 stated:... *"up to the end of March the estimate of £25,000 has been exceeded by £3,184.14s.8d., due to the deep foundations required, the site having been filled from 15ft. to 20ft. with town refuse. The extra cost of getting this out and putting in concrete foundations is £6,120."*

Longsight now had accommodation for 164 locomotives. Webb had retired in 1903 to be succeeded by George Whale, a man who had very different ideas on locomotive design to his predecessor. A minute dated October 10th 1906 shows acceptance of a tender from Kirk & Randall, Woolwich (£30,370) for: "new carriage shed, office, store room, etc., at Longsight." These buildings were brought into use in 1907. The carriage shed being a commodious affair-comprising thirteen roads and some 950 feet long; it was built between the new sheds and the main line. The new accommodation was built on the site of the old M&B works, the earlier carriage shed and the fire-ravaged 8-road engine shed. One record shows that some undamaged timbers, salvaged from the fire, were sent to Llandovery to be incorporated in a new shed under construction there at the same time. The LNWR were a most resourceful company! A single line of track ran between the north and south loco sheds and the later carriage sheds. Inexplicably, it was know ever after as 'Burton's Road.'

One curiosity surrounding Longsight was the lack of a large turntable provision. A new table, 60ft. in diameter was installed in 1934 under the LMS modernisation programme; but nothing larger than that ever came the shed's way. Visiting LMS Pacifics were dispatched to nearby London Road station to be turned there. After this was removed in 1958 to make way for the new power signal-box, "Duchesses" and "Princess Royals" were sent all the way out to Stockport to be turned on the triangle formed by the junctions at Edgeley No.1, Davenport and Cheadle Village junctions before

Longsight, c.1957. An elevated view from the gantry at the north end of Longsight looking south. Access to the depot was improved in the early years of the Twentieth Century along with major redevelopment of the facilities. The signal box, Longsight No 4, an LNWR Type 5 design - in this instance all-timber and first introduced in 1904 - gives a clue to the date of these improvements. It was the final development of signal box design by the company. From left to right, the lines (to the right of the signal box) are Up Loop, Up Slow, Up Fast, Down Fast, Down Slow and Down No 1 Loop. Down No 2 Loop (out of the picture), served one side of the excursion platform across from the depot.. Beyond the signal box were the Up Marshalling sidings with a capacity for 528 wagons.

Martin Welch

return to Longsight. Asking a former employee who worked at London Road why the engines could not have used the far nearer combination of Gorton, Hyde Road and Fairfield junctions, he replied: "Good heavens, no! That was the Eastern Region!"

FROM M&B ENGINES
TO EARLIER LNWR MOTIVE POWER

The first engines to John Ramsbottom's own design came to commence work at Longsight on June 1st 1864. They were No **531** *Lady of the Lake*, No **563** *Combermere*-both single wheelers and No **902** *Onyx* an engine of the 2-4-0 'Samson' Class. No.531, with driver Thomas Cheetwode, worked the 9.30 am Manchester to London on Mondays, Wednesdays and Fridays; Cheetwode returned on Tuesdays, Thursdays and Saturdays with the 2.45 pm from Euston, due into Manchester London Road at 7.45 pm.

No.902, with driver David Pennington, worked the 7.45 am Manchester to Crewe, the 9.0 am Crewe to Stafford, the 11.30 am Stafford back to Crewe, the 1.33 pm Crewe to Manchester, the 4.50 pm Manchester to Crewe, returning finally with the 7.21 pm Crewe back to Manchester. No.563 Combermere was the relief engine for both these two workings.

After a few years, the through running to London ceased and No.531 then worked the 9.30 morning London train as far as

Crewe; this was followed by working the 10.45 am Crewe to Stafford, the 12.40 pm Stafford to Shrewsbury, the 5.50 pm Shrewsbury to Crewe before returning to Manchester with the 7.35 pm from Crewe. *Onyx*, No.902, was set to work on the 1.40 Crewe to Manchester after working the 11.30 am down from Stafford; this was followed by 4.40 pm from Manchester back to Crewe, returning finally with 6.44 pm train to Manchester.

On April 3rd 1876 a new train began to run from Manchester to London. Leaving London Road at 7.45 am the express ran via Macclesfield, Congleton and Stoke-on-Trent and was due in Euston at 12.30 pm; the train returned at 4.00 pm and was due back in Manchester at 8.45 pm. No.127 *Peel*, with Driver David Pennington, and No.667 *Marmion*, with driver Leigh Bowden, worked this service on alternate days. So began driver Bowden's long association with this train. He afterwards had No.196 *Leander*-a Ramsbottom7ft. 6in. 'Problem' 2-2-2 built in 1860-on the same job. No.60, *Tantalus* and No.612 *Princess Alice*-both 'Problems'- were also engaged in working this same train afterwards.

ENTER CHARLES DICKENS

March 1st 1882 is the point that Longsight's most famous locomotive came on the scene. From then on, engine No.955

Charles Dickens, one of F.W.Webb's 2-4-0 'Precedent' class, worked the 7.45 Up Euston express from London Road daily from Monday to Saturday in the charge of drivers David Pennington and Leigh Bowden. The feat was maintained for twenty years: after July 1888 the morning departure was altered to 8.15 and subsequently to 8.30 after July 1889. *Charles Dickens* returned daily with the 4.00 pm Down train from Euston. Turned out from Crewe on February 6th 1882, No.955 was sent straight to Longsight for sole duty on the London service. So seldom was it absent from these trains that, on September 12th 1891, it had accomplished the rare feat of running one million miles.

The little engine's work was not entirely without travail, however. Writing in his memoirs, Stockport fireman W.H.Wood (the famous *Private W.Wood, V.C.* whose name appeared on 'Claughton' and 'Patriot' Locomotives), described the firing of the famous engine-from tales related to him by colleagues. On one occasion whilst hauling the Up train, *Charles Dickens* had slipped violently on frosty rails before reaching Stockport. Here, the driver examined the engine but could find nothing wrong. Between Stockport and Macclesfield the fireman had made his way along the moving engine and noticed excess movement in the spring over the driving axle. Still unconvinced that nothing was seriously amiss, the driver nevertheless decided to play safe and a replacement engine was obtained. On dismantling the motion it was discovered that the crank axle had broken inside the eccentric sheaves. "I have often thought how lucky we (sic) were to find it out there, and what an extraordinary occurrence it was," Wood reflected in his writing.

On August 5th 1901, soon after passing Bramhall station (between Stockport and Macclesfield), on its 5,312th round trip between Manchester and the Capital, *Charles Dickens* had completed its two millioneth mile. Just for good measure, 186 shorter trips were included in the total! Owing to the heavy mileage the engine had been handled by two sets of men: each crew taking charge three days per week. Again, the drivers were David Pennington and Leigh Bowden. Sadly, Pennington's eyesight failed him, and on March 11th 1886, he was succeeded by Josiah Mills, another Longsight worthy. Thus, driver Bowden had the amazing record of having driven *Charles Dickens* during the whole twenty years of its existence. After 1902, the weight and speed of the London trains was increasing and No.955 was given a lighter job. Its place was taken by Webb four cylinder Compound No.1959 *Revenge* of the 'Alfred the Great' Class. The celebrated Victorian writer's name passed to a 'George The Fifth' 4-4-0 in 1913, before returning to Longsight in 1953 on BR Standard Pacific No.70033 which was allocated there until 1960.

One final note concerns the 7.45 Manchester to Euston train itself. Driver Leigh Bowden had, prior to getting *Charles Dickens*, worked this train since April 3rd 1876. This means that, prior to the departure of his beloved No.955 in 1902, Bowden had an unequalled record of service as one driver on one train, from one shed; something unparalleled anywhere in the annals of railway history.

F.W.Webb's engines at Longsight

The year 1881, ten years after Webb ascended to the LNWR throne, is a fortunate one for observers of the Longsight scene. One, Arthur Nixon, who began his railway career as a telegraph boy at Stockport North (sic) box on April 4th 1878 maintained an extensive correspondence up to around 1933 with Walter Laidlaw, a Manchester draper who lived in Withington, a suburb of the city. Early in his career on the LNW Nixon had struck up a friendship

with a young man by the name of S.S.('Sam') Scott who worked in a similar position at Heaton Norris Junction box. Nixon moved on to work as a guard, worked at Manchester's Exchange station as an inspector and completed his service as stationmaster at Stalybridge before retiring in 1929. The duo seemed to have gleaned extensive knowledge of Longsight allocations and links. Nixon wrote to Laidlaw stating that he began to record numbers of LNW engines as far back as 1875.

For the year 1877 Nixon recorded a total of 238 engines stationed at Longsight. The shed was then coded "16" and the allocation included the satellite, or sub sheds, controlled by the parent depot. Sub sheds at this time were Buxton, Chelford, Oldham, Ordsall Lane and Stockport. Longsight's biggest allocation then consisted of 85 "DX" 0-6-0 goods engines; there were four solo examples at the shed then: an 0-4-0 saddle tank No.1206 which lasted, amazingly, until 1947; 1101-a 2-4-0 goods engine which had been Lancaster & Carlisle Railway No.3 *Sedgewick*; a 2-4-0 long firebox goods engine No.480 dating from 1855; and a 2-2-2 No.1810 (duplicate) which first saw life in 1852 as No.290 *Rocket*.

The 1881 Longsight Links

We are supremely fortunate in that Nixon and Scott's records survived and have come down to us. It is worth mentioning also that 1881 was a census year and thus it has been possible to trace many of the Longsight drivers of the period-a valuable social record. The extracts that follow are from Nixon's records of Longsight links for the year stated. The links were (total engine numbers in brackets): **No.1**-Ramsbottom 7ft. 6in. Singles (2) **No.2**-Ramsbottom 6ft. 6in. 2-4-0 'Newton' class (12); **No.3**-Ramsbottom 6ft. 0in. 'Samson' class (12); **No.4**-6ft. 0in Trevithick locomotives (7); **No.5**-Ramsbottom 7ft. 6in Singles (9) **London & Birmingham Goods link**-Ramsbottom DX 0-6-0 (12); **Carlisle, Hereford, Birmingham, Garston, Liverpool & Leeds goods link**-Ramsbottom DX 0-6-0 (9); **Buxton & Macclesfield goods link**-1 17in. 0-6-2 tank, 10 Webb 0-6-0 coal engines; **Assisting engines link**-(10 locos made up from Webb 'Precedent' & 'Precursor' 2-4-0s, 1 ex-L&C 2-4-0); **Clifton Hall coal train**-1 Webb coal engine; **London Road station shunter**-Crewe 2-4-0 saddle tank; **Shunting engine link**-2 Ramsbottom 0-6-0 special saddle tanks; **Heaton Norris yard shunter**-Ramsbottom DX goods engine.

Space precludes details of all the engines and men, but two complete examples are given below:

Link No.1-Ramsbottom 7ft. 6in. Singles:

1434 *Eunomia*	driver David Pennington
565 *Napoleon*	driver Leigh Bowden

Link No.2-Ramsbottom 6ft. 6in. 4-coupled ('Newton' class)

393 *Brougham*	driver Isaiah Holcroft
1141 *S.R.Graves*	driver David Greenhalgh
1513 *Shakespeare*	driver Edward Smith
1667 *Corunna*	driver Samuel Cook
	(Cook drove 1484 Telford previously)
1672 *Talavera*	driver Thomas Lee
1673 *Lucknow*	driver John Hallam
1679 *Bunsen*	driver James Taylor
1680 *Livingstone*	driver James Allman
2002 *Madge*	driver Joseph Burrows

Looking through the 1881 census records tells us much about the

Longsight men of the period. We discover that almost all of them lived within walking distance of the shed; for we must remember that this was an era where even the mass-produced bicycle had yet to arrive-let alone the motor car. Almost all the addresses fall within a three-quarter mile radius of the shed. Gorton Lane; St.Johns Road, Rusholme; Glebe Street and Elizabeth Street, Gorton-all consisted of neat rows of terraced houses: the "two-up, two-down" residence was a commonplace in most of Manchester's working class districts at the time. All the men were married. First we look at Moses Allen (driver of DX 0-6-0 No.1551 in the London & Birmingham goods link); he lived at No.12 St.Johns Road with his wife, Margaret; she is described as "Engine Driver Wife." Leigh Bowden, of *Charles Dickens* fame, lived at No.13 Tank Row-a thoroughfare almost on top of the shed-see below. His wife, Sarah, is described merely as "Wife"- why the difference, one wonders? Leigh had fathered six children, ages 2 to 19 years old. In terms of local geography, Longsight shed sat within the borders of West Gorton-witness the addresses of many of the drivers and the boundary marker for the district that stood aloft on the wall of Ainsworth's Jewellers at the corner of Kirkmanshulme Lane and Stockport Road for many years-a small fact unknown to many.

Tank Row was directly on the north-east side of the shed and was still standing in the 1950s. On the 1881 census 43 of the 138 inhabitants of the 30 houses (only 29 appear on the census) set along this rather drab-sounding thoroughfare had occupations as either railwaymen or some kind of associated engineering job. Leigh Bowden, mentioned previously, was but one. The Longsight shed foreman, Peter Holcroft, lived at No.1 Tank Row; with five children to feed it is no surprise to find the Holcrofts taking in a lodger, one Woodville Rigby who is described as "Ry Engine Cleaner". James Boswell, boiler maker, was at No.2; Richard Hough, a fitter, lived next door at No.3 with his mother Ellen, an Irishwoman hailing from Dublin. Engine Driver James Kitchen, aged 43, lived at No.4 with wife Harriet and six children aged 10 months to 19 years. Two more engine drivers, George Bearders

and Edward Wood lived at No.9; Next door, at No.10, we find drivers James Dickinson, aged 39 and Thomas Greenhow, aged 62. Their neighbour at No.11 was John Allen listed as head of household. Aged 33, John, too, was a driver. Oddly, Thomas Emery, living at No.15, is described as a "Stoker (Rly)", instead of the more usual "fireman." It was between Nos.18 and 20 Tank Row that the rail connection from the shed to the Belle Vue pleasure gardens was sited. It is listed on an LNWR private siding diagram under an agreement dated August 23rd 1905 with J.Jennison & Co. (Belle Vue actually pre-dated the shed, having been founded by John Jennison in 1836.) Before leaving the Longsight characters of the period we pause across at No.39 Hyde Road where Gabriel Watson, driver of the famous Ramsbottom Single No.531 *Lady of the Lake*, lived with his wife, Mary and no less than seven children. Perhaps family finances were eked out by his wife's earnings: Mary is shown on the census return as a "Tobacco and Fancy Goods Dealer."

AFTER WEBB AND INTO THE TWENTIETH CENTURY

After the departure of the Ramsbottom Singles and the Webb 'Precedents'-amazing little machines by any standards of railway operation-the era of the 4-4-0 arrived at Longsight. The turn of the century would see the arrival of the bigger Webb Compounds-the 'Alfred the Great' and then, from 1904, the Whale 'Precursor' 4-4-0s and the celebrated 'George the Fifth' in 1910. Come 1913 and the four-cylinder 4-6-0s-the 'Claughtons'-would ensure transformation of the Manchester to London motive power out of all recognition from the days of drivers Bowden, Pennington and Watson.

LONGSIGHT CHARACTERS

Harold Gorton, a friend of the writer's, recalled starting work at Longsight-on March 11th 1918. Born in December 1902, Harold (always known as "HG") remained at the shed until his retirement in 1967. One of his first memorable firing trips was on a Webb

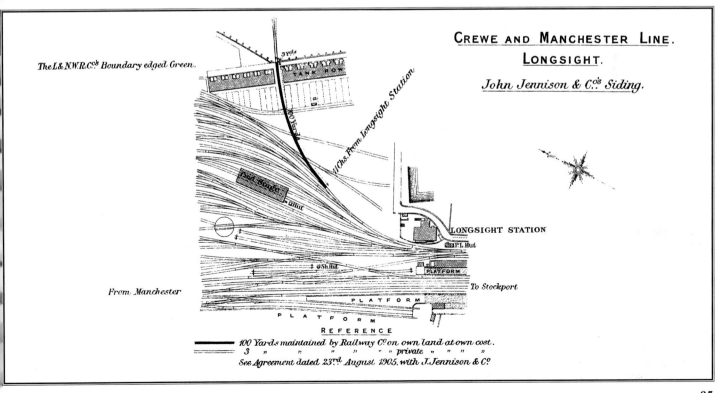

REFERENCE
100 Yards maintained by Railway Cᵒ on own land at own cost.
3   „   „   „   „   „ private „   „   „
See Agreement dated 23ʳᵈ August 1905, with J.Jennison & Cᵒ.

Longsight, c.early 1930s: "Build 'em cheap and Pile 'em high" seems to be a fair summary of the LNWR's locomotive building philosophy. But perhaps this is a cheap and something of a throwaway remark: Crewe was a centre of excellence and a world leader in its time in production engineering, sound organisation and standardisation techniques - all founded on principles laid down by the redoubtable F.W.Webb. Seen at the south end of Longsight shed is such a Crewe product: Whale "Experiment" Class 4-6-0 No 5525 *Byzantium*, one of 105 engines turned out from the famous works between 1905-1910 and now rebuilt with a Belpaire firebox. Steam hisses sharply from the cylinder drain cocks as Byzantium waits at the shed outlet signal before moving south. Alongside is a mess room which belonged to the Carriage & Wagon department. *Author's collection*

'Benbow' 4-4-0 with George Bazley, curiously enough over Woodhead, with a special coal train around 1923. Starting as a cleaner, Harold recalled some of the old LNW drivers as still wearing white overalls and some sporting earrings. Engineer Manchester-a Webb 'Waterloo' class 2-4-0, formerly No.2156 *Sphynx*, was at Longsight in Harold's early career when he fired the little curiosity to driver Ted Whitehead who had signed the road as far as Leeds. Longsight's association with the locomotive dubbed Engineer Manchester began back in October 1888 when Trevithick Single No.323 *Greyhound* assumed the mantle. A second engine then took the title: this was a Ramsbottom 'Samson' class 2-4-0 ex No.631 *Hotspur*-the *"Engineer"* title passing to the engine in November 1901 and lasting until 1914 when the erstwhile *Sphynx* arrived. This last *Engineer Manchester* survived at Longsight until 1927 after which no more engines carried the name.

Other personalities at Longsight during HG's early years were George Hulmes who drove 'Experiment' 4-6-0 No.1689 *Monmouthshire* and Joe Linley who worked on ex-L&Y 4-6-4 'Baltic Tanks' on the Buxton trains-engines the Buxton men detested, it seems. Joe was famous at the shed for his use of the word "however." Ex-Midland 0-4-4 tanks came to Longsight in 1932 and were motor-fitted to work push-pull trains over the Styal line. Willie Jones is well remembered as one their drivers.

Joe Linley had an unfortunate experience in his later years when he had ascended to top link work. On December 31st 1934 he and fireman Wood, also of Longsight shed, were working the 11.50 am express from Euston to Manchester. They had prepared the engine-"Royal Scot" No.6167 *The Hertfordshire Regiment*, themselves and noted nothing amiss until they had passed Tring (31½ miles out) when steam started to blow up between the front edge of the footboards and the boiler back plate. The situation grew

steadily worse until, when the train was approaching Welton (70 miles out), there was a loud explosion. Travelling at about 60 mph, the footplate became enveloped in steam and boiling water. Joe stopped the train by means of the vacuum brake with the regulator still open-badly scalding his right arm and wrist in the process. It was decided that fireman Wood would have to go to Welton box with a wrong line order for assistance. Returning to the footplate Wood, too, received severe scalds to his right arm.

The fault was traced back to a defective steadying bracket stud in the bottom of the firebox back plate. Incredibly, the same engine had thrown an identical fault with the same stud just five days earlier whilst hauling an express past Madeley, south of Crewe, causing its driver similar injuries to those sustained by Joe Linley and his mate. Inspector J.L.M.Moore for the Ministry of Transport traced the accidents to defective work at Crewe North shed. In future, all such brackets would be fixed by rivets and the studs done away with. A small incident perhaps, but one that showed how steam locomotive development was an empirical process via lessons learnt from the machines working in traffic. Alas, footplate crews had to pay the price for such events.

Harold Gorton was passed out as a driver-on an LMS Compound working an afternoon train to Crewe in 1933-a fifteen year "apprenticeship", something that seems amazing by today's reckoning. He possessed one of the widest ranges of route knowledge of any man at Longsight. Much of this had been acquired by walking the track and visiting signalboxes. Looking through the notebooks he compiled is to gaze back on the life of a man who was an engineman through and through. Each signal marked with notes on whistling codes and speed restrictions carefully marked down. Harold graduated to Longsight's top link, eventually driving Bo-Bo 25kV electric locos. He finished his career in the calmer waters of suburban work: driving diesel and electric units, turns that gave him more regular hours-surely a welcome relief after almost 50 years of strenuous shift patterns.

TOWARDS THE GROUPING

After the arrival of the 'Claughtons' from 1913 onwards, no new LNW express designs appeared to grace the Longsight motive power scene. Between this point and the Grouping came the appalling hiatus that was the First World War; its attendant drain on men and resources, the forced growth and pressure of traffic all taking a dramatic toll. As is well known, LMS motive power was in a muddle from Grouping in 1923 and with Midland influence in the ascendancy, old rivals found themselves strange bedfellows. As a fireman, Harold Gorton recalled a lodging turn to London in the 1920s; the Camden barracks were out of use for repairs and the men were dispatched to Kentish Town instead. Here the "foreigners" from the LNW-as it was still perceived-received a very frosty reception! George Hughes, a former Horwich man, had succeeded Captain H.P.M.Beames as locomotive supremo on the LNWR in 1922; the LNW itself having amalgamated with the L&Y that same year. Hughes held the reigns until the arrival of Fowler in 1925. But another five years would pass before anything dramatic happened at Longsight-certainly as far as express engines were concerned. Here we pause to look at the shed's allocation for the year 1927-a point usefully looked upon as something of an interregnum.

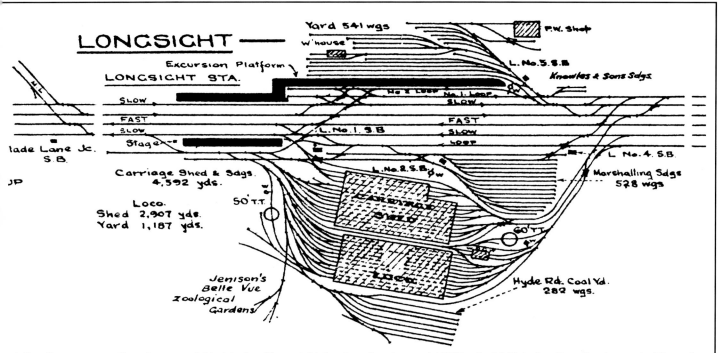

A line diagram - sometimes known as 'sidestrips' - of Longsight depot produced around 1926 by the LMS, before the redevelopment of the early 1930's. The 'Hyde Road Coal Yard' was in fact the sidings installed for the storage of loco coal wagons. Draughtsman's licence has prevailed during preparation of the diagram in as much as the carriage and engine shed buildings ran parallel with the main line.

LAST DAYS OF THE "CLAUGHTONS"

The shed was home to both varieties of rebuilt "Claughtons" from 1928 onwards. The first rebuilds retained the Walschaerts valve gear, while a further ten engines were fitted with Beardmore-Caprotti gear. It has been recorded that all the second batch were based at the shed in 1928. Subsequently the Caprotti "Claughtons" were dispatched to Holyhead and Longsight received Walschaerts engines in return. The "Claughton" rebuilds were 9A's top link motive power until the arrival of "Royal Scots" Nos.6164-6166 in September 1930. Even after that event the "Claughtons" were handling all the London expresses via Stoke-on-Trent. More "Royal Scots" arrived in 1932 which left just one London turn for the "Claughtons"; this was the Up "Lancastrian" which left London Road at 12.15 pm and travelled via Stoke. The engine returned to Manchester on the 8.55 pm (SX) 7.50 pm (SO) parcels train from Euston. Other London expresses (via Stoke-on-Trent) that were hauled by "Claughtons" at this time were the Down "Mancunian", the 2.50 pm from Euston and the 8.30 morning express from London Road; but these were all Camden engines, not Longsight inhabitants. Longsight "Claughtons" also worked trains to Crewe where engines were changed.

However, the most interesting engine diagram involving "Claughtons" was a two-day roster for two locomotives. The diagram entailed working an evening stopping train from London Road to Crewe followed by the "York Mail" from there to Leeds. Using Farnley Junction men, the engine worked from Leeds to Liverpool and back before finally returning to Crewe with the York to Swansea mail train. In September 1931 the daily diagram using two locomotives was as follows:

05 pm	Longsight to London Road (light engine)
30 pm	London Road to Crewe
2.30 am	Crewe to Leeds (men lodging)
30 am	Leeds to Liverpool (Lime Street) using Farnley Junction men
00 pm	Liverpool (Lime Street) to Leeds (crewed as above)
10.10 pm	Farnley Junction shed to Leeds (light engine)
10.40 pm	Leeds to Crewe (Longsight men)
2.15 am	Crewe to London Road
4.15 am	London Road to Longsight (light engine)
1.30 pm	London Road to Crewe (stopping passenger)
4.45 pm	Crewe to London Road (stopping passenger)
6.37 pm	London Road to Longsight (light engine)

NOTE: In similar form, this diagram lasted up to the end of the 1950s latterly using "Royal Scots" and "Britannias".

By 1935 all the Rebuilt "Claughtons" had left Longsight, their place being taken, as described, by the popular "Baby Scots" or "Patriots". The last rebuilt "Claughton", No.6004 the erstwhile *Princess Louise*, soldiered on working out her life on a variety of tasks until withdrawal in April 1949. She was cut up at Crewe, her birthplace, on August 10th that year.

LONGSIGHT MOVES TOWARDS THE STANIER ERA

Augmenting the 'Royal Scots' at the shed in the 1930s were the so-called 'Baby Scots' or 'Patriot' 4-6-0s. Based at Longsight up to the outbreak of war were no less than 21 of these '5X' machines at one time or another; this from a total number of 52 in the class. First 'on shed' was No.5501-from 28/10/31; the last was No.5518 on 7/10/39-just after war broke out. 'Patriot' "namers" at Longsight in this period were the celebrated No.5536 *Private W.Wood, V.C.* (QV); No.5537 *Private E.Sykes, V.C.*; and No. 5541 *Duke of Sutherland*.

Stanier began to make his mark his mark at Longsight with the arrival of the 'Jubilees.' 1934 saw five of the handsome 4-6-0s arrive as new engines: 5610/5626-29 between July and early December. Eight further 'Jubilees' arrived on 9A as transfers, mostly from Crewe, between October 1934 and February 1938. 'Black 5' 4-6-0s came to Longsight in the shape of No.5256 which arrived at the shed, brand new, on October 5th 1936. She was followed, eight days later, ...*continued on page 99*

Longsight shed coaling plant c.1937/38: One of the single biggest improvements in steam locomotive preparation was, without a doubt, the introduction of the mechanical coaling plant. Longsight acquired theirs in 1934, part of a major modernisation of large depots by the LMS from the early 1930's onwards. Made from reinforced concrete and electrically-operated, two types of coaler were introduced: No.1 pattern - for bigger, more important depots - consisted of two 150-ton bunkers; No.2-for less important depots - had two 75-ton bunkers. Naturally, Longsight was equipped with the former. 9A's coaler was erected on the east side of the depot, towards the top of the North engine shed. Below was the Hyde Road coal and mineral yard to where the fuel was delivered. Harold Gorton recalled coal from Dalton Main and Grimesthorpe collieries as being good fuel; but, of course, the shed would have procured coal from many different pits within its lifetime. In the immediate pre-War period "Royal Scot"

No.**6111** *Royal Fusilier*, in one of its two brief sojourns here, is seen in steam outside the top end of the North shed in the shadow of the massive bulk of the coaling plant. Notice the loco has received its Stanier 4,000 gallon tender, but is in original, parallel boiler form-rebuilding not taking place until 1943. As 46111 Royal Fusilier returned to Longsight for brief periods: two in 1953 and finally, from June 1957 until September 1960. *Author's collection*

*Today, anyone needing to climb up an 80ft.high or so structure would need safety training and equipment and a risk assessment would have to be carried out prior to the operation. Just under sixty years ago things were rather more free and easy. A young Stockport railway enthusiast, **Eric Kearns**, visited Longsight shed one Sunday in May 1948, climbed half-way up the coaler and took two photographs seen below (facing north) and opposite (facing south).*

Looking north, May 16th 1948: From the top of the North shed the tracks curve down from the junction with the main line out of London Road. Below, a pair of 2-6-4 tanks are in steam while a "Crab" busies itself with a line of loaded coal wagons-fresh fuel for the mammoth coaling plant. Across at the top of the photo can be seen the old "coal hole" with water tank on top. In front, two former Midland 2F 0-6-0s appear to be out of steam amidst all the usual shed clutter.

(Above) Looking south, May 16th 1948: Facing in the opposite direction this view looks down on the top of the North shed where work on rebuilding the severely dilapidated roof has begun. The work was not completed until 1957 when BR finally rebuilt the south engine shed. Once more, 2-6-4 tanks and 3F 0-6-0s form the bulk of the visible motive power with the line-up of loaded coal wagons waiting to fill the two ever-hungry coal bunkers.

(Left) Longsight, inside South shed, pre-WWII: "Patriots" or "Baby Scots", as 9A men referred to them, seemed to have been popular engines at the Manchester shed. This striking view of the front of No 5545 was taken inside the South shed during the six-year period May 1935 to 1941 when the loco was a Longsight allocation. 5545 became *Planet* from November 1948 and returned to Longsight later that month for just two weeks before moving to Bushbury – *Planet* did not re-appear as a Manchester allocation and was withdrawn in May 1964.

continued from page 97............by Nos.5257 and 5258, also as new engines. The sequence of 'Black 5' arrivals at 9A was then: 5054 (ex-Kentish Town) on 28/11/56; 5295, new engine-same week; 5296 on 28/12/36 as a new engine and 5184 (ex-Willesden) on 2/1/37. The Stanier 'Black 5' saga continued into the BR era when, in 1951, 44686 and 44687-the fourth batch of Caprotti engines-were allocated to the shed until they moved away from April 30th and September 10th 1960 respectively. (Monument Lane and Llandudno Junction).

Another notable arrival at Longsight in the 1930s was 4-6-0 No.6170 *British Legion*. This engine was rebuild from the infamous high pressure *Fury* and paved the way for the rebuilding of the parallel boiler 'Royal Scots'-though 6170 had a slightly different taper boiler to the rest of the 'Rebuilt Scots.' *British Legion* came to Longsight on November 23rd 1935 and went

A
LONGSIGHT
GALLERY

(Left-top) This undated view shows Ramsbottom 0-6-0 saddle tank No **263** is seen acting as coal stage pilot in this lovely little study in LNWR days prior to the First War. A Crewe product-works number 1449 of December 1871, the engine was renewed as No 3130 in October 1891. She was restored to the capital list as No 263 in April 1907 (thus helping to date the picture) and put back on the duplicate list in January 1919. She became LMS No 7251 in March 1927 and was cut up in October 1932. "Precursor" 4-4-0 No **1723** *Scorpion* stands in the background. *Authors collection*

(Left-second from top) Longsight shed, 1935: An ex-LNWR stalwart rests inside the old south shed. Cold, lifeless and out of steam, is Webb "Coal Engine", 0-6-0 tender locomotive No **8271**. The photographer exhorts us to: "note LNW lining on tender". Noted also is the observation that, as No 28271, the engine became extinct in 1944. *G H Plat*

(Left-third from top) March 20th 1937: Wonderful effects of light and shade play around Webb 0-6-2 tank No **6936** as she rests in the south shed. This was the last of 80 such engines built in the period 1898-1902 with 5ft.coupled wheels and Joy valve gear. LMS "Dobbin" (Jinty to others) No **7400** keeps company at the front; a box van and a 6-wheeled coach-maybe part of the Longsight breakdown train-can be glimpsed in the background. *G Harrop*

Longsight shed, October 1950: LMS "Jinty" 0-6-0 tank No **47601** displays its pre-1948 ancestry as it stands alongside the former coaling stage. With water tank aloft, this stood at the south end of the shed, near to the rather inadequate 50 ft turntable. Houses on the rather un-salubriously-sounding thoroughfare, Tank Row, mentioned in the text, can be glimpsed in the background. *Authors collection*

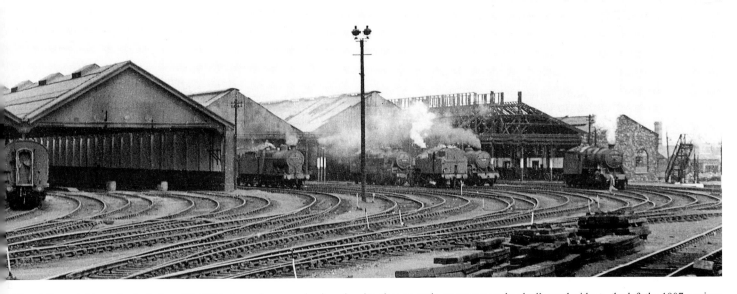

(Above) Longsight, south shed, June 9th 1951: A good panoramic view showing the two main structures on the shed's south side: to the left the 1907 carriage shed with its distinctive hipped roof. In front, 'Dobbin' 0-6-0 tank No 47395 barks away with a couple of vans. Over to the right-hand side is the dismal sight of the south shed, the second part is in near ruins being minus roof. In front, to the left, a 4F 0-6-0 is seen waiting at the top of the track that passed between the carriage shed and the south engine shed. Known as "Burton's Road", the line got its name because of its associations with the Staffordshire brewery trains. A Fowler 2-6-4 tank and another tank, also a 2-6-4; a "Crab" and a Stanier Mogul complete the line-up. Spare a thought, just for a moment, for the poor souls-drivers, firemen, cleaners, fitters and labourers for whom this was their *working environment*. In the meantime, the south shed would be rebuilt and long-term things were to improve. Alas, it was all a very slow process.

Tom Lewis

Longsight, South shed, early 1950s: We have mused on the dilapidations of this shed elsewhere, but this close-up view shows how bad the problem really was. The destruction of the roof is now known to have been caused by an incendiary bomb attack in 1941. But, meanwhile, doubtless everyone grumbled about the conditions endured, but money was tight and capital investment would have to wait a few more years yet before things got better. In this undated picture nothing more glamorous than 0-6-0 tank engines are on view; essential workhorses nonetheless and we must not overlook them. On the left can be seen a Longsight stalwart – "Dobbin" 0-6-0 No 47369 on number 8 road. Simmering away to the right is another of the same class, No 47343 standing on number 11 road. Both locos had been at 9A since at least 1948. Notice the uprights and the raised roof portions, once part of a very neat roof – all covered in and with copious numbers of slats to aid ventilation, a thing hardly necessary then!

M.Bland

(Right-lower) September 4th 1954: A spot of bother on shed? The duties attached to 8F No 48046 seem to centre around reversing a set of coaches. But a fitter appears to be wiping his hands, so maybe the loco has been the centre of some attention-alas, we will never know. Alongside, the fireman of a Stanier 2-6-2 tank "puts the bag in" the side tank of his engine. All par for the course and just one of the myriad parts of humdrum daily life "on shed."

Norman Jones

straight into the top links, becoming responsible for hauling the prestigious Up 'Mancunian' and the Down 'Lancastrian'. This required average speeds of 61.7 mph and 60.3 mph respectively. 6170 moved away to Crewe North from on February 5th 1937 but was back at Longsight on November 5th 1938. By then, though, the fireworks had ceased; British Legion sojourned in Crewe Works for no less than 81 days, before being taken out of 9A's hands and handed back to Crewe North on July 29th 1939. It was not allocated to Longsight again. However, as 9A's Joe Linley would have said, whilst at Longsight No.6170 became something of a film star-appearing in the title role of the LMS's 1936 film 'Engine on the Shed'. This superb film shows *British Legion* leaving London Road station and undergoing all the stages of engine shed disposal routine. It must be the only professionally-produced film ever shot at Longsight! (The film survives on video in the B.T.F.Omnibus series and is highly recommended.)

We complete 9A's first years with Stanier's passenger locomotives by looking at its pre-War allocation of the designer's most prestigious engines: the 'Princess Royal' and 'Duchess' Pacifics. The associations were somewhat brief-almost fleeting; they were:

No.	Name	To Longsight	From Longsight
6201 - *Princess Elizabeth*		15/07/1939 (ex-Camden)	16/09/1939 (to Camden)
6206 - *Princess Marie Louise*		15/07/1939 (ex-Camden)	1/12/1939 (to E.Hill)
6207 - *Princess Arthur of Connaught*		21/10/1939 (ex-Rugby)	2/12/1939 (to Camden)
6208 - *Princess Helena Victoria*		21/10/1939 (ex-Camden)	2/12/1939 (to Camden)
6209 - *Princess Beatrice*		16/09/1939 (ex-Camden)	2/12/1939 (to Camden)
6228 - *Duchess of Rutland*		16/09/1939 (ex Camden)	30/09/1939 (to Rugby)
6235 - *City of Birmingham*		16/09/1939 (ex Crewe)	30/09/1939 (to Rugby)
6236 - *City of Bradford*		16/09/1939 (ex Camden)	30/09/1939 (to Rugby)
6237 - *City of Bristol*		16/09/1939 (ex Camden)	30/09/1939 (to Rugby)

Readers may wonder if No.46246 *City of Manchester* was ever stationed at Longsight. Not so; it was at Crewe North from 1948 until 1960 and may well have visited the shed when engaged on running-in turns from Crewe works-a regular feature at Manchester London Road by both 'Princess Royal' and 'Duchess' Pacifics alike.

Longsight, 1949: Early on in its BR career, 1937 Armstrong-Whitworth-built "Black 5" No **45307** - a Chester (6A) engine-stands outside the end of the old South shed, the latter yet to be rebuilt. Despite the widespread allocation of this popular Stanier mixed-traffic engine, Longsight was seldom allocated more than a handful of the 842 examples. A "snapshot" allocation taken from the famous Ian Allan "Locoshed" book and dated December 1st 1956 shows a mere ten examples; of these, seven were Caprotti variants-Nos.44741/42 & 44748-52. Referred to elsewhere, most of these were later transferred away from 9A, though one more example-No.44747-had returned by 1964 to accompany 44748.

Gordon Coltas Photographic Trust

The last word on Stanier's engines at Longsight goes to the celebrated 8F 2-8-0, introduced in 1935. With ex-LNW 0-8-0s holding sway, Longsight had to wait until August 13th 1949 when 8Fs48425/48429/48500/48601&48516 joined the 9A fold-not that the shed did any considerable amount of freight work. A further 12 engines came on shed until the last 8F-No.48310-made its appearance on September 17th 1960. It should be added that some allocations were only of short duration; some were also loaned out to Northwich for periods of 2/3 weeks at a time. The longest 8F stay on the strength was 48389 which was at the shed from 1949 until November 26th 1960.

LMS DAYS AND INTO BR

The sheds were re-roofed in the early 1930s; while 1934 saw the arrival also of the mechanical coaling plant-a revolutionary innovation that allowed for the coaling of four locomotives simultaneously-along with two ash disposal plants. The shed escaped bomb damage in WWII, but wartime dilapidation ensured replacement of the shed roofs-work that was carried out in 1948. The Longsight "south shed" remembered by most readers had been re-built and re-roofed between 1955 and 1957 at a cost of £120,000. New pits and lighting were installed in anticipation of the arrival of electric and diesel locomotives and units. At this time the number of roads was reduced from eight to six while retaining the four through roads. Known today as "The Diesel Shed", the six roads were reduced to two in each part to enable fork lift access for Diesel Multiple Units. In 1960 a new 2-road electric maintenance depot was built at the end of the south yard. This was built from brick with laminated timber roof trusses. With the "overhead" energised to Crewe early in September 1960 steam here was bound to be an early casualty; concentrated now in the north shed, the steam locomotive left Longsight for good on February 14th 1965.

9A'S REMIT POST-1948

Longsight's authority widened not long after Nationalisation when, from May 22nd 1950, it took Heaton Mersey, Northwich and Trafford Park under its wing. Hitherto, these depots had worked under the control of the Trafford Park motive power district (code 13); they now became 9F, 9G and 9E respectively. Stockport (9B).

Buxton (9D) and Macclesfield (9C) were already under district 9's control. To complete this note on district ownership it should be mentioned that Longsight had absorbed neighbouring Belle Vue (ex Midland/LMS) on April 14th 1956. Derby (district 17) took control of both Heaton Mersey and Northwich from January 1957, the two sheds being renumbered as 17E and 17F.

Regional boundary changes brought Gorton (an important ex GC/LNER shed in East Manchester) under Longsight's remit from February 1st 1958. Gorton had already absorbed and had the Reddish electric traction depot and the Dinting out-station under its control . Later on in 1958, on April 20th, Heaton Mersey and Trafford Park returned to Longsight's control, although Northwich was switched to Liverpool's Edge Hill. A last major re-organisation, effective from September 9th 1963, saw the creation of a Manchester motive power district. This major change saw Agecroft, Bolton, Bury, Newton Heath, Lees (Oldham) and Patricroft brought into Longsight's empire. (Lees had passed from 9A's control in 1931 when it was transferred to the LMS Central division). MPD district 9 then encompassed sheds A-P, the three "B" sheds being Bolton (9K), Buxton (9L) and Bury (9M), a total of 13 depots. Only Longsight, of course, and Newton Heath which is little more than a stabling and re-fuelling point for DMUs are with us today.

A 1950 SHED 'BASH'

Of the many shed visits made by enthusiasts, comparatively few records survive giving precise details of engines seen. Fortunately, Howard Turner, a long-standing and much-travelled member of the RCTS Sheffield branch has provided a copy of a record he made during a society visit to Longsight on Sunday, April 16th 1950. The following were 'on shed' that day. ('Foreigners' are in brackets; named engines thus*)

41905	42935	41159
2772	46149*	42355 (9C)
47341	42887	42308
47369	46131*	48501
48268	42775	42814
47347	539	40136
47343	40693	42936
42430	44271	42381 (9C)
42467	44308	42788
40107	43275	42854
42322	44303	40674
42399	46129*	42580
46169*	41906	42858
44749	42979	47673
45570*	42937	48429
42776	42369 (9C)	46150*
45669 (1B)	48326 (9D)	48516
41168	46114*	44357
44937	41113	47528
43717	49428	42608
41907	48631 (8C)	42398
45593*	48389	46122*
45638*	47395	**Total=68 engines**

Points of interest from Howard's records are the large number of 'Crab' 2-6-0s-11 in all, with just one Stanier 2-6-0 on shed-No.42979. Notice, too, by this time that just one ex-LNW engine was present: 7F No.49428. Just two engines: Nos.539 & 2772 were still carrying their LMS numbers. Interestingly, Longsight

drivers tended to refer to their engines by the pre-Nationalisation numbers, eschewing the "4" added from 1948.

RCTS VISIT 27TH SEPTEMBER 1959

A series of shed visits arranged by the RCTS for the Manchester area - Stockport Edgeley, Trafford Park, Patricroft - also included Longsight, illustrating that five years on from Howard Turner's trip, effects of the Modernisation Plan were taking effect, the diesels had definitely arrived! From the diaries of Wallace Sutherland, the following engines were noted on shed, numerous of which were visitors.

In rows east of the shed were:-

47431	47395	48613	48429	44138	42416
42318	42398	40107	42470	42304	42443
41221	40122				

All apparently stored were:-

47346	47291	41907	40125	40674	40084

On north end shed were:-

44752	73091	45556	70033	45601	73034
46135	44678	42348	45536	44842	45540
45505	45631	45606	45078	42938	

On south end shed were:-

D214	D217	D3765	D3766	D3768	D3770
70021	44185	46108	47369	42772	47395
42889					

THE 'BRITANNIA' ERA

Largely absent from the shed from pre-War years onwards, Pacific power came back to Longsight in the shape of the, then, new 'Britannia' 4-6-2s. Though none of the class 7 engines arrived as new motive power, several arrived for various periods in the 1950s. The longest serving BR Pacifics would appear to be Nos.70031 *Byron* & 70032 *Tennyson*; also the eponymous *Charles Dickens* (No.70033) which served from 1953 to 1960. Other notables during the 1950s were Nos.70043 and 70044 - the two Westinghouse-fitted engines and originally un-named which came on shed late in 1953 and 1954 respectively. Pacifics aside, Longsight appears only to have acquired one other BR Standard engine of its own-Class 4MT 2-6-4 tank No.80039 which arrived in December 1953 and stayed until February 1955.

FURTHER AFIELD

During the late 1940s/early 1950s a Class 6 or Class 7 engine from Longsight worked the morning Manchester to West of England express as far south as Pontypool Road. Another regular working took a Class 6 or Class 7 locomotive from Longsight as far as York, reaching that city on the overnight Swansea to York mail train. The balancing working brought the engine back the following evening. In between these duties the 9A engine worked a slow train from York to Leeds. From here it returned as pilot to an Edge Hill 7P locomotive from Leeds to Liverpool on the 9.55 am Newcastle-Liverpool express before returning to Leeds during the evening.

During the summer of 1953 a Longsight Class 5 engine was rostered to work the 11.40 am (FO) London Road to Hastings train as far as Brighton, returning to Manchester the following day with the balancing working-the 1.50 pm from Brighton. On August 8th of that year "Jubilee" No.45595 *Southern Rhodesia* was noted on this duty.

The shed's Class 5 engines were noted frequently on excursions from Manchester to Stratford-on-Avon via Crewe, Wellington,

Longsight, August 1953: Another un-named "Patriot" – this time No **45547** – with tender brim full and a haze at the chimney, waits at the top of the North shed for its next call to duty. Never a 9A resident, 45547 was stationed at Crewe North when this photograph was taken. Further peregrinations saw the locomotive move to Willesden (twice), Carnforth, Llandudno Junction and Edge Hill before withdrawal from there in September 1962.

Photomatic collection

Wolverhampton (LL) and Birmingham (Snow Hill). A Western Region pilotman was picked up at Crewe with the engine being serviced at Tyseley after reaching the Shakespearean town.

Fast goods work fell to 9A's engines in the form of the overnight fitted freights from Manchester to Willesden. Caprotti Black 5s, Nos.44748-52 were often seen on these workings. The "Caprottis" worked as well as on "The Pines Express" as well as the Euston expresses-including at least one spell on "The Mancunian" (Q.V.)

These far-flung exploits of the sheds' locomotives recall the writer's conversations with ex-Longsight driver Harold Gorton who is referred to elsewhere. Harold was well known at Longsight for his outstanding route knowledge, something he had gained in many cases by walking the track and talking to signalmen, so keen was he to become acquainted with "foreign" routes. Harold recalled taking the Northampton Parcels trains south via the former North Staffordshire Churnet Valley route from North Rode Junction and south past Rudyard Lake. It was alongside the Staffordshire lake that the poet and writer Rudyard Kipling was conceived-thus arose the famous name. (Did 70035 ever pass this way?) Whether romantically-inclined or not, Harold spoke fondly of the route and always referred to the glow worms that could be

seen at the trackside there. A nice story from a wonderful man.

ALLOCATIONS IN 1954

Having dealt with steam at Longsight from its earliest days we complete coverage of the shed's motive power by taking a look at the allocations there on January 30th 1954.

Stanier 2-6-2T: 40077, 40107/36. **LMS 2P 4-4-0:** 40539, 40674/93.
LMS Compound 4-4-0: 41113/59/68. **LMS 0-4-4T:** 41905/6/7.
Fowler 2-6-4T: 42308/22/50/51/97/8/9.
Stanier 2-6-4T: 42427/30/61/67/78,42542/75/80/94/99,42608.
'Crab' 2-6-0: 42772/75/76/78/88,42814/48/54/58/86/7/9.
3F 0-6-0: 43275, 43457, 43717.
4F 0-6-0: 44271, 44303/8/49/57.
'Black 5' 4-6-0: 44748-52/59/60, 44837/38, 44935/37.
'Patriot' 4-6-0: 45500/1/20/30/34/36/39/40.
'Jubilee' 4-6-0: 45556/93,45603/17/31/32/38/55/80/88,45709/23/34/40/42.
'Royal Scot' 4-6-0: 46114/15/20/22/29/31/43/45/49/50/60/67/69.
'Jinty' 0-6-0T: 47267, 47341/43/45/47/69/95, 47400, 47528, 47673.
'8F' 2-8-0: 48389, 48425/28/29, 48500/1/16, 48633.
Ex-LNW 7F 0-8-0: 49322, 49428/39. **Total=128 engines.**

Longsight, July 8th 1962: Enter the Diesels. The writer still remembers the shock of seeing his first Diesel-the "box" that was a Type 4 heading towards London Road with a Down express in the summer of 1959. Though separate accommodation was to be provided for both Diesel and electric power at Longsight, the new traction had, perforce, to rub shoulders with the old for some time. Flanked to the left by an English Electric Type 4 and in front by a Type 2 Diesel No **D5138**, is "Crab" 2-6-0 No **42804** from 6C (Birkenhead). With 1160 hp and a Sulzer engine, the Diesel became one of Class 25; this loco had only a short life-being withdrawn in August 1969. Little has been made of the enormous upheavals faced by loco crews at this time - an interregnum between the passage of the old motive power and the dawn of the new. *Gordon Coltas Photo Trust*

Longsight, April 18th 1956: Appearing at the south end of the shed yard, close by No.1 signalbox, is brand-new BR Standard 9F 2-10-0 No **92080**. Seen in glistening unlined black, the engine was then less than a week old, having entered traffic just four days previously. 92080 had worked in to Manchester London Road Goods with the 8.27 am freight from Crewe. Having been watered and turned she will shortly be en route light engine to Heaton Norris to work the 11.17 morning freight from there back to Crewe. Like so many of her Standard compatriots, 92080 had but a short life; she was withdrawn on May 6th 1967.   *R.E.Gee*

END OF STEAM AND A NEW BEGINNING

Gradually, a new dawn came at Longsight as modern facilities replaced old and new technologies of driving, maintenance and repair had, perforce, to be embraced. DMUs appeared on Styal line local services in the mid-1950s and as early as 1957 electrification work was well under way on this stretch of railway; the Styal line having become the training ground for electric traction with East Didsbury as a temporary 'depot.' (Q.V.) 'Type 4' Diesels (later Class 40) began to appear on London services in the summer of 1959-Nos.D227/228 arriving at Longsight in August of that year. In 1960 the first 25kV Bo-Bo electric locos made their debut having been based previously out at East Didsbury. How quaint those blue-liveried locomotives with their red buffer beams seem now!

Beginning in January 1959 the new electric traction depot at Longsight took shape. In the main this consisted of a new shed 300 ft.long by 57 ft.6 in. wide. Laminated timber frames were used, being laid at 15 ft.centres. Inside were two tracks with inspection pits 278 ft. long. A new workshop and stores were added along with new mess accommodation and an up-dated carriage washing plant. Unfortunately, on November 5th 1983, somewhat ironically, a fire caused serious damage to the roof and walls of the electric depot. Two particular casualties were a Glasgow 'Blue Train', set No.059 and one of the 1,500V dc EMUs used on the Glossop and Hadfield route, No.006. Fortunately, at that time, these sets were in the last year of their life, but even so the unit was damaged beyond any economical repair.

So, with Diesel traction having been in the ascendancy at Longsight since the mid-1950s, the Crewe electrification coming onstream the year after and the impending completion of the Euston programme, it was inevitable that the days of the steam locomotive at Longsight, as indeed elsewhere, would be numbered. But steam hung on for a few more years yet-surviving, as mentioned previously, up to February 14th 1965.

Longsight station-along with the famous Belle Vue excursion platform-had already closed to passengers on September 15th 1958. The celebrated neighbouring zoological gardens which had brought so many rail passengers over the years survived until 1977 while the remainder of the old Belle Vue amusement park closed in stages up to 1987. Over on this side of the station, on the site of the excursion platform (which still exists!) and to the side of the former Freight terminal, the shed's newest addition, post-steam, arrived: the wheel lathe depot. Installed in 1988, the lathe-a Hegenscheidt type 106 Mark II-re-profiles wheelsets from a wide variety of locomotives, EMUs and DMUs. The depot, 200ft. long, is equipped with a 10-ton travelling crane and inspection pits. Ultrasonic testing equipment is installed for ready detection of flaws in either wheel or axle. A far cry indeed from the days of the wheel tapper!

Longsight ceased to be a signing-on point for train crews from midnight on July 23rd 1994. That same year work began on what was probably the shed's biggest-ever addition, the new 'Eurostar' maintenance depot-something.....................*continued on page 107*

(Above) Longsight , July 8th 1962: Longsight's new era. No less than eight Class AL5 Bo-Bo electric engines (later Class 85) including Nos.**E3058** and **E3014** are lined up "under the wire" at the east side of the shed. Delivering 3,300 hp, the 25kV ac locomotives were a revolution in British electric locomotive traction; hitherto, dc power was picked up, either via third rail or overhead catenary. Now, on-board transformers and rectifiers were used to enable power to be delivered at the lineside straight from the "grid" at 25kV. Entering service with "Electric Blue" all-over livery, white cab roofs, stainless steel numbers and red buffer beams-the new locomotives were a complete revolution, both in terms of appearance and tractive power. Familiar on the east Manchester skyline are the outlines of Stuart Street power station in Bradford - a sight long departed and dominated nowadays by the National Cycling centre.

(Centre) Longsight TMD, c.1960. **E3005** stands outside the then new depot. Classed originally as AL1 (later) Class 81) and numbered E3001 E3023, these were the first of the various Bo-Bo types to appear successively from 1959 through to 1966-Classes 81-86. The houses in the background stand on the thoroughfare prosaically named "Tank Row". Hard to believe that the same dwellings overlooked this spot in the Ramsbottom era-long before the advent of electricity and when gas and coal were the kings of fuel. ***Authors collection***

(Left) Longsight depot, c.1960: Harold Gorton (right) and a colleague receive instruction in the finer parts of the workings of a 25 kV AC EMU later Class 304. The steam locomotive - a simple, rugged beast was light years removed from its successors in terms of technicalities and it is a tribute to the dedication and application of the likes of Harold that railway managers were able to put the wonders of the latest electric technology into such skilled hands. Collection of ***Sylvia Hampson***

........of a white elephant, alas. Until 2005 a banner proclaiming *"Le Eurostar habite ici"* was displayed on a blue ground aloft of the building. Alas, this apotheosis of the EMU never got further south than Bletchley on its numerous test runs and has long departed the Manchester scene, so perhaps the blandishment should have been prefaced by... *Il-y-a déja longtemps!* In 2004 HST sets were seen again on the depot, appearing now in the rather pallid green and grey of Midland MainLine. Their arrival was connected with "Project Rio", the short-term provision of an alternative London route while the Potteries Loop Line via Stoke-on-Trent was being up-graded. For a brief period it had been possible once again to travel to London St.Pancras from Piccadilly. MML services to St.Pancras ended in September 2004.

In 2006 the HST's successors, the Virgin 'Voyagers' and 'Pendolinos' ('Pendolini'?) in their brash red, grey and yellow liveries are the staple fare of the depot, now under the stewardship of Alstom. Facilities in the erstwhile carriage shed enable the 9-car Pendolinos to be lifted off their bogies while refurbishments are rolled in. "Voyagers" arrive for overnight stops, largely for re-fuelling and cleaning. All marshalled now on the same ground where Leigh Bowden, Wallace Chalmers, Harold Gorton, Joe Linley, and Harry Price prepared their charges for daily journeys south. Longsight, still alive and well, has entered its third century.

(Right) Manchester Piccadilly, September 27th 1960. Not Longsight depot but a view of motive power which would be familiar for decades to come. On this occasion however, a 'new' Piccadilly witnesses a pair of locomotives with a potential 6,600 horsepower - which does at first seem a little excessive for a train of six main line coaches - arriving at the station! The 'pan' is down on the second engine (E3002) so there is every possibility that AEI Bo-Bo **E3048** could have been returning the loco to its Manchester depot as a balancing exercise. Even so, the sight of two blue electrics was clearly worth this superb shot as the duo run alongside platform 8 with the 8.55am train from Cardiff. It is a moot point to compare the train length of four decades past with the two and three car offerings of today. Small wonder one lady passenger was heard to remark a couple of years ago: *"Whatever happened to **real** trains ? **Michael Mensing***

(Centre) Longsight, 9th July 1964. Despite Manchester being one of the earlier recipients of AC electric traction, steam still played a prominent part in the proceedings. Mutual Improvement Classes, (M.I.C) which were attended by footplte and shed maintenance staff to gain an understanding of locomotive mechanics, were catered for in specially modified vehicles, in this instance L&NWR Wolverton built 12-wheeled carriages. Transferred into departmental stock, they contained a variety of features including a cinema (right) and classroom (below) which contained a replica locomotive back plate, exhaust and live steam injectors. The 'trains' toured depots throughout the region on planned schedules. When a course had been completed, cleaners from the respective depots were given the task of cleaning the brass fixtures and fittings. *J W Sutherland*

(Left) Longsight, 9th July 1964. More than five decades after entering service, these vintage carriages, now in use as 'Motive Power Instruction Cars' (see pages108/109), occupy one of the through roads between south and north sheds (engine facing Manchester). These former sumptuous 12-wheeled vehicles were, above (left), Car No 3B (BR-**M198851**) of 1908 and Car No 3A (BR-**M198852**) of 1913. The former was one of twelve built for the American boat trains on the Euston to Liverpool route whilst that to the right (also the picture opposite-left), served as a former 'Club Car' on the Llandudno 'Club' trains. *J W Sutherland*

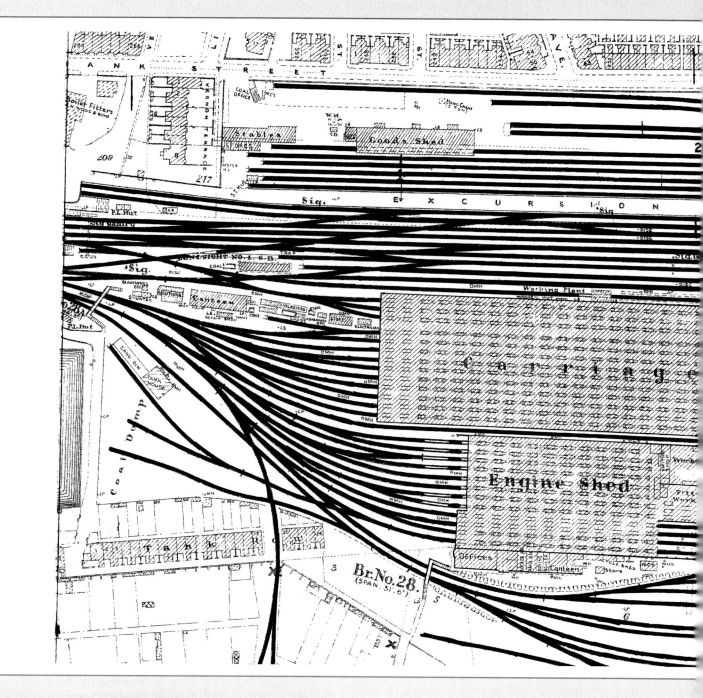

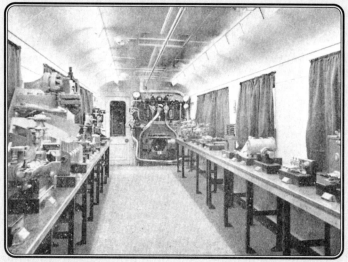

British Railways (L.M.R)
Motive Power
Instruction Cars

The two photographs that appear on page 107 serve to illustrate th[e] practical use applied to these specially converted vehicles when tourin[g] the steam depots. From *The Locomotive* magazine of January 15, 1949 [it] has been possible to add more detail of the refinements and requirement[s] needed in understanding the functions provided to train staff about th[e] technical equipment fitted to locomotives.

Described as a "School-on-Wheels", the former passenger carriage[s] were *"Fitted with up-to-date equipment including cinema projectors an[d] working models, and staffed by lecturers who will live and sleep on boar[d] when required, being in service for the training of enginemen and artisa[n] staff in the technical equipment fitted in locomotives.*

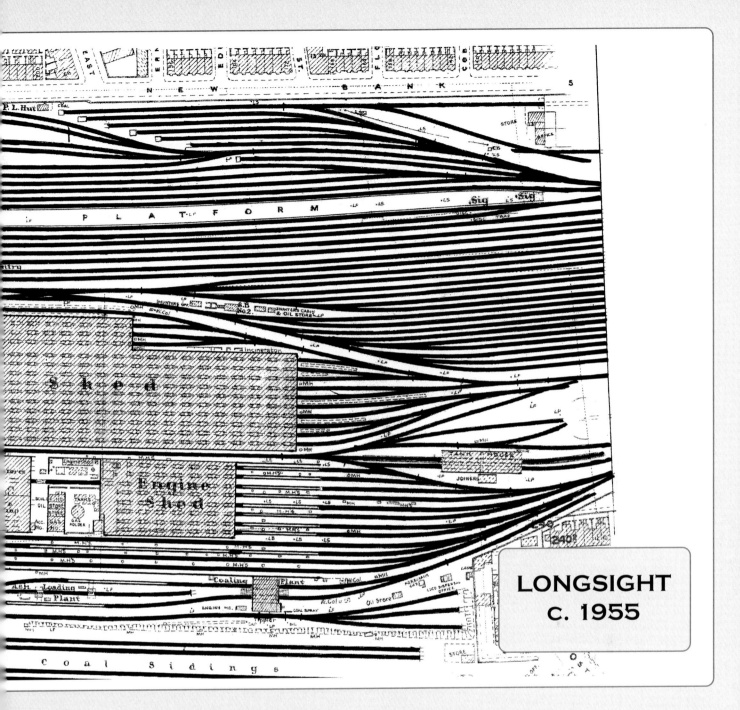

LONGSIGHT
c. 1955

Each lecture coach has seating accommodation for 31 students and is equipped with projectors and a screen for the display of films, lantern slides, etc., fitters' vice, bench and tools. An ordinary blackboard and a magnetic blackboard for displaying symbols for demonstrating rules dealing with signal operation and protection, etc., are also provided.

The demonstration coach has working models of water gauges, vacuum brake arrangement, test gauges, etc., steam brake arrangement and automatic train control.

In addition to the working models a number of components, mostly in section, of the various parts of steam and diesel locomotives are exhibited together with diagrams.

Models of both Walschaerts and Stephenson's Valve Gear are provided. The cylinders on both models are half sectioned to show the steam ports and cylinders. The piston valves and piston heads are in full diameter. The motion gear is of a light weight metal alloy and the whole is mounted on a metal back plate. Screw reversing gear is provided on each model to enable fine adjustment of the port openings to be explained.

Each train is self-contained. Steam supply for working models is obtained from a small 'Oil fired' boiler, placed at one end of the demonstration coach, behind the back plate carrying the water gauges, etc., A diesel driven electric generator is installed in the boiler room to provide current for the lighting of both coaches and for working the film projectors, epidiascope, etc., Tungsten lighting is provided throughout the train, with the addition of Fluorescent lighting over the models.

Fuel oil for the oil burning boilers and the diesel units for the electric generators will be obtained at the Motive Power depots during the visit of the train, the grade of oil required being the same as that used for diesel locomotives and for cleaning purposes. The capacity on each train of the main fuel tanks is 100 gallons, and the service tanks 50 gallons.

The total water supply on the trains is 380 gallons, 50 to 60 gallons of which is drinking water for use in the lecture car. the trains will be cleaned and watered at the Motive Power Depots.

Itineraries of the visits to be made by the train have been supplied to the Divisional Operating Superintendents and suitable workings have been arranged for each train".

(Above) Longsight depot, April 24th 1980: The Class 83s were the third generation of 25kV loco-motive and were introduced in 1960. An English Electric design, the 83s were of lighter weight (at 73 tons) and incorporated several innovative ideas. Notable amongst these was the use of single-anode rectifiers of the "Ignitron" type. It was this, princi-pally, which affected the locomotives' reliability, though the rectifiers were ultimately replaced. Two of the class, Nos **83 015** and **83 008** are seen at the depot's north end. One class member, 83 012 sur-vives in preservation at the Barrow Hill roundhouse near Chesterfield. *John Hooper*

(Centre) Longsight depot, August 15th 1980: A Manchester stalwart-Class **86 242** is caught on camera outside the electric shed. As "AL6" the class was developed jointly by BR and GEC/AEI from 1962. The class was variously modified from inception; one such and easily identifiable alter-ation is seen here: the application of the helical spring or "Flexicoil" suspension applied to E3173 (86 024) in 1969. 86 242 became *James Kennedy GC* in November 1981 and subsequently *Colchester Castle* in October 2002. *John Hooper*

(Right) Longsight depot, August 15th 1980: Incredibly, it is now approaching half a century since the first main line Diesels, in the shape of the, then, Type 4s appeared in South Manchester on a regular basis. Here, Class **40 113** stands in the yard below the footbridge at the south end of the shed, an unidentified class mate peeps out behind. Blue livery, if one can call it such, was then standard along with the BR corporate logo, yellow front and headcode discs. Other appendages of the modern era-fuel tank, "Zebra-fronted " shunter and DMU appear in the background. *John Hooper*

Longsight station, May 4th 1956: The delights of the shed aside, Longsight was a wonderful place from which to view passing trains. From the Down platform an excellent vista of the line along to Ardwick could be obtained and the excursion platform, seen off to the left gave a broader vista still. With No.1 box dominating the scene 9A's "Rebuilt Patriot" No **45540** *Sir Robert Turnbull* looks in fine shape at the head of the 11-coach 4.05 pm express to Euston. Travelling via Stoke-on-Trent, arrival in Euston was at 8.00 pm. With the advent of the winter 1957 timetable this train became "The Lancastrian" reviving a title from pre-War days, though only managing a modest two minute gain on the schedule.
R E Gee

Longsight shed, mid-1950s: Whatever the shortcomings of the nationalised British Railways, the system of yesteryear had an undoubted character-much of it of course a direct inheritance from the pre-1948 companies. Outside of the 1907 carriage shed a Stanier "Black 5" is coupled to a set of ex-GWR 'Toplight' corridor coaches, maybe these have been drawn through the carriage washing plant; dirty-looking trains were a rarity in those days. Standing off to the left, this was an LMS innovation from the 1930s. One of 9A's "Jinties"-No **47347**-simmers in the afternoon sun whilst a set of Stanier 57ft. suburban coaches have been marshalled-probably bound for a local or semi-fast working out of London Road later that day. Guarding all is the unmistakable sight of the LNWR semaphore signals standing aloof on their gantry and worked by Longsight's No.1 signal box.
Teddy Gorton

(Above) Longsight shed, early 1950s: Taken from the north end of the Down station platform this picture gives a splendid view, uncluttered by trains, along the line towards Ardwick. Dominating the scene is the splendid LNWR signal gantry with those familiar corrugated steel arms mounted on posts topped by plain caps. The steel girders of the gantry with their square lattice sections had become a standard design for the LMS. Two Stanier engines- a Caprotti "Black 5" and a "Jubilee" can be seen in the shed yard, while further along Longsight's No.1 box and the carriage washing plant are prominent sights. Notice the locoman-sporting the familiar shiny "grease top"- walking down the platform ramp, no doubt going over to "book on" at the shed. All once familiar sights: yet within a few years, the steam locomotives, signal box, signals and even the station would be gone. **G H Platt**

(Right-centre) Longsight, shed yard, c.1956: An interesting shot providing some fascinating details of the Longsight gantry for signalling aficionados: notice the calling-on arms below the main home "boards", the planking, handrails and smoke troughs. The footbridge in the background led right down outside the foreman's office-trespassers beware! The water tower-seen in other views-shows in detail, while Tank Row stands prominent in the background. **G H Platt**

(Left) Belle Vue, miniature railway, 1962: Longsight's other railway! Long before the days of Alton Towers and the ubiquitous "theme parks" up and down the country, Manchester's Belle Vue was the mecca for the family day out in the north of England. The locomotive is Bassett-Lowke Atlantic No **32** *Prince Charles*, later to become *Synolda* and happily still at work on the Ravenglass & Eskdale Railway. Our picture shows the Atlantic on what was Belle Vue's third 15in. gauge line, though four had existed at different periods. When this picture was taken the trains were propelled from the station towards the Belle Vue lake close to Hyde Road. A frequent service was run with trains returning smokebox-first. **N.R.Knight**

Longsight station, May 11th 1938: From the excursion platform we look across to No.1 signalbox and the two platforms of Longsight station; note the extensive station canopies. Rattling through on the Down Fast line is Stanier 2-6-2 tank No.137 with a three-coach train carrying "express lights"; bringing up the rear on the Slow line is a Fowler 2-6-4 tank at the head of a "stopper." Watching the proceedings, the Permanent Way gang, three men plus the lookout, lean on their tools-just enough time for a quick draw on a "fag" before work resumes.

E.R.Morten

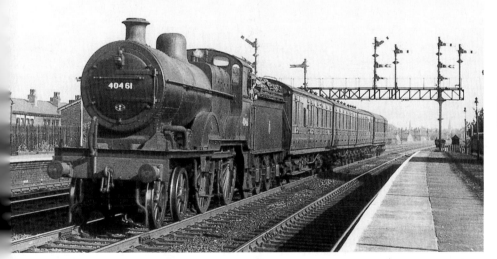

Longsight station, July 9th 1955: Just how far the British railway system of the early 1950s had to go to modernise itself is well illustrated by this picture. Class 2P 4-4-0 No 40461 - a rebuild of a Johnson Midland Railway engine built in 1893 heads a truncated set of close-coupled suburban stock. These first three coaches were parts of sets built for the Midland Railway's suburban services in Manchester and Birmingham by James Clayton in 1903. Longsight station officially closed to passengers on September 15th 1958 but saw a brief renaissance during the Spring of 1959 when for a short period, normally on a Saturday, the station was brought back into use as a temporary 'Manchester' terminus to accommodate trains from Stockport, Buxton and the Macclesfield /Stoke directions during the modernisation of London Road Station. On Staurday 30th May for instance, Manchester bound trains terminated at Longsight and were met by buses which transported passengers to London Road. Passengers from Manchester for outward bound trains commencing at Longsight were required to be at London Road some fiteen minutes before normal train departure times. A truncated platform serving the Down slow line survives today and is used as a staff halt. It found public use for a brief period in 1988 when services, truncated by the new Manchester Piccadilly signalling scheme discharged their passengers here.

R.E.Gee

Longsight station, May 28th 1960: The Down side buildings as viewed from Kirkmanshulme Lane almost two years after 'closure' to passengers. Beyond the station buildings and off to the left, a subway (bridge No.28) connected the two sides of the station. In this late period, some traffic is known to have emanated from visitors to the nearby Belle Vue entertainment complex, but how much and for how long is not certain. One such special remembered was a Saturday evening excursion from the Stoke-on-Trent area, comprising a 'Derby Four' 0-6-0 and nine bogies. Originating at Cheadle in Staffordshire and picking up at stations between Cresswell and Stoke, the special would arrive alongside the excursion platform at Longsight about four o'clock in the afternoon, disgorging several hundred already inebriated individuals. The train soon became known by rail staff as the 'Cheadle Boozer', and to the relief of all concerned, departed back to the Potteries about ten o'clock in the evening.

Graham Whitehead

(Above) Longsight station May 11th 1960: Viewed from the excursion platform this was the station's Up platform building now shorn of its canopy, its demise ensured by the presence of the all-pervading overhead electrification masts. To the far left can be glimpsed part of the modernised former steam shed; seen behind the station building is the front of the, then, new electric traction depot - the doors of which were destined to be regularly damaged by a generation of careless drivers - sited close to where a former coal stage and reservoir had stood.

Graham Whitehead

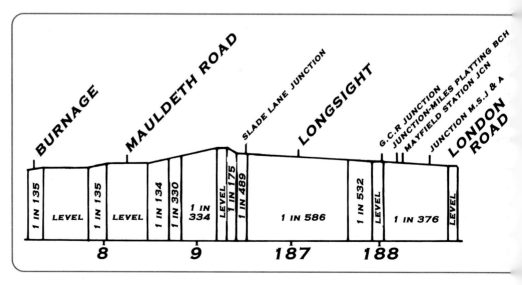

Manchester London Road, early 1920s: An attractive, yet odd, combination. "Precursor Tank" No **6819** pulls sharply away from platform 1 with an express. Odd, because the engine is in the LMS livery of lined crimson lake while the coaches remain in the "plum and spilt milk", two-tone LNWR passenger livery. The use of "Express Lights" suggests a London train hauled as far as Wilmslow or even Crewe. Immediately after Grouping the 8.10 am London Road to Euston, calling at Wilmslow, Alderley Edge and Crewe travelled over the Styal line and used Longsight engines on Mondays, Wednesdays and Fridays. The 9.45 Euston was also known to be tank engine-hauled as far as Wilmslow in the 1920s. No.6819 was withdrawn in February 1937.
Author's collection

LONGSIGHT to SLADE LANE JUNCTION

With the smog and smoke of industrial Manchester now being left behind, southbound trains are travelling on a continuously rising gradient-nothing too severe, a mere bagatelle of 1-in-929 to around 1-in-1178 as far as Levenshulme North, the first station beyond Slade Lane Junction on the line towards Stockport. Before reaching the Stockport Road, the present-day A6, the railway is flanked to the west by the former township of Gorton and on the east by the township of Newton. Land here was owned by the Dean and Canons of Manchester to whom the railway paid a perpetual yearly rent of £200.00. Over Stockport Road the railway is carried on bridge number 23. A two-part structure: the first was built with cast iron arches, this carried the Down lines-fast and slow and dated from 1840. The second part, carrying the Up lines, was constructed from wrought iron-the difference in materials is significant-and dated from the widening of the line here in 1880. With approaching modernisation and electrification looming in the 1950s and half of the bridge now well over 100 years old, renewal was considered a necessary priority.

The new bridge No.23 consists of post-tensioned concrete box girders, each carrying one track. Each girder comprised 16 pre-cast box units, each unit weighing 30-35 tons. The box units are joined by diaphragms and post-tensioned with 16 cables each containing 72 wires of .276" diameter giving a total pre-stress force of 3,600 tons. The girders, each supported at four points on steel and rubber bearings, are 7'-6" deep and 107' across, giving maximum width for the roadway. Installation of the new bridge

was a massive operation. The pre-cast units for each beam were erected on staging spanning the road alongside the existing bridge. Cables were dropped in and stressed, the finished beam then being jacked down and rolled onto temporary reinforced concrete columns.

Existing bridge sections had been replaced by temporary beams during the preparatory site work and these were lifted out of each track in turn as the new concrete beams were rolled into position. All work was carried out during weekend possessions between July 8th and August 24th 1958. To enable traffic to keep running whilst work was proceeding at bridge 23, diversions were put in place: trains travelled via the "Lanky Branch"- London Road to Ardwick, up to Midland Junction, then Philips Park No.2, and Baguley Fold to Droylsden. Down via Ashton Moss Junction to Denton Junction and then over Heaton Norris Junction into Stockport Edgeley. A bit tedious, but it all worked! Because of the revolutionary new techniques being used for the new bridge No.23, considerable interest was aroused, with many "top brass" paying visits to the site as the work progressed. The contractor for the new work was Leonard Fairclough of Adlington, Lancashire. Faircloughs aroused further interest by their use of a mobile 70 ton road crane, "Lorraine" which they had bought from the USA. "Lorraine" made short work of lifting the pre-cast diaphragm units onto the staging ready to be stressed together. As one of the leading BR engineers said: *"just like threading cotton bobbins on a string!"*

Longsight, bridge No.23 - Stockport Road; August 31st 1944: Wartime Manchester; life is hard for the young mothers and their children waiting for their tram (or is it bus?) outside Lea & Mellor's fish and pie shop. Little traffic moves along here - a major highway; come modern times and it will be brave man who can stand on this spot with a camera! In the distance a Stockport Corporation bus-a number 92, followed by a horse and cart, ambles south towards its parent town. Notice the interlaced tram tracks between the narrow confines of the bridge. Close to here, about 50 yards south along Slade Lane, was the "lost" village of Rushford. A station was built by the M&BR at roughly this point and grass-covered stone steps leading up to the possible site were reported as having been found about 1920. Rushford had a station – opened on June 4th 1840 and closed as far back as April 1843 (another source gives 1854), but the name of the village lives on in the names of nearby Rushford Park, Rushford Street (off Stanley Grove) and Rushford Avenue in neighbouring Levenshulme.

Manchester City Engineers' Archive

(Centre) Longsight, corner of Attwood Street and Stockport Road - A6, 1958: Preparations are well in hand for the rebuilding of bridge No 23. The huge trestles, comprising steel girders and supports, carry the concrete sections for the new bridge. Once aligned, these will be slid into position - one track at a time, each over the duration of a single weekend possession. No "rail replacement buses" or wholesale closures for weeks on end in those days! "CAUTION-DEAD SLOW" warns the sign in the middle of Stockport Road as a cart, heavily laden with sacks, heads towards Ardwick. Approaching the camera, a No 92 bus belonging to Stockport Corporation and wearing the familiar red and white livery of the Cheshire town's fleet ambles along, bound for Stockport and subsequently Hazel Grove.

Martin Welch

(Right-lower) Bridge No 23, June 8th 1958: As mentioned in the text, replacement of this structure involved a considerable degree of technical innovation. Though staged for publicity purposes, this photograph - taken to record the positioning of the first new span - recaptures a now lost generation of civil engineers, railwaymen and operating practices - to say nothing of their attire! From left to right are: Arthur.N.Butland, *Assistant Chief Civil Engineer, LMR Euston* - later CCE for the BRB; John Calf (looking at the camera) *New Works Resident Engineer, Manchester CCE dept*; Arthur Lloyd-Owen, *District Engineer, Manchester (CCE dept)*; Lord Rusholme, who was *Chairman of the BR (LMR) Board* leans forward to shake hands with J.Taylor-Thompson, *Chief Civil Engineer LMR, Euston.* **British Railways**

Slade Lane Junction, 1957: Only the Lampman ever saw the junction from this viewpoint! Taken from one of the bracket signals on the junction's south side, the view looks towards Longsight and Ardwick. Some track relaying and re-ballasting has been done while freshly-spiked baseplates and sleepers await their turn on the left-hand side. Coming south from Longsight the keen-eyed may notice the LNW lower-quadrant arms, after half a century's use, have been replaced by BR standard ones on the far signal gantry. From right to left the tracks are: Up Slow, Up Fast, Down Fast and Down Slow. Noticeable are the two crossovers; one enabling trains to access the Styal line from the Up Fast line; the other enabling trains coming off the Styal line to transfer over the Down Fast line. After modernisation the layout would change completely, the tracks becoming paired by direction to and from Manchester. (Q.V.) *Martin Welch*

It is at Slade Lane Junction that trains bound for Crewe have a choice of routes. Straight ahead is the original route of 1842 via Levenshulme and Heaton Chapel to Stockport; while right forms the "new line" of 1909 - the Wilmslow & Levenshulme Railway, or "Styal Line" of the LNWR. Slade Lane itself had been something of a country backwater up until the mid-1920s when its southern end became the site of the starting point of Kingsway-now the A34 with an electric tramway running via a dedicated central reservation as far as East Didsbury - less than a mile from the Cheshire boundary. Leaving the old Manchester to Stockport Turnpike road in Longsight, the lane passed Slade Hall one of the oldest buildings in Manchester with origins going back to the middle of the 13th century. The Slade family occupied the hall until the reign of Queen Elizabeth I when the house and estate was sold to the Siddalls. Slade Hall was rebuilt in 1585 and an inscribed lintel exists to this day bearing testimony to this. It must have been a blow to the Siddalls to have their land sliced in two when the M&B built their railway-the LNW line plan bearing the words "Trustees of John Siddall." Further land was relinquished early in the 20th century by the family when the Styal Line was constructed. Beginning from a junction with the A6 Stockport Road, Slade Lane passes Slade Hall, then meanders under the overbridge bearing the "New Line" before taking a sinuous curve past Old Hall Lane and eventually forming a junction with Kingsway. Now turning sharp left, Slade Lane eventually becomes Burnage Lane

forming a continuing thoroughfare that takes the traveller on to the boundary with the Borough of Stockport.

Until the re-signalling and associated power box working the four tracks at Slade Lane Junction followed the conventional pairing of slow/fast/fast/slow lines. With modernisation this was

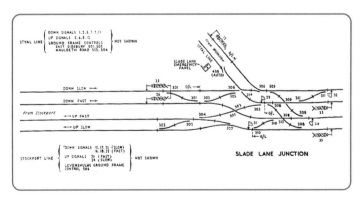

altered to give pairings of the tracks from Manchester Piccadilly by speed as opposed to direction. This transposition brought the slow lines to the west side of the terminus and enabled the fast lines to serve the longer platforms in the middle. Thus the four tracks became Up fast and Down fast and Up slow and Down slow respectively; pairing reverting to direction on the south side of the

CRASH AT JUNCTION

Pines Express and diesel

Extracts from the Manchester edition of The Guardian for Tuesday November 24, 1959 describe the accident which occurred the previous afternoon at Slade lane Junction. To quote their own reporter, *"Seventy passengers escaped serious injury when the* **Pines Express** *from Bournemouth to Manchester collided with a stopping train from Buxton yesterday afternoon. Only three passengers, all in the express, were hurt. The locomotive of the express train and the first three of the seven carriages were derailed, as were the second and last carriages of the six-car diesel stopping train.*

The crash was at Slade Lane junction, three and a half miles south of London Road station, Manchester.

At the time of the crash both trains were travelling at about 30mph; the Buxton train on the slow line and the express on the fast line alongside it. Railway officials refused last night to comment on the cause of the accident. From the appearance of the wreckage, the heavy Castle class locomotive of the express seemed to have been taken by the points into the rear of the first car of the diesel train. Those hurt were Mr Harry Ryan, aged 32, a train driver, of Mulgrave Street, Salford, who was a passenger in the first coach of the express, and Mr and Mrs Michael Isaacs, both aged 69, of Waterpark Road, Salford, who were in the rear coach and were slightly injured by falling luggage. Uninjured passengers were taken by buses to London Road Station. The accident occurred on a stretch of line where recent damage to the tracks and embankments has worried the railway police. British Railways last night were not prepared to comment on the possibility of sabotage by children".

junction through Levenshulme and Heaton Chapel towards Stockport. The re-modelled junction had 19 pairs of points and four moveable switch diamonds.

It was in the last days of Slade Lane signalbox's life when one of the junction's two recorded accidents occurred. As part of the re-signalling scheme, block working between Heaton Norris Junction and Slade Lane had been done away with and trains were "belled" along only, though block instruments remained for the section from here to Longsight No.1; Colour light signals and power points were controlled now by the route relay system known as "one control switch". This had been installed in November the previous year. On the evening of Monday, November 23rd 1959 two trains were converging on the junction from the Stockport direction. One, the 3.59 pm Buxton to Manchester London Road DMU travelling on the Down Slow line was scheduled to wait at the junction home signal, while the second train, "The Pines Express" hauled by "Patriot" No **45520** *Llandudno* and running about four minutes late, was booked to run in front of the DMU by crossing over from the Down Fast to the Down Slow line for the last 2½ miles into London Road. The Ministry of Transport report maintained that the Buxton driver misread the green signal on the Fast line for his own, which he claimed had changed from red to yellow with a "feather". The two trains collided side-on at a point some 170 yards short of Slade Lane box. Fortunately, speed was low and the two trains travelled only about 100 yards before coming to rest. There was no loss of life and only two passengers and one railwayman were injured. The Inspecting Officer, Colonel D.McMullen placed the blame on the Buxton driver for having mis-read the signals. He had criticism also for the guards of both trains for failing to observe signals at an important junction. A rather comical

side on this accident appeared in the following morning's issue of "The Guardian", repeated above. *"From the appearance of the wreckage, the heavy Castle class locomotive of the express seemed to have been taken by the points into the rear of the first car of the diesel train."* Manchester Gricers should have been so lucky!

Slade Lane Junction, August 10th 1954: The LNWR, being the highly-standardised and efficient railway it was, built its signalboxes to a clearly-defined range of standard sizes. Slade Lane box fitted in to size code 'H' with a length of 26ft.6in with 2 X 2 window units, sitting along with 2 X 3 window units in between. With 36 levers the box controlled the sections between Longsight No.1 and Levenshulme on the Stockport line and to and from Mauldeth Road on the Styal Line. Signalman Albert Hall poses at the north window for fellow "Bobby" Ronnie Gee. Slade Lane Junction signalbox survived until Stage 1 of the introduction of the new power box at London Road station. The change-over was carried out on the weekend of Saturday to Monday 12th-14th December 1959. *R.E.Ge*

Slade Lane Junction, May 7th 1953: From a low angle the paunchy boiler of Longsight's "Crab" 2-6-0 No **42886** is seen to advantage as she heads the 8.42 morning train from Manchester to Crewe, first call Stockport Edgeley(arr 8.53) along the Up Fast line in the direction of Levenshulme. After stopping at all stations, arrival at Crewe was scheduled for 9.54am to connect with Blackpool and Windermere portions forming the 10.09am Crewe to London Euston (arr 12.55pm) service. Restaurant Car facilities were provided in the 8am departure from Blackpool Central and Through Carriages were attached en route at Wigan The squat, bold arms of ex-LNWR semaphores are in charge of things this side of the junction with both Up Fast and Up Slow homes being "pegged" off.

R.E.Gee

Slade Lane Junction, August 10th (Tuesday) 1954 : The photographer stands in the centre of the track of the Down Styal line. Coming smartly along the Down Fast (Stockport) line is Fowler 2-6-4 tank No **42306** - a long standing 9D (Buxton) engine - at the head of the 6.40 pm Buxton to Manchester train. During the week, this train ran fast line from Stockport but on Saturdays was required to call at Levenshulme North (7.41pm), adding some four minutes to the schedule. The semaphores read (L-R) Down fast home, Down Slow to Up Fast home, Down Slow home; distants for Longsight No.1 box are beneath all three signals.

R.E.Gee

THE STYAL LINE
THE LONDON & NORTH WESTERN RAILWAY'S
WILMSLOW & LEVENSHULME RAILWAY

"Commencing by a junction with the Crewe and Manchester Railway at Wilmslow in the Parish of Wilmslow, in the County of Chester, and terminating by a junction with the Crewe and Manchester Railway at Levenshulme in the Parish of South Manchester, in the City and County Borough of Manchester, in the County of Lancaster". The London & North Western Railway (New Railways) Act 1899

INTRODUCTION

The comparatively few photographs that exist showing the railways in South Manchester in the years before the Grouping depict a landscape utterly different from that extant today. Open views across vast tracts of sparse-looking farmland are broken only by the ribbons of steel that were the railway lines heading into the distance. It was across such a landscape that surveyors working for the LNWR would have made their assessments and worked out the alignment for one of the company's last railways, certainly its last main line: the nine or so miles from Slade Lane Junction over the farmland of South Manchester towards the River Mersey and on to the market town of Wilmslow in Cheshire where a junction would be made once again with the old M&B line south to Crewe.

RAISON D'ÊTRE

It has been written that the Styal Line was built with a view to opening up the residential districts north and south of the Mersey. But even the most optimistic railway company could have not have expected to generate significant traffic from such a region as a sole case for a big investment in a new railway, for there was indeed a paucity of souls living in and around the farms and districts south of the city at the turn of the nineteenth century. Farming in those days was a low-level activity, hard work indeed for those engaged in it, but far removed from today's high-yielding, factory-type operations. In the districts closer to the city - Ardwick, Longsight and Levenshulme there was already an established railway complete with well-used stations. So, to get a realistic glimpse of the raison d'être of the new railway it is necessary to look at the goings-on at Manchester's London Road in the last twenty or so years of the nineteenth century. The joint station had been expanded by the LNW and even the hard-pressed MS&L had squeezed in another platform, eking out their meagre share of the space allocated to them under the Act of 1861. Hemmed in by the presence of the MSJ&A, in which the LNW held joint tenure, the company chose to build another station on the opposite side of Fairfield Street. This, of course, was the building known eventually as Mayfield* which opened in 1910, just one year after the first trains ran over the Styal Line. However, problems at London Road aside, it was at Stockport, some six miles down the line that more serious difficulties were being encountered.

*An LNW minute dated July 13th 1910 refers to "Fairfield Street Station, Manchester".

CONGESTION AT STOCKPORT

As was mentioned elsewhere, the lines from London Road to Ardwick and from Longsight through Levenshulme and Heaton Chapel to Stockport had been quadrupled by the early 1880s-indeed, authority for the first widening between London Road and Ardwick had been given as far back as June 1860. Commensurate was the widening of the Stockport viaduct-from 1887-1889, such was the growth in traffic between Manchester and Crewe. By the late 1890s there were some 700 trains on average every 24 hours passing through the Edgeley station. Of these, around 450 were passenger trains including some 90 or so that either started from or terminated at the station.

THE NEW LINE IS PROPOSED

The railway was proposed in a Bill-The London & North Western Railway (New Railways) Act of 1899. Aside from the Styal line, the Bill also sought to authorise a new railway from Holland Arms to Red Wharf Bay in Anglesey-opened in 1908/1909- and an obscure short line known as the Netchells Junction Railway in Aston, Birmingham. Despite the new line not really encroaching on any existing districts-only a handful of properties required demolition-the Bill did not go through Parliament unopposed. Seemingly, the residents of most of the areas through which the proposed railway was to pass were opposed to it. One piece worth quoting comes from the Burnage area-in the days a sparsely populated district, albeit with some very select houses along the Burnage Lane. Burnage people claimed that the new railway might spoil their peace and seclusion and bring into the district.... *"undesirable residents in the shape of a working class population."* Clearly, Nimbyism is nothing new!

Fortunately, the local press were on the side of the railway. "The Manchester City News" writing on March 25th 1899 thundered *This (the proposed new railway) is a serious alternative. It remains now for the opposing residents of Burnage and Didsbury and the Levenshulme, Withington and Cheadle District Councils to carefully consider their course of action. The working class population in these districts and in Manchester generally, who are always benefited by improved means of communication which bring new industries in their wake, may also wish to be heard in this matter, as may also the Styal and Gatley populations who don't care to be cut off from easy communication with their leading market. In conclusion, it must not be forgotten that this is a question which should not be settled off-hand by a few select suburbs. It is rather one for Greater Manchester, with its population of 1^{1}/2million.*

But the opposition, such as it was, had no success and the LNW's Bill received the Royal Assent on August 1st 1899. The contract for the line's construction was awarded to Messrs.Naylor Brothers of Huddersfield, though Robert Neil & Co. of Manchester were appointed to undertake some construction at

Slade Lane Junction, August 17th 1954: The signal, "Up Fast to Up Branch" reads "Off" as "The Mancunian", drawn by "Royal Scot" No **46140** *The King's Royal Rifle Corps*, clatters over the junction with its 45mph speed restriction from the Up Fast line before heading south, round the corner and en route over the Styal line; thence to Wilmslow, Crewe and beyond. By today's standards, the 75mph maximum permissible speed applied to the Styal Line seems rather cautious, but then advances in track and rolling stock design have transformed what was essentially a railway of Victorian origin into a system to compete with the competition from air and road travel, where time and speed have priority . A pity that the appearance of the 9A engine did not match the pristine condition of the train.   ***R.E.Gee***

Wilmslow station. In precise terms the line was described as being 9 miles, 3 furlongs, 5 chains and 95 links (100 links per chain). As ever seems to be the case, the line ran over budget. An LNWR minute recording thus: Cost of Wilmslow and Levenshulme Railway:

Works and permanent way (double line)	£285,160
Stations and accessories	£59,759

	£344,919

(being £19,385 over estimate.)

Figures when up-dated can be misleading. Put into modern perspective we can reflect that the entire electrification of the (almost) 400 miles of the East Coast Main Line in the early 1980s cost around £200-odd million pounds. At the time of writing the government has refused to finance the planned extensions to Manchester's Metrolink system, the so-called "big bang" running, in the early summer of 2004, to a total cost approaching the £1 billion mark. Within the "big bang" package, the 2½ miles of projected new Metrolink from Chorlton to Didsbury was estimated at no less than £93 million pounds. With hindsight it is safe to say that the LNWR got a bargain.

THE ALIGNMENT OF THE RAILWAY

Work began at the southern (Wilmslow) end in October 1901 with an immediate obstacle in the form of the Bollin Valley where a new viaduct was required to take the line over the void. Wilmslow station itself had to be rebuilt to provide four platform faces and the goods yard was moved to a new site south of the station on the Up side of the Crewe line. A new signalbox was provided hereabouts; this consisting of an overhead pattern on a gantry frame. The Bollin viaduct, set 60 feet above the river and comprising eleven arches, was one of three such structures required by the new railway.

ENGINEERING FEATURES

Somewhat less than a mile further north, the River Dean was crossed, this time at a height of 50 feet from ground to rail level. A third viaduct took the railway over the River Mersey. At 660 feet long, the arch over the river was built on the skew and constructed throughout in blue engineering brick. Twelve arches in total form this viaduct, the bridge register recording the structure as bridge No.28 with an overall length (on the square) of 172 ft. 10 in. Arches nos.9-11 are set on the skew which alters the total length. An addendum notes that a concrete side retaining wall was added in 1922 to prevent erosion of the river bank. Set before the viaduct was bridge No.27, 51 ft. 6 in. on the square (60 ft. 9 in. on the skew) where the railway crossed the CLC's Glazebrook to Godley line. This was one of four railways traversed by the new route: immediately north, between mileposts 5¼ and 5½, bridge

THE
STYAL
LINE

Wilmslow, c. 1907/08. There may well be a degree of speculation as to the exact location of this picture, but by the nature of the curvature of the line, it is to the south of bridge No 7 at Lacey Green, shortly before the line converged with the route from Stockport. The bridge is faintly visible in the right background. The steam excavator is removing spoil from the bottom of the cutting. The small four-wheeled contractor's trucks looks barely adequate but it was this spoil that was moved forward to provide materials from which the embankments were formed for much of the line north of Heald Green.

Authors collection

No.26 took the line over the Edgeley Junction to Northenden line-another LNW railway. Stepping over the Manchester boundary the Styal Line had to span the Midland's 1880 Manchester South District line via bridge No.33 between mileposts $6^{1}/2$-$6^{3}/4$. Further south, at mileposts $8^{1}/2$-$8^{3}/4$, bridge No.43 spanned the former GCR's Chorlton Junction to Fairfield line, itself a later development and opened throughout in 1892.

Bridges 27, 33 and 43 were innate curiosities. At widths in excess of 50ft. they were designed to span a future four-track railway. The dimensions were prescribed in the Act of Parliament and the same was laid down for future railway bridges in South Manchester-notably over the former Midland South District Railway. All this is manifest today where redundant four-track spans sit splendidly over an alignment bereft of track at Chorlton Junction, Princess Road, Parrswood Road and Kingsway. A severe case of over-optimism if ever there was. With later structures added on, the Styal Line contained no less than 54 bridges on a railway of just under $9^{1}/2$ miles in length.

Beyond Wilmslow was the parish of Styal-set in the rural district of Bucklow-through which the new line had to run in a cutting north to a point between Heald Green and Gatley-at almost exactly between mileposts $4^{1}/2$ and $4^{3}/4$. Fortunately for the LNWR this convenient dividing point enabled the formation of the remainder of the line. For from this point, right along to the junction with the Stockport line at Slade Lane, the railway had to be carried on an embankment-save for the

Wilmslow, c.1907/08. This and the picture above are at the same location although this view illustrates the excavator going through its repertoire of working positions as it gouges away at the earth to form a cutting for the new railway. Considering the lateness of construction of the Styal line, views of such occurrences are as rare as the proverbial 'hen's teeth'. The contractors, Naylor Brothers of Huddersfield were very much involved in railway construction at the turn of the Twentieth Century, having completed some years before the heavily engineered Ashbourne extension from Buxton. The crudity and small size of the spoil wagons should be noted although they had to be capable of being manhandled in the broadest sense. *Authors collection*

river and rail crossing points mentioned previously. Building the embankment must have been a formidable task, especially at East Didsbury and Mauldeth Road where a formation had to be provided to accommodate a goods yard as well. The contractors were hard put to complete their task on time. A company minute dated June 21st 1905 records that… *"to expedite operations on the Wilmslow and Levenshulme Railway, the contractors began working all night at tipping Didsbury (sic) Embankment. But residents complained, and a Mr.David Moseley of "Scotscroft", Didsbury, threatened to apply for an injunction, so, after legal advice, the contractors are tipping 7.00 am to 8.00 pm only."*

The Styal line was built with a ruling gradient of a modest 1-in-135. Largely undulating, going north a summit of sorts was reached at Styal, whereupon the alignment fell at 1-in-135 towards the Mersey before climbing again to East Didsbury. The photographer William Lees (Q.V.) accompanied some of his excellent pictures on the line with the phrase "on Burnage Bank." But such references are really illusory when speaking of a ruling gradient of no more than 1-in-135 prior to a level stretch. It has been said that, due to the line's undulating nature, some Camden crews had refused to "sign the road" for the line. Following a curve near Styal and another at Gatley the Styal line is more or less straight through East Didsbury down to beyond Mauldeth Road where two gentle curves, north-east, then north-west bring the railway to Slade Lane junction.

THE STATIONS

Only four stations were planned in the original scheme of things: going north, these were to be at: Styal, Gatley, East Didsbury and Mauldeth Road. The 400 or so inhabitants of the hamlet of Heald Green were decidedly unhappy about being left out. In consequence, they sent a deputation to the LNW headquarters at Euston. A body of Cheshire farmers-names recorded include Francis Cash, John and Matthew Royle-spent a week in the Capital arguing their case, guaranteeing the company a steady market in agricultural traffic. Interestingly, of the stations planned-only one was required under the Act; clause 15 stating: *"The company shall upon the opening of the Wilmslow and Levenshulme Railway provide and shall maintain a sufficient station for passengers at or near the Wilmslow Road."* Thus was born the station known today as East Didsbury, in those days East Didsbury and Parr's Wood. Left out, too, at first was Burnage, the station there not opening until July 1st 1910. An interesting observation shows that planned stations were provided with awnings over the platforms; the two built by petition were not similarly endowed!

Styal station comprised substantial accommodation and the platform buildings were brick-built. As at East Didsbury, the station was equipped with separate classes of ladies' waiting room, the only two stations on the line to be so endowed. The area around Styal, in like manner to East Didsbury, contained several large dwellings. In Styal, noteworthy developments were the Styal Cottage Homes and the famous Quarry Bank Mill, owned by Samuel Greg. The Cottage Homes were a more or less self-contained development and were owned by the Guardians of the Poor of Chorlton Union (to use the full title). Chorlton Union were landowners in the area, having sold land around milepost 2¾ to the LNW in 1902 and 1905 for the construction of the railway. Sited on Styal Road, just over half a mile from the station and opened in 1898, the homes comprised an initial 14 cottages housing 300 children. This was added to in 1903 when the population rose to 450. Styal Cottage Homes closed in 1956; the property and land has now become part of Styal Women's prison. Samuel Greg's Quarry Bank Mill dates back to the 1780s and in its day would have been the village's largest employer as well as providing substantial traffic for the station. Today, Quarry Bank Mill belongs to the National Trust and is part of what is known as

Gatley, c.1908: Construction of the Down side buildings proceeds apace. Timber is literally heaped around everywhere. By the looks of things, the platform buildings on each side were constructed in turn. The timber platforms, likely to be the extremely durable *jarrah* (Australian mahogany), as well as the sectional buildings, were meant to last, in fact the buildings seen here (or part of them), survive to this day, almost a century after construction. All the workmen, carpenters and joiners - was there a difference ?) - have stopped work while the photographer busied himself. Notice that all wear white shirts, caps and aprons. The man standing aloft on the building close to the awning clutches a saw in his right hand-no Working at Height Regulations in those days! Hand tools would have been the norm then-none of your chop saws, gas-powered nail guns and SDS drills all screeching away! The track, distinctly rough and laid on thin sleepers has the rail merely spiked down. But such "temporary way" was just that-to enable the contractor's vehicles to move materials about. Collection of *H.D.Bowtell*

"Styal Country Park". Alas, only a meagre percentage of its many visitors arrive by rail.

SERVICES BEGIN-THE EARLY YEARS

Construction of the Styal line, over budget as mentioned earlier, was completed by January 1909. Colonel Yorke, for the Board of Trade, inspected the line on February 4th and, as is usually the case with new railways, freight services began first-these commencing just four days later-from Monday February 8th. LNWR records, however, show an anticipated opening for goods traffic in December 1908. Passenger services were held off for just under three months, the first train-the 6.30 am from Manchester Oxford Road to Wilmslow-steamed out on Saturday, May 1st drawn by two Webb 5ft.6in.2-4-2 tanks, Nos.1156 and 1763. Twelve trains were provided each way by the LNWR in the first timetable. In 1910 (May) this had shifted to 10 down and 12 up stopping trains; with little exception, all called at every station-Burnage had yet to open (on July 1st 1910).

A PIECE OF AVIATION HISTORY

Burnage station has one small claim to fame. In a field close to the line here the French aviator, Louis Paulhan, landed his Farman biplane on completion of his celebrated London to Manchester flight in April 1910. It was the newspaper magnate, Lord Northcliffe-owner of the Daily Mail-who had offered a prize of £10,000, a colossal sum of money a century ago, for the pilot of the first successful flight from London to Manchester. Northcliffe's conditions were stringent: the flight, of 185 miles, had to completed in 24 hours, only two landings were allowed and the competitors were required to both start and finish within five miles of the Daily Mail's offices. The LNWR put on a special train to act as a support. Thought to be drawn by "Jumbo" 2-4-0 No.619 *Mabel*, the train carried two Daily Mail reporters, M.Paulhan's wife, M.de.Kersanan, Paulhan's partner in the enterprise, M.Farman, the plane's designer and his wife, two mechanics, an official of the Aero Club and a young boy, one Alan Buchanan, who Paulhan had adopted as his mascot.

Paulhan, taking off from Hendon Aerodrome, had to contend with Claude Grahame-White, an English pilot who had set off from Park Royal, London, in hot pursuit behind the Frenchman on the evening of April 27th. (A previous flight by Graham-white four days earlier had to be abandoned when his plane was forced down by high winds into a field at Hademore, between Tamworth and Lichfield).Upon nightfall, both pilots were forced to land. Night flying had never been attempted before, but, notwithstanding the risks, Graham-White decided to chance flying by moonlight, his supporters using their automobile headlamps to aid his take-off and thus making the world's first-ever night-time flight. Alas, though, the Englishman's machine landed short of the target landing again near to Lichfield.

Wisely, Paulhan decided to wait until daybreak and, despite facing strong winds, ascended to around 1,000 feet and managed to complete the flight, landing in Burnage at 5.32am. The plane touched down in farmer Bracegirdle's fields where oats and potatoes were grown, causing considerable damage. Paulhan, ever the gentleman, had telegraphed beforehand asking permission to land here. Bracegirdle had consented, with the proviso that he was to be compensated for any damage caused. We can assume that the large crowd of onlookers, most of whom must never have seen an aircraft before, can only have added to the damage to both field and hedges-which was estimated at £100. Perhaps the farmer should have charged an entry fee! Paulhan and his entourage were taken by train into Manchester and on to the Queen's Hotel on Portland Street. The Frenchman's celebrated aircraft was dismantled in situ and stored in the works of Hans Renold across on Burnage Lane. Paulhan Road, close to Burnage station and lying parallel to the Styal line, commemorates the Frenchman's heroic flight-a truly epic journey that took no less than 4 hours, 18 minutes. On April 28th 1985 several aircraft, including a Chipmunk, Cessna 172 and a helicopter, landed at Hough End fields, in Chorlton, to commemorate the 75th anniversary of this aviation landmark flight. In his home country, Paulhan's feat lives on-a college in Sartrouville bearing his name was opened in 2002. Louis Paulhan died in St.Jean de Luz, France, on February 10th 1963 aged 79.

Site of Paulhan Road, Burnage, April 28th 1910: The scene in farmer Bracegirdle's fields as preparations are made to dismantle Louis Paulhan's Farman biplane prior to it being dispatched back to London. In the background the Styal line, then a new railway, can be made out clearly, its bland embankment cutting through a landscape then still unspoilt by the post-First War housing estates. Immediately to the right of the plane's wings can be seen bridge No.35, then spanning a footpath leading in a north-westerly direction towards Pytha Fold farm. From around 1926, when Fog Lane park was developed and the present-day housing estates evolved, the path would have become the present Brayside Road. Farmer Bracegirdle's land, together with that on the railway's east side around the area was then owned by the Earl Egerton of Tatton. A covenant placed on the lands between Burnage and Mauldeth Road stations stated that.. *"The railway company are not to manufacture bricks or tiles, or to erect engine sheds, or manufacturing works on these lands."* **Collection of Brian Robinson**

Manchester London Road, c.early 1920s: Motor train (or "push-pull") services over the Styal line are thought to date from soon after the line's opening in 1909. Though Webb 2-4-2 tanks had been used from the outset, in 1920 three Webb 0-6-2 tanks arrived to help handle the four-coach trains. The engines employed were LNW No.2028 (LMS 6896), LNW No.16 (LMS 6890) and LNW No.55 (LMS 6919). Seen here running alongside the GCR's signalbox is the latter of the trio, No.55, still carrying its LNWR numberplate. The engine was fitted for motor working in August 1920, this and the numberplate helping to date the picture. The coach seen behind the engine, was to LNW diagram D57 (in the motor book). A 3rd class 50ft.vehicle, it was one of nine built between 1903-06, being converted from D285 for push-pull working. The 0-6-2 tanks continued in service along the Styal line until the Spring of 1932 when one of the driving coaches was badly damaged in a shunting accident. The were replaced by the ex-Midland 0-4-4 tanks (Q.V.)   *P.F.Cooke*

MOTOR TRAINS

It was around 1912 that the so-called "motor" train services began, Longsight shed having two motor-fitted 4'-6" 2-4-2 tanks-Nos.383 and 2065; No.529 followed in 1913. Records for February 1913 from the collection of Walter Laidlaw show 11 Up and 9 Down regular weekday stopping trains worked by motor trains. Most of these were to and from Wilmslow, though the first working (at 7.00am) was from London Road to Styal. Other Styal line local workings at this time were handled by LNW 5'-6" 2-4-2 tank engines with a 12 year or so stretch by Webb 0-6-2 18" side tanks. The noted photographer William Lees (Q.V.) wrote that the Longsight men who worked the motor trains were known by their colleagues as "clean slop" men, due the disposition of driving the train in the clean environment of the leading coach. Laidlaw records that the same men (in 1913) were paid at the rate of 7/- per day (35p).

Around September 1932 the ex-LNW engines that had charge of the Styal line motor trains were displaced. In their place the LMS sent Longsight three ex-MR 0-4-4 tank engines which were fitted with vacuum control gear for auto working. Officially, the engines were Nos.1274/76 and 78, though there is evidence that at least one other locomotive (No.1286) was used. Normal operating practice was for the engine to be sandwiched between the four coach sets

on weekdays. On Sundays the stock was slimmed down and the Tanks ran with just two coaches. Longsight diagram (No.56) for the motor trains (Summer 1937) shows them working just three Up and three Down trains over the Styal line on weekdays; this increased to six each way on Saturdays. This Saturday service was pure shuttle: beginning from Manchester Mayfield at 10.25 am and then working Down-Up-Up-Down throughout the day until 9.20 pm when the last train left Wilmslow-due Mayfield at 9.46. Mayfield seems to have been used throughout the period Monday-Saturday with London Road being used on Sundays. Sundays show a generous provision: nine push-pull trains in both directions; four each way continued to Alderley Edge, due no doubt to the attractive walks in the area and to the famous copper mines.

Motor trains aside, other motive seen on Styal line locals in the 1930s were the LNW "Precursor" 4-4-2 tanks-stalwarts, though all gone by around 1935. In the latter half of the decade, various tank engines of the former North Staffordshire Railway were noted on locals; known identities being 0-6-4 tank engines of Class "C" and "F", 0-6-2s of Class "L" and 0-4-4s of Class "M". A former L&Y Aspinall 0-6-0 tender engine was also noted (Q.V.), unfortunately Bill Lees, who managed to photograph it, only records the occasion as May 1938. An even rarer observation (by Eric Dalton) was the sight of ex Furness Railway 4-6-4 ("Baltic") tank engine which was seen at Mauldeth Road on July 17th 1926. More modern offerings came with the introduction of Fowler and Stanier LMS 2-6-4 and 2-6-2 tank locomotives. That scholarly observer of the Manchester scene, the late lamented David Tee, wrote that he believed motor train working from London Road ceased on the outbreak of war in September 1939 with 0-4-4s Nos.1278 and 1286 being moved from Longsight in early 1940, though others of the class did appear there later. Longsight's affair with the former Midland 0-4-4 tanks lasted until October 11th 1947 when No.1420 left the depot to be transferred to Rugby.

EAST DIDSBURY STATION AND DAD'S ARMY 1939-45

Though within the areas close to the east of the railway, i.e.around Fallowfield, Burnage and Didsbury, were sited two factories, Hans Renold in Burnage and Fairey Aviation in Heaton Chapel, little bomb damage ensued. Renold's, inter alia, were engaged on work for the Admiralty while Fairey's were concentrating on aircraft production including components for the Lancaster bomber. A Home Guard battalion was stationed on Cringle Fields, close to the Stockport line and hard by the Fairey Factory in Heaton Chapel. The machiavellian Lord Haw-Haw had even sent his wishes to the girls engaged in biscuit production at Mc Vitie & Price's factory behind Fairey's on the other side of the Manchester-Crewe line!

At East Didsbury "B" (Didsbury) Company 46th County of Lancaster Battalion had two positions installed in 1941: at bridge No.32 (Q.V.) over the Wilmslow Road; the other at bridge No.31, south of East Didsbury station spanning Gawsworth Avenue. At bridge 32 three sandbagged walls, each 5ft.high and 30in.thick were loopholed (sic) 2ft. 9in to 3ft. 6in. from base. These were built in excavations varying in size from 24 ft.by 12 ft. to 8 ft. by 5ft.at the base of the bridge wing walls. Bridge 31 had only two sandbagged positions; these were on the east side of the railway. A sand bunker was provided at the south end of the Up station platform by the entrance to the goods yard. At both bridges, on either side of the line, wooden platforms, 6ft. long by 18in.wide were constructed. These were set by the trackside at the bridge centre 3ft. 6in. below the top of the parapets. Clearance between passing trains and the occupants of the platforms must have been minimal. One wonders what Captain Mainwaring would have made of this?! Behind East Didsbury station itself, on the fringe of the embankment behind the present-day Parrswood Court flats, the same Home Guard battalion was provided with a trench 50 ft. long.

Thankfully, as mentioned, the area in the line's immediate vicinity received no heavy bombing. The nearest the blitz reached the railway was on October 11th 1940 when the house at 518 Kingsway, not far from East Didsbury station, was destroyed by a bomb. Alas for Manchester city centre, the evening of December 22nd 1940 brought havoc from incendiary and HE bombs causing devastation and fires not seen in an English city since the Great Fire of London. Warehouses in the Piccadilly area and in particular, Exchange station, were all but destroyed that night.

LOCAL SERVICES IN MODERN TIMES

As mentioned later, tank engines provided the bulk of the motive power for local services after the Second War. We are fortunate in having a record of engine workings for about two years from

October 1946 for the 8.10 am Wilmslow to Manchester (Mayfield) train. Normally worked by 2-6-4 or 2-6-2 tank locomotives from Stockport, the following locos appeared:

CLASS	NO.	OCCASIONS WORKED
4-6-0s		
"Royal Scot"	6160 (5A)	1
"Jubilee"	5592 (12A)	1
"Black 5"	5287	1
4-4-0s		
2P	531 (9A)	5
	539 (9A)	6
Compound	1122 (9A)	6
	1166	
"CRAB" 2-6-0		
	2778 (9A)	1
	2859 (9A)	5
	2923 (9A)	1
	2936 (9A)	1
0-6-0 (4F)		
	4074 (9B)	4
	4340 (9B)	1
	4385 (9A)	1
	4444 (9B)	9

From October 8th 1956 Diesel Multiple Units took over the stopping services between London Road, Wilmslow and Alderley Edge. At first, no improvement was attempted over the existing steam schedules due to the start of engineering work over the line prior to electrification. Indeed, for the whole of the first month of operation the DMUs terminated at Styal-the section between there and Wilmslow being closed completely for this period to enable track lowering prior to erection of the overhead line. A brief glance back at fares in those days shows a cheap day return from Mauldeth Road to London Road as costing 10d, East Didsbury 1/2d and Wilmslow 2/6d. First Class was still available in these "good old days" at 50% extra.

Elsewhere, changes were manifest in Manchester local workings as, from this date, DMUs appeared also on Buxton and Macclesfield line trains out of London Road. This began a gradual cycle of improvements to local services on the Styal line: electric traction appeared from September 1960 on workings right through to Crewe; then this was followed, albeit ten years later, when 25kV working was instituted from Oxford Road via Styal and Stockport to Crewe. Thus began the first major change in stopping services over the line since its inception, with the MSJ&A line becoming opened up to through journeys from all six stations, something well overdue.

Only Gatley and Burnage stations were without goods yards. Goods handling was available at all the others, though neither Mauldeth Road or Heald Green was equipped with a crane. Surprisingly, Heald Green had no facilities for handling livestock, a strange omission given the pressure put on by local farmers for the LNW to provide a station there in the first place. None of the stations were provided with footbridges-access for both Up and Down sides being supplied independently via sloping wooden approach ramps. These lasted until the line was electrified when they were replaced by structures made from reinforced concrete.

CLASS 303 EMU THE BLUE TRAINS

Mauldeth Road, July 25th 1984: Something that distinguished the 303s from their 304 and 305 partners was the provision of sliding doors, a feature possessed by their predecessors on the Glossop services, the Class 506 1500v dc EMUs. Appearing in the, then, BR two-tone blue and white livery, 303 067 pays a call on an evening stopping service to Wilmslow. Notice the LNWR buildings still extant on Mauldeth Road's Down side and the "switchback" nature of the line as it dips down in the distance towards Burnage. Finally, notice the twin cables-inductive loops-running in the "four foot" between the rails. These were part of an experiment for the abortive "driverless train" and were laid down over the entire length of the line from Slade Lane to Wilmslow. *Author*

Though the Class 304 EMUs covered the initial bulk of the services on the two routes from Manchester to Crewe, their appearance in the GMPTE area became more widespread when the Manchester-Glossop-Hadfield route was converted to 25kv working after December 1984. In the meantime, "foreign" EMUs, in the shape of the Class 303 units were seen working around Manchester. Built for the Scottish Region's North and South Clyde services by the Pressed Steel Company at Linwood, Paisley in 1959 the 91 three-car sets had electrical equipment by Metropolitan-Vickers ("Metro-Vicks" to Mancunians). Known as "The Blue Trains", due to their Caledonian-like blue paintwork, these quite attractive-looking trains held great promise for a modernised suburban network. Sadly, the Class 303s suffered a near-catastrophic inauguration when two explosions in separate MBS cars, occurred in December 1960. All the 77 units so far delivered were withdrawn and a subsequent MOT enquiry traced the problems to a build-up of oil and air vapour in the equipment compartment between the guard and passenger sections. Problems occurred too, with water leakage in the wrap-round design of the front windows. However, after modifications, carried out by Metro-Vicks at Dukinfield Works, the units re-appeared (the rest were modified in Scotland) and after proving trials on the Styal line they re-entered service. The first such to be noted was at Heald Green on March 13th 1961. The modified power cars were sent out from Dukinfield in pairs to East Didsbury and from here they were marshalled between driving trailer cars, forming an effective 4-car train. With testing complete, six power cars were marshalled between two Gresley brake coaches with a 20-ton goods brake van at either end. Drawn by an 8F travelling tender-first, the ensemble ran to Wilmslow where reversal took place before running back towards Stockport. From here the train proceeded via Heaton Norris Junction, Denton Junction and Ashton Moss Junction. Then "over the Snipe" (the Droylsden Branch) to Droylsden Junction and along towards Manchester Victoria. Thence out via Blackburn and the Settle & Carlisle line and home to Glasgow. A long, tedious and slow trip!

A youthful observation noted that the new ramps were steeper than the old due to the re-siting of the platform entrances.

ANALYSIS OF STOPPING SERVICES OVER THE STYAL LINE-1922-2004

(Monday to Friday and SX services; train services labelled "SO" are omitted)

1922 (July)
Down-19 trains.   Up-14 trains.

1938 (July)
Down-35 trains.   Up-34 trains

1945 (May)
Down-18 trains   Up-16 trains

1955 (September)
Down-16 trains   Up-16 trains

1957 (Summer)
Down-16 trains   Up-15 trains

1985/1986 (whole year)
Down-32 trains   Up-32 trains

Present day (July-September 2004)
Down-40 trains   Up-39 trains

DETAILS OF BUILDINGS

Awnings or not, Styal line stations were nothing if not functional. Plain, standard LNWR timber buildings were set on wooden platforms erected on timber piles driven straight in the embankment, though Heald Green and Styal were, as mentioned, in modest cuttings. All the buildings survived until modernisation of 1958-60; those on the down side at Mauldeth Road lasted beyond this before succumbing to an arson attack on October 27th 1985. On April 5th 1991, the buildings on Gatley's down platform were fired also, though, thankfully, this time the damage was minimal and restoration was possible. Modernisation had ushered in buildings that were up-to-date, airy, light and functional. Electric heaters took over from coal fires-something unthinkable in the era of minimal and, later, de-staffing. Wooden platforms were replaced by concrete ones of sufficient length to accommodate 8-car trains, a hopelessly optimistic gesture. Though, in September 1960, when electric services began, the new Type AM4 (later Class 304) EMUs-comprised four cars, these were later reduced to three. This has left the present-day operators with a maintenance headache and, today the platform extremities on the Styal line are cordoned off with the warning "passengers must not pass this point, or cross the line." Thankfully, there are plans in hand currently to replace the platforms. These will, of course, be nothing like the original length, as in most cases, 2-car DMUs and 3-car EMUs are the commonplace service providers nowadays. An occasional luxury turned up when the Airport to Blackpool and Barrow stopping services presented themselves as a 2-set Class 175 ensemble!

EXPRESS WORKINGS OVER THE LINE

In the formative years of the line the LNW's "Precursor" 4-4-0s, introduced from 1904, were the biggest express engines allocated to Longsight; the November 1912 allocation being 10 locomotives. In 1913 the first express along the line was the 9.45 morning express to Euston which stopped at Wilmslow to connect with the portion from Manchester Victoria and Stockport. The 9.45 was hauled by a Longsight "Precursor" 4-4-0 and was crewed by the shed's No.1 link men. Walter Laidlaw records their pay as being the highest at the shed-8 shillings per day. After working the morning train to Euston the same engine returned to Manchester with the 4.05 pm departure via Stoke-on-Trent. The big 4-4-0s, naturally, worked the bulk of the expresses to London with odd use on semi-fasts and, occasionally, local services. William Lees, then in his early teens, recorded seeing a "Precursor" piloted by a "Precedent" 2-4-0 in regular service around this time on the 6.05 pm express from Euston. He noted the train doing an estimated 70 mph through East Didsbury with the Precursor's white hot smokebox glowing brightly on a dark night; "slap on time at 9.26 pm" to use his own words. Lees noted drivers Tommy Blacow, Bill Simpson and Lee Bowdon working expresses along the "Styal Branch"-as he termed it-in the pre-WWI period.

After the First War, in 1921, express services over the Styal Line consisted of, firstly, the morning 9.45 and evening 6.15 trains from London Road to Euston. In later years these similarly-timed expresses would become "The Mancunian" and "The Comet" respectively. Both trains stopped at Wilmslow where carriages worked over from East Lancashire-Colne, Burnley and Blackburn were attached and detached. Secondly was the 4.30 pm (SX) to Birmingham-first stop Crewe and the 5.43 pm (SX) train to Crewe calling at Wilmslow and then all stations to Crewe itself. In the Down direction the only express was the 10.30 morning train from Euston. This was due into London Road at 2.30 pm after the Wilmslow stop where, again, the East Lancashire portion was detached. Finally, a service appearing strange by today's standards, the 8.32 morning train from Chelford, Alderley and Wilmslow, which then ran non-stop into London Road, appeared in the timetable.

The summer of 1922 saw a new addition to the timetable in the shape of a 6.30 evening train from Euston to Manchester which ran non-stop to Wilmslow to arrive at 9.46. At Wilmslow the train was split into two portions: the front portion going forward to Stockport and then Manchester Victoria where it was due to arrive at 9.30. the rear portion hung around at Wilmslow for 14 minutes and was then allowed a leisurely 30 minutes for its journey into London Road over the Styal line. Beginning after Grouping another London service was suing the Styal line; this was the 8.10 morning train from London Road which called at Wilmslow, Alderley Edge and then Crewe.

From 1923 the 9.45 am Up and 6.05 pm Down London expresses were accelerated and given a 3_ hour schedule. Using the Styal line, both trains called at Wilmslow. Interestingly, the morning train carried a former L&YR 5-coach Restaurant Car set; this worked back to Manchester in the afternoon via Stoke-on-Trent. Another pre-Group oddity at this time was the appearance of an ex-Midland Railway 6-coach Restaurant Car set which put in an appearance on the 6.05 pm. The formation had worked up to Euston as part of the 12.05 pm express from London Road, again travelling via the Potteries. Through workings to Halifax and Colne (using ex-L&Y stock) were a feature of both trains.

THE ROYAL SCOT

AT ....EAST DIDSBURY !

(Left & Opposite top) East Didsbury, March 5th 1961: Two photographs showing the usefulness of the Styal line as a diversionary route when the WCML between Wigan and Crewe is out of action. **(Left)** At 4.25 pm none other than "The Royal Scot" appears drawn by **D288** with 14 bogies, growling past in typical and well-remembered fashion. A local landmark, the clock tower of the Manchester Corporation bus depot, stands out in the background. Surviving today, it is now a feature of the local Tesco supermarket. *W.A.Brown*

As noted, the sight of a "Duchess" working over the Styal line was a fairly common one in the early 1960s. Pictures, though, are rare so we are fortunate that Allan Brown was at East Didsbury to record this splendid sight. Sunlight graces the scene as Carlisle Upperby's (12A) **46255** *City of Hereford* passes through with a Glasgow to Birmingham express. The train was made up twelv coaches and three vans Ahead is bridge No.32, manned as a Home Guard position in 1941.

W A Brown

It was in 1928 that trains would appear whose titles at least would be familiar to modern generations. In 1928 the 9.45 morning express from London Road to Euston had the title "The Mancunian" bestowed upon it. At the same time the 6.05 evening train down from Euston to Manchester was endowed with the name "The Lancastrian." In the summer of 1932 many LMS expresses were being accelerated: this resulted in the two Styal line celebrities having their overall time cut to 3¼ hours. The Up Mancunian was not non-stop, though, as it still called at Wilmslow to pick up through coaches from the East Lancashire towns that had come in via Manchester Victoria and Stockport. Coming down from Euston, "The Lancastrian" had its departure time altered to leave the Capital at 6.00 pm. To keep within the "XL" limit the train no longer carried coaches as before and the division at Wilmslow was therefore not required. A mere two minutes was allowed here before the train, again travelling via Styal, departed to arrive in London Road at 9.15 pm.

Another named train with Styal line connections, at least in its early years, was the Up "Comet". A corruption of the words "COTTON-METROPOLIS" ("COMET"), the train entered service in September 1932 and was given a 3¼ schedule to Euston. Departure at first was 5.40 pm from London Road and, running over the Styal line, the first stop was Stafford to detach two coaches for Birmingham, after which the train ran the 133.6 miles to Euston in no less than 127 minutes. At an average speed of 63.6 mph this made "The Comet" the second fastest train on the whole of the LMS. Always a heavy train and a popular one, "The Comet"

was rostered to a Longsight "Royal Scot", though "Princess Royals" were used briefly just prior to the outbreak of WWII.

At the time of writing this feature "Pendolino" services have started with a great flourish between Euston and Manchester Piccadilly; on September 20th 2005 such a train covered the Down journey in a record-breaking 1 hour and 53 minutes. The red, silver and yellow-liveried trains are regular visitors along the Styal Line due to frequent diversions away from Stockport. Consisting of nine vehicles, it is interesting to look at the make-up of our "Lancastrian" service of 72 years ago by comparison. Consisting of eleven or twelve coaches this train comprised:

One Corridor brake 3rd
Two open thirds (56 seats each)
One kitchen car
One open first (42 seats)
Two corridor brake composites (18 first, 24 third class seats)
One corridor brake first
One restaurant car composite (12 first and 18 third class seats)
One open third (56 seats)
One corridor third (42 seats)
One corridor third (42 seats-Fridays only)

On occasions" The Lancastrian" would be loaded with more stock-in which case it would be divided at Wilmslow. This was necessary as, in those days, the platforms at London Road could not handle trains of more than 12 coaches. The second portion would be normally be taken forward from Wilmslow by a tank engine.

EXPRESS MOTIVE POWER

As a main line constituent of the LNWR the Styal line would have witnessed the whole gamut of the company's motive power. True, on its inception in the first decade of the twentieth century, the heyday of the Ramsbottom and Webb engines-the amazing "Jumbo" 2-4-0s and the pretty and remarkable "Lady of the Lake" 2-2-2s had passed. Now it was the turn of the "Precursor" and "George the Fifth" 4-4-0s and the "Experiment", "Prince of Wales" and "Claughton" 4-6-0s to show their prowess. When the line opened, back in the first months of 1909, the debut of the first "Royal Scots" was still 18 years away.

USE AS A DIVERSIONARY ROUTE

Going back to our introduction, one of the reasons for the line's construction in the first place was as an alternative railway to the original route to Crewe via Stockport. Thus, when in the Summer of 2004, the entire railway between Slade Lane Junction and Stockport was closed for up-grading as part of the WCML, the Styal line came very much into its own. Stockport aside, though, the line has seen, on many occasions, diversions in both directions of trains to and from the West Coast line. By dint of using Piccadilly's through platforms, 13 and 14, trains can travel via Castlefield Junction, along the former Liverpool & Manchester mainline to Parkside (of Huskisson fame), then north via Golborne Junction to Wigan and Preston. Since the opening of the Windsor Link in 1988 diversionary scope has been widened further since trains can now access Bolton and Euxton Junction (where the WCML is joined) as well.

ADVENT OF THE TRAMCARS

From the mid-to late 1920s massive changes began to creep over the south Manchester landscape. Substantial housing estates-built by both private and council developers-began to appear north of the Mersey. Names of small farms that had existed for hundreds

of years became transposed into titles for roads both major and minor: Pytha Fold, School Lane, Hyde Fold and Parr's Wood, to present just a few examples. Though these estates would offer the railway more potential passengers, another development would actually deprive them of traffic. Continuing south from Slade Lane, at a place known as West Point where this ancient thoroughfare turned off to become Burnage Lane and reach the Stockport boundary, Manchester Corporation constructed the highway known as "Kingsway". By the standards of the day Kingsway was something of a revolution. Built throughout as an almost dead straight dual carriageway, the road was lit and-almost certainly to the railways' chagrin-had a central reservation carrying a tramway.

Electric tramcars had appeared in Manchester as far back as 1901, though the city council was not the first operator in the area that honour going to the Oldham, Ashton & Hyde company who began their services in June, 1899. The southern half of Kingsway opened in stages throughout 1926: to Mauldeth Road on July 18th, to Fog Lane on October 4th and, finally, to East Didsbury on December 13th. Kingsway proper begins at a junction with Slade Lane in the area known as "West Point". A resolution dated February 1st 1921 by the Manchester Town Planning Special Committee notes: *"Resolved: That for the purposes of finding additional work for the unemployed, the construction of a portion of Road No 25 between West Point and Moseley Road be proceeded with, subject to the Ministry of Transport agreeing to bear 50% of the actual cost of the work".* It was also noted that agreement with the Great Central Railway be sought (and sealed-sic) in connection with works for the new bridge over which would be laid lengths of Decauville trackwork. This bridge, numbered 25, took over the embryonic Kingsway over the GCR's Chorlton Junction to Fairfield line between Fallowfield and Levenshulme; the new bridge works were completed in 1922. A photograph dated 1921 looking south from Moseley Road shows the site for the new road sprawled out alongside the Styal line with pieces of trackwork laid in random fashion. Decauville track was essentially for a light railway and was usually laid to 600mm gauge. It had been extensively used for military purposes elsewhere and its application

Kingsway, looking south, 1920s: This view is taken close to the junction of Homestead Crescent in the south Manchester suburb of Burnage. Approaching the cameraman a No.40 tram-East Didsbury to Albert Square-is seen; the popular red and cream livery shows up well. Burnage station lies across to the right over the fields awaiting the second batch of council-built houses. In the distance notice the road rises to cross the former Midland South District line en route to Stockport and Cheadle Heath. Looking at this view showing state-of-the-art trackwork, laid dead straight with sleepers and ballast formation, it is hard to believe that such a system was abandoned after little more than twenty years existence. Today, at the end of 2005, Manchester is fighting hard to acquire the very thing it once jettisoned.

Collection of *J.H.Turner*

Kingsway, April 26th 1938: Long before the days of Metrolink, a No.38 tramcar drops a lone passenger off outside the Kingsway Hotel. Off to the left the tram rails snake their way along to West Point where Slade Lane joined the new thoroughfare of Kingsway. The Styal line is out of sight to the left behind the row of semi-detached houses. Behind the photographer is Moseley Road where the tram (which began its journey in Cheetham Hill in North Manchester) will turn right. Along Moseley Road the service will cross the major highways of Wilmslow Road and Princess Road before running along Barlow Moor Road to the terminus in Chorlton. *H.B.Priestley*

there would have been for the continuation of Kingsway down towards Mauldeth Road station. Though these days the term "tramway" is often freely interchanged with "railway", it can be said that the Kingsway scheme was-effectively a "light railway." It was certainly planned and laid down as such, the track along the central reservation being carried on wooden sleepers with a ballast formation. Though all this is now almost eighty years behind us, it is interesting to note that the concept of "rapid transit"-insofar as Manchester was concerned-was dreamed up as far back as 1913 by John Moffatt McElroy, the tramways' General Manager from 1900 to 1922. McElroy envisaged a whole network of fast tramways throughout the city. In 1914 he had presented to the city council a report envisaging the need for rapid transit railways. A prophet indeed.

The railway gradually responded to the Kingsway tram scheme and by 1939 the Styal Line had an excellent timetable. Despite its low speed, the convenience of the tramcar had undoubtedly lost the railways a considerable amount of passenger traffic both here and elsewhere in South Manchester. But in the meantime, the depression of the late 1920s and '30s and the Second War cast a shadow over any further developments à la McElroy's scheme of things. Manchester gradually abandoned its tramway system and the last car ran on January 10th 1949. Styal Line services had been reduced in the war and would not see a real revival, despite the advent of DMUs in the meantime, until the electric services began in September 1960.

THE STYAL LINE, SOME PERSONAL MEMORIES

I was born within sound, though not sight, of the Styal Line. My earliest memory of train travel was being taken by my mother and sister to Burnage station where we caught an afternoon train to Styal. Long before the phrase "Styal Country Park" was coined, the area in the Bollin Valley was known simply as "Styal Woods." The attraction for my mother was blackberry picking, though I only have clear recollections of the train journey. Standing on the wooden platforms of Burnage station I remember vividly staring down the line towards Mauldeth Road and willing the train to

come. A dark blob appeared on the horizon; nearing us it manifested itself as the rear bunker of a tank engine. I cannot remember what class it was and I shouldn't think that any four-year old could-however keen his later interest proved to be!

Trips to Styal continued and my interest in railways abounded. My father was a Manchester Police Sergeant and worked a more or less steady 8-hour shift pattern including night duty. Weekends off were always at a premium and it was one of dad's few grumbles about Police life that the men had to work 6 or more weeks before qualifying for the precious weekend prize. So, when late turns or weekends off allowed, I was offered the choice of a Sunday morning station visit: "Burnage, or Mauldeth, Ted?", he would ask. I invariably replied "Mauldeth" as the station had its own sidings where we could wander around amongst the wagons. It mattered little to this five-year old child that there were no trains on the Styal Line on Sundays until midday or later in those days; it was enough just to wander amidst the wagons, crunch our feet over cinder ballast, tread over creosoted sleepers and just soak it all up. Unworried by the trespass laws we simply walked across the open tracks, over the running lines and up onto the Down platform. "Why are the signals all down?"-asked the inquisitive child; "they leave them like that on Sundays"-dad replied, unaware, bless him-for he was never the enthusiast that I was-of a process called "switching out".

THE MANCUNIAN

1953 was the year of the bike for young Johnson. A black roadster with rod brakes acquired in early summer from Mr.Herring's shop in Burton Road, Withington, meant mobility had arrived. School holidays and weekends now provided opportunities to cycle to railway observation points that had been inaccessible before. The first port of call of the day was to reach a spot where the Up "Mancunian"- 9.35am from Manchester London Road-could be seen. From home in Heathside Road the quickest point of access was the top half of Briarfield Road where an unobstructed view could be had over the school playing field towards Mauldeth Road station. Sometimes a relief train was put on to augment the non-stop named train, for "The Mancunian" was the only Euston express that did the journey without a stop. Very much a "celebrity" train, it was always regarded as something special by passengers and enthusiasts alike. Usually hauled in the mid-1950s by a "Scot", "Britannia", or a "Jubilee" the ensemble was invariably well turned out and had the distinction of carrying carriage destination boards with the "LONDON-MANCHESTER" legend set on a light blue background. Sometimes Mauldeth Road station itself was the chosen point for observation of our favourite express-though alas with never the benefit of a camera or any thought of carrying a notebook.

APPEARANCE OF STANIER PACIFICS OVER THE LINE

Notes on motive power for the prestige train later in the decade shows at least half a dozen well-documented appearances of Stanier Pacifics on the Up "Mancunian". February 28th 1959 saw the celebrated *Duchess of Hamilton* hauling the train (Q.V.) The following year, on February 23rd & 24th real "cops" for the Manchester spotters were achieved when "Princess Royals" Nos.46204 and 46203 respectively appeared. Later on, in 1962, on both March 30th & 31st, 46225 *Duchess of Gloucester* appeared at the head of the train, followed, on April 2nd, by No.46231. These records for Stanier Pacifics are crowned (literally!) by the use of none other than 46220 *Coronation* on the Up "Mancunian" on February 27th 1963. Sadly, this magnificent locomotive was withdrawn in the week ending April 20th 1963 and was cut up at Crewe Works before the end of May.

Other sitings of "Duchess" Pacifics over the Styal line in the early 1960s are worth a mention. At Heald Green on February 26th 1961, 46240 was noted with the 6.55 am Heysham-Euston; 46242 with the 11.10 am Birmingham-Glasgow and 46232 at the head of the 9.20 am Glasgow-Birmingham. A week later, at East Didsbury on March 5th, 46255 appeared with an Up Birmingham train. Into May that year and, on Sunday, May 5th again at East Didsbury-46230 on a Down Birmingham-Glasgow, 46249 on an Up Glasgow-Birmingham and 46250 *City of Lichfield* were noted. 46250 was at the head of "The Royal Scot" and was noted as being made up to 16 coaches. The records for this truly vintage year for "Duchess" sitings conclude on Sunday , November 5th when, at Heald Green, 46234 passed through with the 7.57pm Aberdeen-Crewe and 46232 with the 11.10 am Birmingham-Glasgow.

And, finally, at East Didsbury on Sunday April 7th 1963, these diverted Euston-Glasgow trains were noted. They were: 46238 with the 9.20 am Euston-Glasgow relief, 46235-9.40 am Euston-Glasgow, 46256 with 1X90-a Euston to Glasgow express and 46225 with 1X89-a further Euston-Glasgow working. At this time, of course, the "Type 4" 1-Co-Co-1 Diesels were making inroads to WCML motive power and the "Duchesses" were being withdrawn. But, after a gap of over 40 years we were privileged, once again, to witness the sight of one of Sir William Stanier's creations. Late in the evening of Friday, July 7th 2004 crowds thronged the platforms at East Didsbury and nearby to see No.6233 *Duchess of Sutherland* head towards Piccadilly station with a 12-coach special working from Euston. True, she was travelling fairly slowly, a local train was in front, and a Diesel-66 138- was piloting in the rear but what a magnificent sight and one which we are assured may never be repeated.

THE ELECTRIC LOCO ERA DAWNS-ARRIVAL OF E1000

As our teen years approached and our horizons broadened, new rides were developed and further venues beckoned. Now the CLC at Cheadle, close to the River Mersey, became an easy prospect to visit. Here was an abundance of traffic, nearly all freight, plenty of trains, but no "Namers" or expresses of course. On our return home we invariably called in at East Didsbury station where we would wait patiently for a train to arrive. Services were few and far between and more than once an approaching train was thought to be in the offing. Sadly, this was almost always a mirage, brought about by the plumes of steam caught on the distant horizon as trains on the CLC, from where we had just cycled, slogged their way under the Styal Line bridge close to the Mersey. But, as we had observed daily from the top of a number 74 bus en route to school, the railway scene was changing.

Quite how we got to know about the impending arrival of E1000 I cannot remember. We first saw her at East Didsbury in the winter of 1959. She appeared as a black, shiny apparition and was quite unlike anything seen before. Not only was this the country's first AC electric locomotive, but she was appearing before our very eyes-on our very own railway. Over the next year or so we saw her many times: travelling up and down between Mauldeth Road and Wilmslow. Sometimes she was coupled to goods wagons, on other occasions, to coaches. Working alongside her were 4-car AC EMUs from the Fenchurch Street-Shoeburyness line; we noted set Nos.201/203/205 & 207. Both loco and EMUs were based at East Didsbury yard to which there was ready access with little or no restrictions imposed on visitors. Before proceeding, a note about the origins of No.E1000 would not be amiss.

Assembled in Manchester in 1951 by Metropolitan Vickers, the 3,000 h.p. locomotive had started life on the Western Region as Gas Turbine No.18100, the second such type of locomotive ordered by the GWR and built for work on former GWR main routes where it had earned the nickname of "Kerosene Castle" due the enduring smell of paraffin! Correctly titled, 18100 was known as "MG3", but having done little actual revenue-earning service on her home ground, the locomotive had languished at the former GCR Dukinfield carriage works from 1953 to 1957. Withdrawn from BR stock on January 1st 1958 the engine was taken to Metro-Vick's works in Stockton-on-Tees. It might be pertinent to add that in its original form No.18100 was not an entirely Mancunian product. Her electrical equipment was delivered from Metro-Vick's Sheffield works and the massive bogies were made and assembled by the Yorkshire Engine Company. She was rebuilt from gas turbine to straight electric working by removing the original gas turbine power plant and equipment and installing a transformer and mercury arc rectifiers. The bogies, originally conforming to the Co-Co pattern, were modified by removing the centre traction motors; thus the locomotive now conformed to the A1A-A1A conformation. To complete the metamorphosis to 25kV ac overhead working, a Stone-Faiveley pantograph picked up current and fed it via a Brown-Boveri air blast circuit breaker.

Now re-numbered E1000 this was to be the first 25kV ac locomotive to appear on the Styal line and though it is thought that the loco never hauled revenue-earning traffic, it fulfilled a vital role in crew training and familiarisation. Later re-numbered E2001, our black loco departed for Crewe electric depot and we never saw her

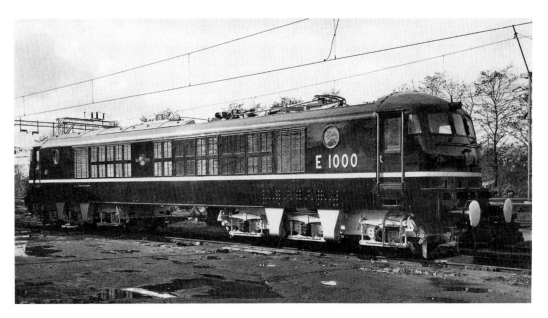

East Didsbury, 1958: The pioneer. The converted Metro-Vick gas turbine locomotive now numbered E1000 stands in the Up sidings at East Didsbury. Judging by the pristine state of the bogies, the picture was taken soon after the locomotive's arrival early in the winter of 1958-59. Soon to be a regular sight on the Styal line, E1000 would remain as the solitary example of a 25kv locomotive until the arrival of the first AL1s the following year. The engine was renumbered as E2001 in August 1959. This was a new scheme utilising the first numeral as the horse power designation; thus: 2001 indicating a 2,000 h.p.traction unit and so on. Collection of *J.Brown*

n Manchester again. It is known that the locomotive was being tested on the famous stationary plant at Rugby on July 14th 1964 for examination of wheel creep and spin with valuable data obtained. After these experiments, E2001 was moved to Aylesbury where measurements were made of lift forces on the pantograph in high cross-wind conditions. Her days as a guinea pig now over, the locomotive was withdrawn in 1968 and sold for scrap.

CONTEMPORARY DEVELOPMENTS

On May 17th 1993 a new railway was opened from a point south of Heald Green station off the Styal Line to serve Manchester Airport. This was the culmination of some four year's work and was a logical extension of the Styal line. The new line and airport station were very much a complementary development to the prestigious and much-vaunted "T2"-Manchester Airport's second international terminal which was opened by the Duke of Edinburgh just over two months earlier-on March 5th.

Sanctioned by the, then, Conservative government in July 1989, the 1½ mile branch from Heald Green North Junction ran due

west in a cutting to end at a point roughly between Terminals 1 & 2. The line runs parallel with the extended Ringway Road-Ringway Road West-which together connect Styal Road with the M56 motorway. Almost immediately it was realised that the new station would be inadequate both in terms of its platform capacity and the fact that the branch was inaccessible from the south. However, things had proceeded smoothly and Manchester Airport's branch and station were officially opened by HRH the Princess Anne on Thursday, May 13th 1993. For the occasion the Princess had flown to Manchester and returned to the city via the branch and the over the Styal line. Unsurprisingly the Royal Tran was not used, her Royal Highness had to put up instead with travel to Manchester Piccadilly in a DMU-actually Class 158 802. Services to the airport began in the small hours of Monday, May 17th with the arrival of the 23.05 from Blackpool North. A slight delay ensued, as the OHL had to be turned off briefly due to a flight emergency.

Quickly, the services became popular with the single island platform rapidly becoming something of a bottleneck. Class 305/2 EMUs, of similar appearance and vintage to the 304 sets, were used on local stopping services at first with the 323 EMUs coming onstream the following year. Longer distance travel was in the hands of Class 158 DMUs and 150 Sprinter sets. But not everyone was happy. Complaints from residents at East Didsbury, whose houses backed onto the line, about increased noise came in promptly and received inevitable press coverage. BR sought to assuage them by diverting some late evening Freightliner traffic via Stockport instead. Looking back to the opening of the Styal line in 1909 when powered flight had only just begun, (Q.V.Louis Paulhan) how rapid the growth of air travel has been! Later on in the decade, in 1996, a second junction, Heald Green South Junction, was provided to enable north-bound trains from the Crewe and Wilmslow direction to access the airport station also-the two sides of the triangle coming together at what is now Heald Green West Junction.

So, inside a few years, the Styal Line had acquired a whole new tranche of traffic with through trains from such hitherto unlikely places as Cleethorpes, Barrow-in-Furness, Blackpool and Middlesbrough running over what was previously a quiet suburban railway backwater. Thus, the "Styal Line" has popularly become the "Airport Line" to today's travellers. In 2005 it was announced that rail passengers using Manchester Airport had topped the million mark over the previous year. As this manuscript is being completed (July 2006) a further programme of expansion, termed "The 25-year Masterplan", has been announced for Manchester Airport. This envisages a doubling of passengers to 50 million a year by 2030. Amazingly, the following day it was announced that the proposed Metrolink extension that would have linked the airport with the existing system would be cut back to Chorlton. Yet another example, surely, of the lack of joined-up thinking that seems to perpetually bedevil the nation's transport system. Doubtless, as with other airport developments-the railway included-all this will be contentious. For the Styal line at least, the airport expansion can only be good news, assuring both local and airport passengers that their railway is safe for the long-term future.

CODA

And that is not quite all in connection with Manchester Airport and the Styal line. The airport itself has grown exponentially since the mid-1960s. To enable construction of the second runway, a hotly-debated and contentious local issue, a railway 1.3 miles long was built. Running from the already new airport branch, the line enabled the bulk movement of stone-estimated at 1.5 million tonnes-from the Peak District to the new runway construction site. Built by Trackwork of Doncaster the line was heavily grant-aided to the tune of £2.2M. Trains began running along the freight branch on December 8th 1997; the official opening was performed by Dr.Gavin Strang M.P., then Minister of Transport on December 17th. A novelty was the use on the opening day of an ex-GWR Inspection Saloon coupled to a 4-wheel hopper wagon and drawn by the preserved L&Y 0-6-0 No.1300. Not that this was the first time such a loco had been seen in immediate area!

Traffic along the branch began on December 17th 1997 when 60 040 arrived with the first train of MEA wagons. As these had no hopper discharge, unloading had to be executed by grabber trucks. These trains continued until February 27th 1998 when 60 008 hauled in the first load of stone conveyed in new RMC wagons which were able to discharge into a stone bunker. Airport runway stone trains ran along the branch until March 25th 2000 when 60 011 traversed the line. The connection to the redundant freight branch is still in today, though with the points clipped and some of the trackwork truncated there would seem little future for this once-useful freight link.

APPEARANCE OF THE FREIGHTLINERS

A prominent feature of modern-day freight workings over the Styal line has been the appearance of the Freightliner trains that pass up and down on a daily basis. The Freightliner concept is popularly linked to proposals by Dr.Richard Beeching's masterly report for the BRB-"The Reshaping of British Railways". In reality Beeching's overview of the amount of traffic that could be won for the railways' liner trains was over-optimistic by a long chalk. Ante Beeching, in 1959, the London Midland Region's "Condor" ("Containers-door-to-Door") service had begun working from Glasgow's Gushetfaulds yard to Hendon, north London. This, the idea of H.P.Barker-a BRB member and others, was spawned back in the mid-1950s when the notion of traditional single wagonload freight was viewed as a doomed prospect. And it was from Glasgow, in November 1965, that the first Freightliner train proper worked south to London. The Railway Magazine of the time stated that, ultimately, 100 routes and some 40+ Freightliner terminals would be in operation.

Be that as it may, Freightliner trains commenced running between Manchester and London, five days per week, on February 28th 1966. Starting from Longsight, the depot was built on the site of the old Down sidings, the electrically-hauled trains ran to London's York Way terminal (Q.V.), the old Maiden Lane station. The Up train left Longsight at 23.08 (London arr.03.10). Manchester-bound, the Down train left York Way at 22.30 and was due in Longsight at 02.30. Services from Longsight to Willesden were still running in 1982, but in the meantime the depot was to be overshadowed by Manchester's second Freightliner terminal, at Trafford Park.

Built on the north side of the former CLC Manchester-Liverpool line, the Trafford Park terminal occupied the site of the former locomotive shed which had finally closed its doors on May 28th 1968. The new terminal saw its first train leave with the departure of the 22.40 to Dudley on September 25th 1969. The depot was officially opened on Monday, October 6th 1969. Subsequently enlarged on its west side to include a new Euro Terminal, the facilities were further enhanced by the extension of the 25kV catenary from Castlefield Junction to Trafford Park itself. Prior to through electric working, stops were made at Longsight Down sidings for crew or engine changes.

SAMPLE WORKINGS

We are fortunate in having records available showing sample Freightliner operation over the Styal line from the fairly early years. Observations were at Heald Green (HG) and East Didsbury (ED).

DATE	LOCOMOTIVE	TRAIN
9/7/1969	D1825	Up to Parkeston Quay (HG)
10/7/69	D1851	As above (HG)
21/7/69	D1956	As above (HG)
23/7/69	D435	To Crewe (HG)
29/7/69	D418	As above (HG)
1/8/69	D415	As above (HG)
11/8/70	E3124 &Class 45	T/Park-Sudbury (Kelloggs) (ED)

Mauldeth Road, July 25th 1984: Typifying latter-day freight operations over the Styal line is this picture showing Class **85 005** approaching the station at the head of an Up evening train of cargo vans out of Trafford Park. Notice the ground frame controlling the crossover and the access to the remaining single siding over the land where B&Q will arrive in the next decade. Signal LR9 shows its usual double yellow aspect, guarding the approach to Slade Junction on the Down line. *Author*

5/8/74	47441	Up Swansea (ED)
26/9/74	87024	Down Freightliner (No ID) (HG)
3/4/79	87014	Down Kelloggs Empties (ED)
16/6/79	47134	11.30 am Aintree-Tilbury (HG)
11/10/84	47360	Holyhead-Trafford Park (HG)
11/4/88	47349	Trafford Park-Holyhead* (HG)
16/3/89	47280	Melton Mowbray -Trafford Park (HG)

*Noted as being re-routed off the line via Fallowfield, Gorton & Philips Park due to Manchester Piccadilly re-signalling. Freightliner trains to Holyhead were withdrawn in March 1991 and the last one noted travelling over the Styal line was on 19/12/89 with 47307 hauling the 06.13 train from Trafford Park.

Electric-hauled Freightliner trains over the Styal line are today something of a rarity. Normal form being Class 60 and 66 haulage. As an aside, despite the vast sums of money being poured into today's rail infrastructure, there seems a strange unwillingness to progress with further electrification. Given the existence of the 25kV along to Trafford Park, surely the logical extension of this would be to wire from here to Hunt's

Cross, thus linking Manchester and Liverpool via an electrified railway.

To complete the Freightliner picture here is a further piece of the story-a window from the winter of 1992-93 showing the trains (both Freightliner and Company) travelling via Styal thirteen years ago.

DEPARTURE

TIME	TYPE	COMPANY TRAIN
05.31 (MX)		Trafford Park-Crewe
23.25 (Sun) (MO)	FL	Southampton-Trafford Park
22.45	COY	Waterston-Glazebrook
02.10 (MX)	FL	Stratford-Trafford Park
09.20 (SX)	FL	Allerton-Trafford Park
12.03 (MTThO)	COY	Trafford Park-Cardiff
13.03 (SX)	FL	Trafford Park-Allerton
15.03 (SO)	FL	Trafford Park-Southampton
13.15 (SX)	COY	Melton Mowbray-Trafford Park
18.15 (SX)	FL	Crewe-Trafford Park
19.15 (SX)	FL	Trafford Park-Stratford
20.33 (SX)	FL	Trafford Park-Glasgow
22.47 (SX)	FL	Trafford Park-Felixstowe
22.15 (SX)	FL	Crewe-Trafford Park

Mauldeth Road, November 18th 1909: Just over six months after opening and the presence of a ladder indicates workmen still putting finishing touches to the underside of the bridge. All looks pristine: the LNWR's standard nameboards and gates, new platform fencing and sparkling white glazed tiles covering the walls beneath the bridge decking. Observe the muddy state of Mauldeth Road, then just a country lane that ran from Burnage Lane in the east to a point a hundred yards or so beyond the junction with Wellington Road in Withington. The buildings seen beyond the bridge on the left-hand side belonged to a recreation ground where the current Mauldeth Road park is today. This is the small district of Ladybarn, an area that sat between Fallowfield, Withington and Burnage. All had been swallowed up into the city of Manchester in 1904. *Manchester City Engineer's archive*

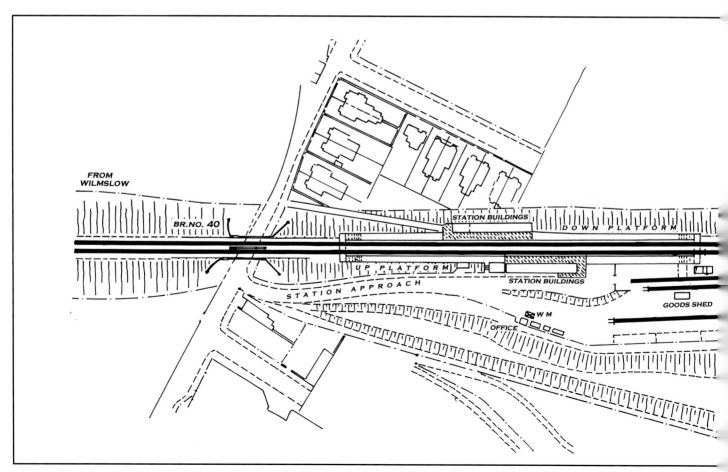

Mauldeth Road for Withington, June 1957: The station, seen almost in the condition it had been since opening around half a century previous. Rolling [in] with a running-in turn from Crewe Works is Edge Hill's (8A) "Princess Royal" No **46210** *Lady Patricia*. Not a wisp of steam anywhere from this magnificent machine which, doubtless, has delighted the two schoolboy spotters on the Up platform. Notice the school cap and jacket: the two bands on [th]e cap, along with the owl emblem on the boy's pocket are hallmarks of Manchester Grammar School. Work has begun on re-modelling the platforms—[th]e wooden LNWR structures being partly removed and will soon be substituted by lengthy concrete ones. A note concerning the station's name is seen [on] the platform seat. The suffix "for Withington" was added by the LMS at an unknown date. Under BR the station reverted in 1974 to plain "Mauldeth [R]oad".

R.E.Gee

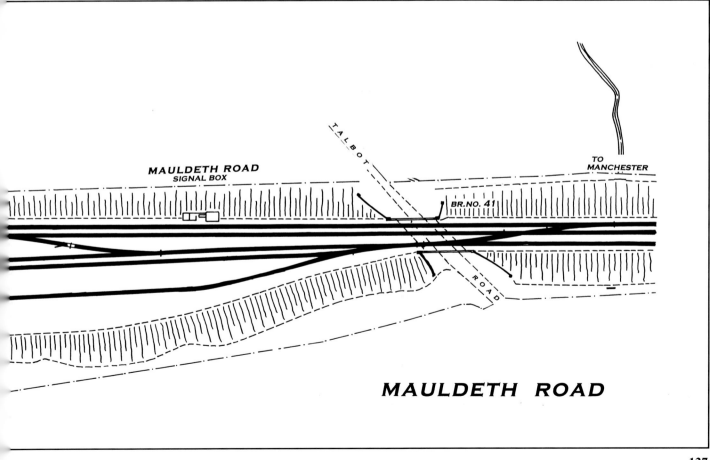

MAULDETH ROAD SIGNAL BOX

TALBOT ROAD

BR.NO. 41

TO MANCHESTER

MAULDETH ROAD

(Left) Mauldeth Road, February 23rd 1960: Though th LNWR Up side buildings were removed, those on the opposit side were completely refurbished. Painted dark green and whit and replete with maroon signs-just look at all those totems!-th rebuilt station might even qualify today for an award from th Railway Heritage Trust. But sadly, it did not last. Whether b accident or design the buildings were gutted by fire on the nigh of November 3rd 1985 and subsequently demolished. Soon after the sidings were removed and the embankment was levelled, thu providing a home for today's B&Q DIY store. In 2006, with i single red, plastic-glazed waiting hut, rocking and shored u platforms which look ever more dilapidated, the station survives handling, it is good to note, a plentiful number of passengers.

British Railway

Mauldeth Road, July 6th 1960: The splendid LNWR awned platform structure where our schoolboys watched 46210 have now been removed. Their substitute is this: a rather functional glass, wood and concrete shelter-cum-waiting room. Doubtless both staff and passengers thought poorly of it at the time, but how welcome would it be today when single arched "bus shelters" do duty as the station's only facilities! Notice the plentiful supply of wagons in the goods yard and a reminder to the writer that this was once his childhood paradise! Now long swept away and levelled, the ground here is occupied today by the B&Q store.

British Railways

Gloucester Railway Carriage & Wagon Co,Ltd: An official pictu taken to record one of the company's products: a 12-ton, 7-plank e door coal wagon. W.H.Kynaston was a long-time user of Maulde Road's sidings; indeed, there was little else handled there aside from t local domestic coal traffic. When the wagon was delivered, Kynasto was supplied with coal from Pinxton colliery, near to Alfreton. *Author note:* Poor Kynaston was the bane of my father's life. Supplies domestic fuel seemed erratic in the 1950s and coal was often of po quality. Time and again Dad had to cycle down to Mauldeth Road plead with Kynaston to call and top up the "coal hole", usually with "drop" of around 5 or 6 cwt. In today's centrally-heated world it is d ficult to imagine how much reliance was placed back then on the op coal fire. The use of "Fallowfield" on the wagon side seems od Residents around Mauldeth Road always referred to themselves living in "Ladybarn" as mentioned elsewhere. *HMRS collectio*

Mauldeth Road, 20th August 199 From 1997-99, "Eurostar" trains tra elled from their Longsight depot bletchley and back on a series of fam iarisation runs. Alas, the whole exe cise, which must have been a cost one, never earned a penny of passeng revenue and the whole concept of ru ning "Eurostar" services from Scotla and the North West was quietly aba doned. But perhaps the ghost of Edward Watkin, a one time resident South Manchester, was having a qu laugh as the silver and yellow appa tion sailed past with an Up working that dull summer's morning. *Auth*

Above) Burnage Station, May 13th 1957: Tempting as it was to consider a plain shot showing all the station buildings here, the author opted to include instead this splendid study of "Coronation" Class Pacific No **46226** *Duchess of Norfolk* watched by three schoolboy "spotters". Notice the wooden construction used at Burnage, universally-applied to both the spartan hipped-roof station buildings and the platforms themselves. Similar buildings and facilities were originally provided at Heald Green, examples that the L&NWR considered sufficient for 'smaller stations'. Another running-in turn with a teatime Manchester London Road to Crewe local, the magnificent locomotive glistens, her Brunswick green paintwork having been freshly applied at Crewe Works. After running-in her bearings, 46226 will be off back to her home shed of Carlisle Kingmoor (12A) fit and able once more to tackle the banks of Shap and Beattock with loads of double or more the six coaches seen here. *R.E.Gee*

Right-centre) Burnage, May 1938: Typifying a form of local train service that had pertained over the Styal line for many years is this picture showing former Johnson Midland Railway 0-4-4 tank engine No.1286. This is the famous "Push-Pull" service, the engine, a work-stained Derby specimen of some fifty years previous, is sandwiched in the middle of its coaches-the vehicle nearest the camera is most likely a former Midland panelled non-corridor, the coach behind the engine is an LMS example. En route to Wilmslow, identified by chimney-first running, the driver will be seated in the (modified) front coach, brake and regulator being operated by vacuum gear. Notice the cord running over the front coach roof to operate the whistle-a vital function! *Bill Lees*

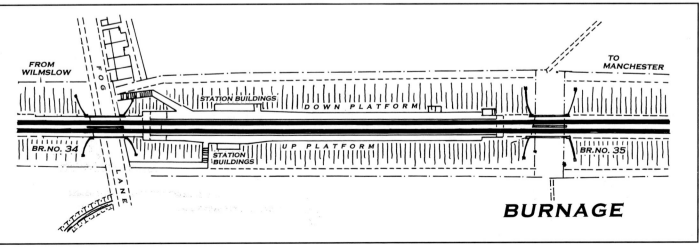

BURNAGE

(Above) **Burnage, c.1950.** From the Up platform at the Fog Lane end of the station, this view towards Manchester belies the close proximity of the city it was built to serve some forty years previously. The overall image is still typical of L&NWR policy towards their 'small stations', predominantly of modular or unit construction using hard durable timber. *Authors collection*

(Centre) **Burnage, May 1938:** Crossing Fog Lane, bridge No.34 and entering the station is ex-L&YR 0-6-0 No **12382** with a stopping train bound for London Road. The 3-coach set, an all 3rd, sandwiched between two brake thirds, is the product of the London & North Western, solidly-built stock which lasted up to modern times (Q.V.) 12382 was an Aspinall engine built at Horwich in the 1880s. At this time, 1938, she was allocated to Bury (26D) and all that is known is that her appearance on Styal line services was brief. As 52382 the loco was still at Bury in 1952; she had been withdrawn by 1956. *Bill Lees*

Southbank Road, Kingsway, late 1920s: This is what became of the farmers' fields along the Styal line. After the First War, Manchester City council embarked on a huge programme of house building in South Manchester. Land both east and west of the railway was bought up and building commenced. The houses, all of which stand today, conformed to a broadly similar outline. All were of brick construction, had slated roofs and most had generous, some would say over-generous-sized, gardens. A particular characteristic was the curved-top front downstairs window frame and the slated porches over the front door. This is Southbank Road, a small thoroughfare off Kingsway, between Fog Lane and Mauldeth Road. In this scene, the brickwork and roofing is complete while piles of double-stacked tongue and grooved floorboards await fixing. The Mann steam wagon in the centre of the picture, number JG 927, appears to be in a spot of bother; bogged down in the muddy morass that will become the

roadway, a second steam wagon appears to be attempting to extricate it. Piles of bitumen are heaped up in the foreground awaiting the "tar boiler" to gro... the jointed concrete slabs used for roadways. Eventually the road here will continue round the back to join Southlea Road. Notice the sparsely-covere... embankment that is the Styal line in the background.
Author's collectio...

East Didsbury and Parr's Wood station, Bridge No.32, July 7th 1909:
A Wednesday, about mid-day-not a soul around, nor even a horse and cart to disturb the rural tranquillity of this Manchester suburb. The second in our series of pictures from the City Engineer and a photograph taken to record the bridge and adjacent highway for the records. An oddity centres around the station's name. All official records show the station opening with the "& Parr's Wood" suffix. Perhaps the answer is that the full title would not fit on to a standard LNWR name board and the company substituted the plain two word title instead. Whatever the explanation, the full title lasted until May 1974 when the station became plain "East Didsbury"-though the celebrated maroon totems had borne the simple two-word designation. In the picture we look beneath the railway towards the junction of Wilmslow Road and Parr's Wood Lane. This was long before the building of Kingsway; back then the road made a simple fork: left towards Heaton Mersey and Stockport and right to Cheadle over the River Mersey. Readers familiar with East Didsbury will doubtless make their own comparisons with today's scene at this spot: Tesco round the corner on the site of the one-time Manchester Corporation bus garage, the endless traffic flow and all the hustle and bustle of the 21st century. Almost unaltered, bridge No.32 still stands; whisking through now are the myriad of services to and from Manchester Airport-a form of transport very much in its infancy when this picture was taken.
Manchester City Engineers archive

EAST DIDSBURY
& PARR'S WOOD

East Didsbury station, summer 1960: Workmen are busy putting the finishing touches to the new station buildings. Glass, wood and concrete have been substituted for the LNWR's standard wooden structures which had stood here for almost five decades. Today, the Up side buildings are out of use and their demise seems imminent. Despite the impending change-over to electric traction, gas lamps cling to life on the Up platform! Gone, too, is the signalbox abolished from December 1959 when this section was brought under the control of the new London Road power box. Notice the siding connections, controlled now by a ground frame; similar condtions existed at Mauldeth Road.

British Railways

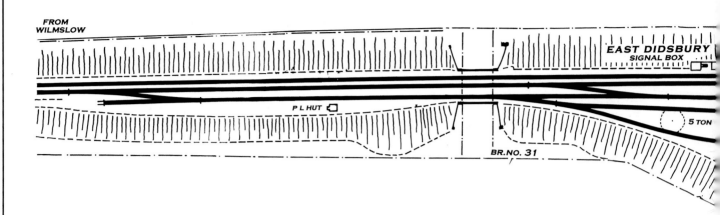

FROM WILMSLOW

EAST DIDSBURY SIGNAL BOX

P L HUT

BR.NO. 31

5 TON

EAST DIDSBURY & PARR'S WOOD

DIESEL SERVICES

between

MANCHESTER LONDON ROAD WILMSLOW and CREWE

9th June to 14th September, 1958

or until further notice

SUBJECT TO ALTERATION

BRITISH RAILWAYS   E 5

East Didsbury, Summer 1959: The DMUs that took over the services from Manchester London Road to Wilmslow and Crewe in October 195 quickly proved popular with passengers and breathed a new lease of life into a railway that had changed little since its inception half a century previou Now, with the wires up, the stations modernised "the Diesels" can be viewed in the context of an interregnum, a staging post between old and new forn of traction. A Birmingham RC&W Co. 3-car unit pauses at East Didsbury on a working to Wilmslow. Features well-remembered from those days wer the first class seats-what luxury! And the view to be had through the front windows giving a whole new vista of the line. This was the summer when th great signalling change-over was pending-an essential part of the modernisation programme. Well remembered from that summer was the sight of teatime stopping train with a "Black 5" in charge rolling in. Signalling was being handled by a temporary telephone centre at East Didsbury, pendir commissioning of Wilmslow power box. (This being done under regulation 25, clause A/3-use of telephone). Emerging from the platform buildings th station "gaffer" called out to the footplate: "You're clear to 'eald Green, driver". Despite all the contingencies, the traffic was kept moving. Paradoxicall today, DMU traction reigns almost supreme over electric in the form of the myriad of services through here to and from Manchester Airport.   *Auth*

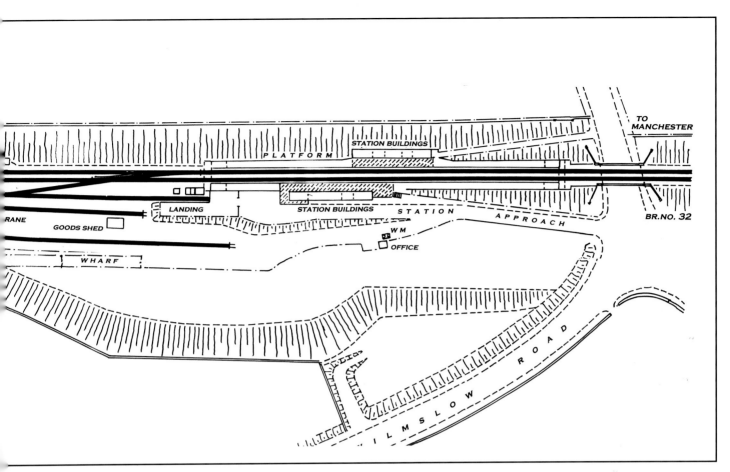

East Didsbury, April 17th 1957: The old order, soon to be no more. An old Longsight favourite, No **43325**, is seen at the head of the 8.12 am Longsight to Alderley pick-up freight. The engine, a definite "foreigner" on this stretch of line, began life on the Midland Railway as No.2048-one of a series of locomotives built by Kitson & Co.in 1892. A hardy survivor indeed, she will soon be rubbing shoulders with traction units powered by a medium still in its infancy in those far-off days. Today the scene here is unrecognisable; the sidings are long gone and a hideous block of apartments towers over the railway, set cheek-by-jowl with a similar structure at the foot of the station approach.

R.E.Gee

East Didsbury, May 22nd 1957: Taken from the signalbox, Fowler 2-6-4 tank No.**42304** is seen pulling away from East Didsbury with a Crewe loca[l] The picture shows the old LNW standard wooden station buildings and platforms, identical in form to those seen at Mauldeth Road and Gatley. The engin[e] was a Styal line favourite and was recorded as a "cop" in young Johnson's ABC. A notice posted by BR and dated September 3rd 1956 stated that th[e] goods yard was to be closed…"for all public traffic". Formal closure and transfer of the sidings to BR's Estate department had come about on May 6t[h] 1957. All a far cry from the time during the First War when the Royal Train was stabled here on two occasions. Some forty years on, with goods traffi[c] gone the way was clear for East Didsbury to become a base for the new traction. Notice the crane busily unloading the steel sections to be used a[s] overhead line masts; some of these are already in place in the sidings.

R.E.Gee

East Didsbury, July 16th 1960: Pending full deployment on their intended home territory, several 4-car 25kv EMU sets for the Fenchurch Stree[t –] Shoeburyness line were brought north in order for crews to gain experience in multiple-unit handling, . Based at East Didsbury, at least five sets we[re] used (Q.V.), though this set-No.310-was not recorded as being seen by the author. Becoming Class 302, 112 of these units had been built at York an[d] Doncaster, the first appearing in 1958. The sets were to lead something of a nomadic existence: appearing not only on the Crewe line, but also on th[e] Clacton, Walton-on-Naze to Colchester line and Liverpool Street - Chelmsford and Southend lines. Unlike their northern counterparts, the AM4s (Class 304[)] these units were equipped for dual voltage working: at 6.25 kv and 25kv. Used thus on their home territory, it was largely due to the unreliability of th[e] voltage change-over apparatus that caused problems, something that led to a re-think of the use of 6.25kv. Sitting in the background, E3016 stan[ds] coupled to a generator car-numbered DM39552 and belonging to the Chief Mechanical and Electrical Engineer's department.

Graham Whitehea[d]

(Right) East Didsbury, June 1961: After inauguration of electric working from September 1960, crew training continued along the Styal line as successive batches of Bo-Bo electrics emerged from their various manufacturers. This picture, showing Class AL5 No.**E3057** and a five-coach test train, was probably taken on a Sunday when the trainee electric drivers would have had the bulk of the day to familiarise themselves with their new charges. On a point of interest: the first coach is an early LMS standard 57ft.vehicle with the distinctive square windows, the third coach looks like a GW specimen. *Fred Walton*

(Centre) Between East Didsbury and Gatley, winter 1971/72: It wasn't just electrification that altered structures along the Styal line. Here, on the south side of the River Mersey, engineers have rolled into place a new underline bridge, numbered 26B, to carry the railway over the alignment of the Sharston by-pass, then designated M56/M63. The bridge sat amidst a veritable plethora of interchange roads-what motorway engineers call a "Spaghetti junction". Hardly recognisable as a motorway, construction of the carriageways and slip roads is some time off yet. Notice the building rising in the background, today's flats known Willow Court. *Mary I Johnson*

(Below) Gatley for Cheadle, c.1926/27: Typifying express working over the line in the early years of the LMS is this shot showing ex-LNWR "Prince of Wales" 4-6-0 No.**1679** *Lord Byron* storming through Gatley with an Up express. The suffix "for Cheadle" is thought to have been added when the LNWR closed neighbouring Cheadle station on New Year's day in 1917 as a wartime economy measure. Notice the open nature of the landscape surrounding the station, a far cry from today's conurbation. Details abound for study: the plain, yet distinctive LNW signals-there was block post here in those days, removed in later years, the boarded foot crossing, trespass sign, the barrow on the far platform ramp and the gas lamps and lamp hut; what inspiration for a model! *L.Hobdey/J.M.Bentley collection*

Gatley, c.1909: Taken, by the looks of things, for the opening of the railway-the scene looking towards Manchester. This may have been a photograph taken on the day the line was inspected. History relates that this was carried out on February 4th 1909 by Colonel Yorke on behalf of the Board of Trade. A train approaches on the Up line headed, possibly, by a goods tender 0-6-0 locomotive. A clutch of people stand in the "four foot" in the distance alongside the train. On the platform all eyes are fixed on the photographer

who has pitched his camera in the centre of the Down line. The man wearing the double-breasted uniform coat may well have been the Gatley Stationmaster, Mr.A.Smith; next to him stands another staff member, maybe a porter. The bowler-hatted gent looks like an official, perhaps he belonged to the inspectorate, while further down the line of men stand workmen-artisans who look like they are putting the finishing touches to the buildings, notice the ladder and planks of wood on the opposite platform. At ground-level the track looks spick and span, a gentle curve being introduced as the rails run south. We should, however, expect nothing else: the LNWR boasted that it had-*"the best permanent way in the world"*.　　　　　　　　　　　　　　　　　　　　　　　　　*Author's collection*

(Centre) Gatley, 28th May 1960. It seems incredible that this view of the Up side buildings was taken almost five decades ago. The timber sectional buildings erected in 1909 by the L&NWR were considered good enough for retention and most certainly blended in well with the concrete component designs which were very much part and parcel of the British Railways Main Line Electrification scheme. The station was well provided for when new with Booking Offices and Booking Halls (Waiting Rooms) serving both platforms. Ladies Waiting Room facilities on the Manchester bound platform were more extensive than those opposite as were Gentlemens' Toilets and Waiting Rooms.　　*G Whitehead*

Gatley, November 10th 1951: A scene just over a quarter of a mile south of Gatley station. The photographer will have walked up Foxland Road to reach bridge No.22, a structure spanning the footpath that leads to the Scholes Park athletic ground to the left of the picture. Tom Lewis's subject that winter morning was the Up "Mancunian", headed today by Longsight's Caprotti "Black 5" No.44750. Lewis was a master of composition and won many accolades within the RCTS photographic circle. We are fortunate that his legacy survives and the author hopes that his darkroom work has done justice to the late master's splendid images. *Tom Lewis*

(Above) Heald Green, c.1910: A winter scene at what was then a remote Cheshire hamlet. A lady, dressed in the attire of the period has stepped off the train. Looking on, a porter stands on the platform with buildings and fencing still looking pristine. Reproduced from a contemporary postcard by C.Severs of Cheadle, the picture shows a Manchester-bound local train pulling away. By the looks of things, the four coaches may well be drawn by a Webb 2-4-2 tank, typical motive power before the advent of the motor trains in 1912. ***Author's collection***

(Left) Heald Green, Spring 1910: "THE NEW LINE WILL BE OPENED ON SATURDAY, MAY 1ST." So proclaims the poster fixed to the wooden wall of the Down platform building. Two members of the station staff seem to have all the time in the world to pose obligingly for the photographer-presumably "the Gaffer", Stationmaster Mr.G.T.J.Taylor, was otherwise engaged! Notice the oil lamps, no electricity here then. Indeed, even in the 1970s, some parts of neighbouring Styal were without mains gas.

Author's collection

Heald Green, 1934: Fowler 2-6-4 tank No.**2358** pays its usual call at the Up platform with a stopping train for either Wilmslow or Crewe. Eleven years into the "Big Four" and the LNW's parentage still shows itself in the platform buildings, signs and semaphore signals. Cloth cap, no cap and a bowler hat features on the figures awaiting their arrival. On the platform seat, a lady leans forward in anticipation of her train. Bovril sandwiches are advertised on the Down platform fencing, a somewhat less esoteric advertisement for this famous British product which had claimed that-"The Pope drinks Bovril" earlier in the century! Notice the wooden stairs leading up to Finney Lane, the footbridge still being a long way off. In 1954 the Renold Chain company opened a large office complex on Styal Road, south of the station. Under an agreement with BR, dated November 11th 1956, a footpath through the goods yard and up the approach road, enabling Renolds' employees to access the station was made on the line's Down side. ***L.Hobdey/J.M.Bentley collection***

Heald Green, May 24th 1957: A nice contrast in motive power for the daily "shunt"-the 8.12 morning Longsight to Alderley "trip" freight. 9A's Stanier Mogul No.**42960** moves forward along the Down line prior to accessing the crossover and single slip leading to and from the small goods yard. Such scenes would have been repeated at hundreds of locations that Friday all over the country. Alas, such workings-seven wagons plus a box van and brake would soon be deemed "uneconomical". Today, the "Shunt's" successor-the modern Freightliner with its Class 66 Diesel at the head-roars over these same tracks to and from the Trafford Park terminal. In the background rebuilding of the station is proceeding apace. Changing times indeed.   *R.E.Ge*

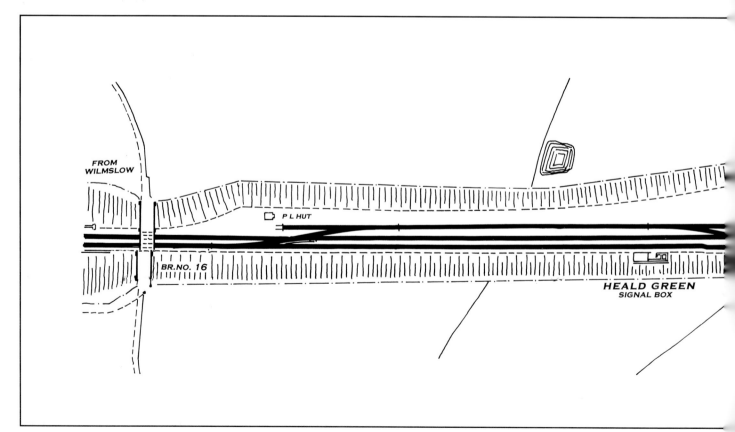

FROM WILMSLOW

P L HUT

BR. NO. 16

HEALD GREEN
SIGNAL BOX

Heald Green, March 3rd 1954: BR Standard Class 4 2-6-4 tank No.**80039** leaves the station behind and approaches the signalbox with the 9.50 am Manchester London Road to Wilmslow. An odd allocation, 80039 arrived at Longsight (9A) from Bletchley (1E) towards the end of 1953. Spending the whole of the following year in Manchester, the engine departed back to 1E early in 1955. So far as is known, this was Longsight's only example of a Standard Class 4 tank. Wooden and steel-bodied wagons, loaded with coal, are lined up in the goods yard. Closure of Heald Green's goods depot came w.e.f. April 26th 1965 with facilities for local traders being transferred to Cheadle Heath, hardly local it must be said. A ground frame, released from Wilmslow signalbox, had provided access to the remaining sidings, but these, too, were removed in April 1966. In modern-day parlance, the land adjacent to the Down line remains today in "non-operational use".

R.E.Gee

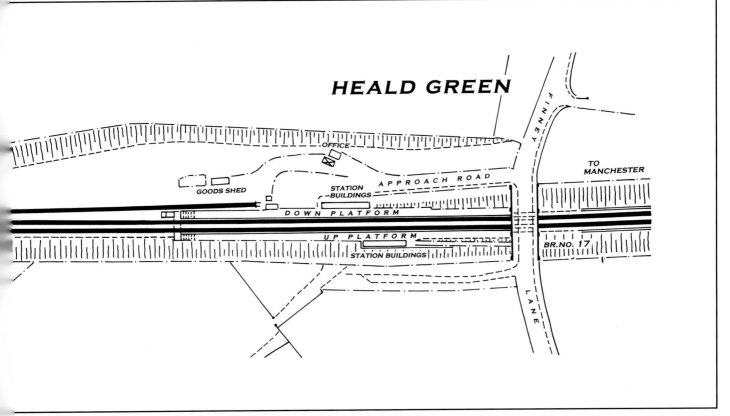

HEALD GREEN

HEALD GREEN

Heald Green, February 12th 1958: The wooden station buildings on the line's Down side had been replaced with brick structures by the LMS in 1938. Twenty years on and some demolition and re-modelling is in progress. Notice the new concrete footbridge; this the only station on the line to be so equipped until a Network Rail initiative of 2006 resulted in Mauldeth Road acquiring a similar passenger, sorry, customer facility requiring endurance testing features. In this view from the Up side, work is well in hand and soon the metamorphosis will be complete. Above, the catenary is strung in place, but not yet energised as some anchor fittings have yet to be installed. The lamp post, a simple fitting from a long line of concrete items emanating from the Newton Heath concrete depot, carries its British Railways (LMR) corporate maroon 'totem'. Who would have believed, back then, that such signs would become prized items, realising in some cases, thousands of pounds each?

(Centre & Below) The shell of the LMS buildings, awaiting the almost 'space-age' transformation, bridges the design 'gap' between the L&NWR timber buildings on the Up platform and the somewhat hybrid features required to convert rather than rebuild. The extension to the right was provided for parcels traffic but latterly served as 'storage' for any unused or surplus item of equipment. The futuristic look of the building remained attractive until the application of a dark green shade of paint which lasted throughout the 1980's, and which, concurrently with the reduction in staffing of stations together with growing graffiti inspired vandalism problems made Heald Green somewhat less attractive to potential users. ***British Railways***

Approaching Styal, May 22nd 1957: Longsight's Stanier 2-6-2 tank No.**40093** at the head of a 4-coach local train meanders along in the cutting between Heald Green and Styal. Now in rural Cheshire, the landscape has changed completely. Gone is the urban sprawl of Manchester to be replaced by green fields and open spaces. This was the rural district of Bucklow in the Parish of Styal. Seen behind the train is bridge No.13 a brick-built, three-arched structure. At a point some 1/4 mile north of here is today's Heald Green South Junction of 1996 enabling access to and from the Airport branch. The bridge carries a footpath from Hollin Lane (B5166), runs close to Styal golf course and emerges at Bolshaw Farm. Before the railway was constructed the LNW acquired the lands here from L.E.Brocklehurst and R.E.Dykes. Under an agreement dated October 24th 1902 and lasting for 30 years, the railway company were liable for any widening of the roadway over bridges Nos.13 & 14 to a width not exceeding 36 feet. ("Vendor to maintain & pay cost of same"). Notice the appearance of masts for the OHL and the troughing alongside the Up line. Modernisation is coming. *R.E.Gee*

Styal signalbox, May 1st 1957: Forty-eight years ago today the Styal line opened! G2 0-8-0 No **49395** is waiting to cross over to the Up line to progress the morning shunt in the goods yard. The reason for the delay is the passage of the Up "Mancunian"-all must wait until then. The box, situated about 220 yards on the north side of the station, was a standard LNWR product, is to pattern "E : 2+3+2 standard window units to the front of the structure-brick base and timber top. Styal's goods yard closed to all traffic on November 4th 1963. *R.E.Gee*

Styal, May 1st 1909: Styal's first passenger train. The 6.30 am from Oxford Road to Wilmslow enters the station drawn by two Webb 2-4-2 tank engines, Nos.1156 and 1763. All looks pristine and well-ordered, but what else could one expect from the LNWR? *Author's collection*

Pride in the railways by those who served them was displayed in many ways. The early days of British Railways proved to be no exception and the ***Best Kept Station*** competition enabled staff to show their skills, particularly when it came to gardening. The views opposite illustrate the efforts Station Master Harry Jackson (top right) and his staff at Styal put in to maintain the high standards. SM Jackson was also in charge of Heald Green station.

The station master of Styal with some of the fine blooms which helped to gain his station a second prize in the Best Kept Station Competition

Bigger prizes—more of them for 1953 best kept stations
Special Coronation Year Competition

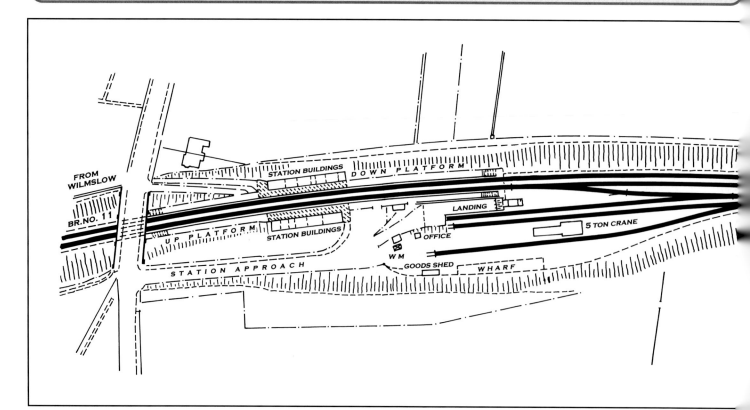

Styal, c.1909: Looking to Heald Green and Gatley, this is almost certainly a picture in the same series as our view at Gatley and, as such, taken to record the completion of the line and its infrastructure in readiness for inspection by the Board of Trade. Though not of an elaborate design, it is the attention to detail that stands out. Signs, lamp hut, platform lamps and awnings; the ornamental brickwork on the Up side buildings and on the chimney stacks-all neatly executed. The Stationmaster here at the time of opening was Mr.J.Henthorpe who had been promoted from Bramhall. Mention should be made of Mr.Albert Brown who began work as a porter here (he may well be the character to the left on the Up side) when the line opened. Albert stayed on at Styal completing an amazing 50 years in the same job. He retired in 1959.

Author's collection

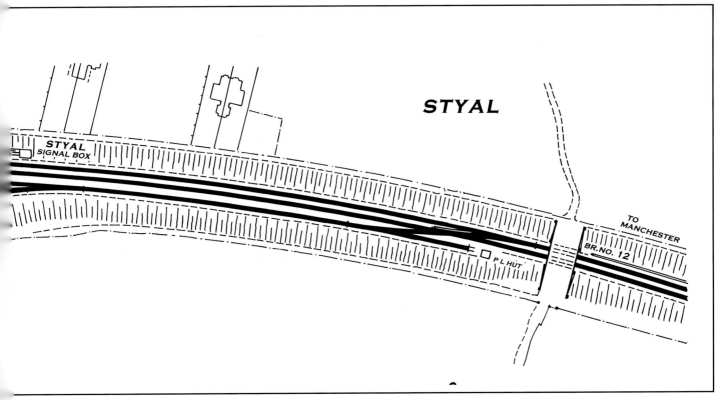

Styal, September 1957: A scene that would be repeated over the next eight years or so at many thousands of similar sites right through from London Road to Euston. At Styal a gang of men are engaged in shovelling concrete into a hand-excavated foundation for a bolted base mast. Single masts-of I-section galvanised steel-were also supported in concrete bases. Holes for these were produced by augers with comparative ease. Though the railway was moving gradually into a "high tec" era, the guts of the overhead wiring required a great deal of brute force and sheer hard labour.   Collection of **David Hibbert**

Styal station, Down side station buildings, June 4th 1960: Given the sub stantial nature of all the Styal platform buildings it seems odd that demolitio was ordered, leaving us with this rather sad sight: the buildings, shorn of the canopies and awaiting the hammer. On this, the Manchester-bound sid accommodation, as witnessed was generous: left to right was a general waitin room, booking office and stationmaster's office, ladies' 1st class waiting roon ladies' 3rd class waiting room, gentlemens' waiting room and "gents". Ho strong social divisions were in the early years of the twentieth century! Th same accommodation was mirrored over on the Up side. Functional glass ar metal-framed buildings were provided in lieu. Don't miss the station clod showing twenty-five past three.   *Graham Whitehea*

Styal, September 10th 1960: Just two days to go before electric services to Crewe are launched and **E3095** sweeps through at the head of an Up t train. Clearly, some refurbishment and tidying-up is still going on here. Despite 'modernisation', the L&NWR retains its presence with one of tho unique platform seats. I wonder if anyone had the foresight to pick up the discarded "Styal" totem lying at the side of the fence?   *Graham Whitehe*

tyal station September 12th 1956: This was bridge No.11 as it appeared 50 years ago, just prior to the start of electrification work. British Railways were untiful photographers of their structures when it came to planning and surveying of work: this is one of at least 21 images taken here before work mmenced. Mother Nature is re-staking her claim to the bridge by the looks of things! Looking to Heald Green and Manchester, Styal station, all intact, pears exactly as it did almost another half-century back. Spanning the tracks is the thoroughfare referred to on the line plan as Sacar's Road (sic). This came Station Road in modern times and Sagar's Road runs further along from here to connect with the present-day Wilmslow Road in nearby Handforth. ne land housing the imposing residence seen on the left-hand side was once the site of a dwelling known as "Horshoe Cottage". *British Railways*

tween Styal and Wilmslow-Lacey Green, Summer 1951: A splendid study of the Up "Mancunian" as Longsight's "Jubilee" No 45633 *Aden* bursts m under bridge No.7 and heads towards Wilmslow. Lacey Green, a one-time hamlet in the Parish of Wilmslow, was a mile north of the Cheshire town. cy (sic) House sat to the left of the railway just by the overbridge. This and other photographs taken around here and Wilmslow are the work of the e Roy Davenport. Roy, who lived in Waldon Road, Macclesfield, was a contemporary of another equally masterful cameraman, Tom Lewis. Sadly, ich of Roy Davenport's material has disappeared, so we should be grateful for the fragments that survive. *R.Davenport*

Wilmslow, Bollin viaducts looking east, c.1909/10: As at Stockport with the Mersey, the M&BR were faced with a large void in the shape of the Bolli[n] valley before they could access Wilmslow and then proceed on to Crewe. Below is the River Bollin, paralleled by a mill stream. The Bollin rises [in] Macclesfield Forest before meandering through the Silk Town, thence via Styal where it once powered Samuel Greg's cotton mills. At Styal the Boll[in] is joined by the River Dean at Twinnies Bridge on Styal Road, below Worms Hill and not far from the station. Here in Wilmslow we are looking at tw[o] viaducts. The first, on the east (far) side, had been built for the opening of the railway from Stockport to Sandbach on May 10th 1842; th[e] structure is listed as bridge No.77. Construction of the first Bollin viaduct required the demolition of Bollin Hall (Q.V.) Today, the Bollin name lives o[n] in Bollin Walk below the viaduct and Bollin Link-the short highway connecting the old and new A34 roads. Bollin Hall Farm once stood roughly on th[e] site of the present-day Wilmslow Park. Near to the photographer is the second Bollin Viaduct-built in the early 1900s for the Styal line and numbered [?] by the LNWR. Off to the far right can be seen the two station Up Home signals with the station itself just peeping out beyond. Unlike the two Stockp[ort] viaducts, which were built hard up one against the other, the Bollin viaducts can be clearly seen as two quite separate structures and are known [to] Wilmslow folk as "The Towering Twins". Tinkling quietly westwards, the River Bollin finds its way beneath the Manchester Airport runways via [a] culvert. Surfacing once more, it crosses Cheshire before quietly expiring into the Manchester Ship Canal at Rixton Junction, 24 miles east of the Quee[n] Elizabeth II dock at Eastham on the Wirral and north-west of the Cheshire town of Lymm. *National Railway Museu[m]*

Wilmslow station, c.1909/10 (Styal line): This picture was taken from the Up Styal line platform and looks north towards the second Bollin viaduct [A] winter scene, this view, station lamps apart, would not change until the modernisation began in the second half of the 1950s. A solitary member of t[he] station staff looks towards the camera as a goods train comes along from Styal; by the looks of things drawn by a Webb 0-6-0 Coal Engine. LN[WR] standardisation is well to the fore here: "Cross the line by the subway", so says the sign under the awning-and heaven help anyone who disobeye[d]. Happily, much of what is seen here is still with us today-the exception being the accommodation on the Up Stockport platform, now replaced by a gl[ass] edifice. *National Railway Muse[um]*

Wilmslow, c.1909/10: Looking north from the, then, new signalbox this was the Wilmslow of yesteryear. In the middle foreground bridges Nos.1 and 76 together take the Styal and Stockport lines over Station Road/Macclesfield Road (the LNW line plan refers to the thoroughfare as "Swan Street"). Along Station Road, to the left of the railway, three cabs and their attendant horses await. A cabman's shelter once existed here for obvious benefit. Pity the poor souls who waited, probably for hours on end and in all weathers, for a fare. Four tracks run through the station. On the right the line from Stockport cuts in, running off the Bollin viaduct. On the far side-to the left-stand the platforms serving the Styal line. 264 yards south of bridges Nos.1/76 the two lines join-the start of the Wilmslow & Levenshulme Railway.

National Railway Museum

WILMSLOW

And so to Wilmslow. In effect the journey we have made is in reverse order, for the Styal line was built from here northwards towards its connection with the Stockport line at Slade Lane Junction. Wilmslow appears in Medieval history in 1287 as "Willmeslawe" and the first mention of the Parish Church of St.Bartholomew in local history appears to have been in 1246. The ancient parish of Wilmslow comprised Styal, Stanilands, Morley, Fulshaw, Chorley, Hough and Dean Row. These were grouped for local purposes into four townships, viz: Pownall Fee - Styal Stanilands and Morley. Bollin Fee - Hough and Dean Row; Chorley and Fulshaw remained as separate townships. St.Bartholomew's Church was re-modelled in the early 16th century.

Two famous characters from English history have Wilmslow connections. Anne Boleyn, surely Henry VIII's most hapless Queen, is reputed to have been born at Bollin/Boleyn Hall. The Hall survived until the construction of the first Bollin viaduct when the Manchester & Birmingham Railway entered the town en route to Sandbach and Crewe. William Ewart Gladstone made his appearance in the town as a 19 year-old in 1828 under the tutelage of Dr.Turner, the then Rector of Wilmslow. Gladstone, of course, proceeded to greater things, becoming Prime Minister no less than four times. His mentor went on to become the Bishop of Calcutta. In modern times by far and away the town's most famous resident was the computer scientist Alan Turing, famous for the development of the modern computer at Manchester University from 1948 and for his work in code breaking at Bletchley Park in WWII.

Tragically, in 1954, Turing took his own life at his home, "Copper Folly", on Adlington Road. This thoroughfare will bring the traveller to Adlington Hall which numbers, along with Bollin Hall, among other large English country houses to have graced the area. Bonis, Fulshaw, Hawthorn, Pownall, Norcliffe (the latter actually in Styal) and Saltersley are examples and some are with us today, enriching the area either by their presence or by the use of their names for thoroughfares and parks.

But no modern description of Wilmslow would be complete without a mention of the man who was its oldest inhabitant by far. This is "Lindow Pete", or "Lindow Man". Found in the peat bog known as Lindow Moss, on the town's south-west side, "Pete" was unearthed in 1984. After the usual Police investigation it was discovered that the well-preserved body was in fact an Iron Age man. Poor Pete had been battered about the head, garrotted and had his throat cut, all dating from around 55 BC. Other human remains were found in the bog at around the same time." Lindow Pete", now an established Wilmslow celebrity, resides in a Perspex case in the British Museum in London.

Wilmslow's first local board elections were held in 1878. A degree of curiosity compels one to ask why five of the twelve proposed board members were put forward by the Railway Hotel committee? The first Urban District Council was formed in 1894 and included Dean Row, Hough, Morley and Fulshaw. In 1974 the town was swallowed by the conurbation of Macclesfield under whose control it now rests.

Study of contemporary maps and pictures of Wilmslow station and the Bollin viaducts taken in the early years of the last century show an area vastly different from modern times. Then a town of around 7,000 inhabitants Wilmslow's population has swollen to around 30,000 today. Wilmslow has long had its fair share of business and affluent folk, but affluence has become a byword for the town in modern times-something easily manifested by taking a walk through today's centre. Beginning, perhaps, by leaving via the station forecourt, walking past the Rectory, now an up-market licensed house. Passing along the old Wilmslow Road by the former Rex Cinema, then continuing along Water Lane and into Grove Street.

The railway had opened in the town on May 10th 1842. Then belonging to the M&BR en route to Crewe and Sandbach, the main station buildings were on the town side, off Station Road. Waiting accommodation was provided as well on the Up (Crewe) side, but this appears on a contemporary map as somewhat basic, consisting of just two small buildings; the two sides of the station were connected by a footbridge. Goods facilities existed as two entities: one, a two-siding goods yard on the station's north side and the other, just below is shown as a Coal Depôt (sic). Early photographs show a signboard bearing the name "Lord Vernon's Collieries" above the yard entrance, his Lordship's collieries being at Poynton a few miles distant. The coal yard comprised seven siding roads, the town's gas works (Q.V.) being a major customer. A lay-by siding is shown on the Up side to the north and a further siding existed to the south of the station where the later goods yard was sited.

Back to 1900, this is a good point, the pivotal time between the old and new railway, to see how Wilmslow's needs were satisfied. An Ordnance Survey map of the town for that year gives us an insight into the local industries. A gas works, sited between Hawthorn Grove and Church Street, would have required copious quantities of coal, likewise a means of despatch of the by-product, coke. Continuing down Church Street and round the corner into Mill Lane, a corn mill-faced by a water works belonging to

Stockport Corporation-sat by the banks of the Bollin. Surrounding the town were numerous small farms-all requiring the passage of livestock and produce at some time or another and all needing movement by rail. In later years, a large timber yard was built on the station's eastern flank, where the present-day Jaguar car showrooms stand. And readers of a certain age who had to endure National Service in the RAF may well remember RAF Wilmslow and the neighbouring depot, 61 MU, at Handforth-both sources of passenger and freight traffic.

Wilmslow, pre-WW1: Station Road in a quieter age. "London & North Western Railway Wilmslow Station", so reads the nameboard spread over bridge No 1 - the underbridge that formed the first numbered structure of the 'new line'. Notice the patterned cast iron parapet, the original bridge - No 76 just behind and carrying the Stockport line was of stone and still there with its 1842 opening! Station Road was then a cobbled thoroughfare and not at all the busy road it is today. Peeping along under the bridge we can see two horse-drawn carts, while two young girls and a cloth capped male amble along by the wooden gates which once led to the goods yard. Notice also the ornamental electric street lighting, a form of illumination then something of a novelty. *Collection of John Ryan*

It was the Wilmslow and Levenshulme Railway, the Styal line that provided the catalyst for an enlarged and thoroughly expanded Wilmslow station. The construction of the second Bollin viaduct was a hugely expensive operation. An LNW minute for June 17 1903 records an acceptance of a tender from Naylor Brothers of Huddersfield for the viaduct's construction; the estimate was £15,400. On July 15th a further tender was submitted by the same company: this time a further sum-£17,994.17/3d (sic) was to be accepted for .."*earthworks and footbridge in connection with the Wilmslow Viaduct*". Thus had the new Bollin viaduct swallowed some 10% of the entire line budget for works and track!

The new station was a commodious affair. With four platform faces, an extended forecourt and a much enlarged goods yard. Consisting of seven sidings, the listing in the RCH book of stations shows facilities for handling goods and livestock, coal, parcels, furniture vans and carriages. A yard crane, with a lifting capacity of 5 tons, was available. A large goods shed was provided and all was overseen by a new signalbox, raised on a gantry on the Up side of the line by the goods yard. A lay-by siding, 1

Wilmslow station, c.1890s: Taken from the Up platform, this was the view looking across to the Manchester (Down) side of the station with the old goods yard seen behind. Little would have changed here, save for the arrival of the LNWR early-pattern semaphore signal and the notice boards, since the station opened under the auspices of the Manchester & Birmingham Railway in May 1842. Notice the prominent footbridge, swept away when the new station was built and replaced by the present subway. The goods yard looks busy with two horse boxes and a mixture of wagons, both low and high-sided seen awaiting dispatch.

Collection of *John Ryan*

WILMSLOW (OLD) STATION

Wilmslow station c.1905: On a winter's day of over 100 years ago this was the scene from the Manchester-bound platform looking south towards Alderley Edge. The Wilmslow station of the early Edwardian era is seen with many trappings, once commonplace, but now museum pieces. Notice the station buildings: those on the Down (Manchester side) platform are built from stone; opposite, on the Up side, a simple wooden structure suffices, but observe that both sides have the familiar "saw tooth" pattern of awning over the platforms. Gas lamps provide the illumination; Wilmslow had its own gas works in those far-off days and houses-even on such far away parts of the town as Adlington Road-were gas-lit at one time. Hoardings show advertisements for Finnigans, once a well-known Wilmslow name, while above it can be seen that land is to be sold on "....Park Estate". Perhaps this was Wilmslow Park, or Pownall Park? Milk churns, barrels and a porter's trolley seem almost anachro-nistic in today's railway age; but ladies had their own waiting room across on the Up side in Edwardian Wilmslow. Whatever would the Food Safety Act and the Sex Discrimination Act make of all this nonsense! Entering the station, a gleaming black apparition barks its way towards the camera: an LNWR "A" Class 0-8-0, a Webb 3-cylinder Compound, heads north towards Stockport with a Down freight train. In all probability this will be a Crewe-Healey Mills working and will leave the Crewe-Manchester line at Heaton Norris Junction, just north of Stockport Edgeley. The engine's centre lamp bracket identifies this firmly as a scene post-1903; note also that the locomotive's middle (low pressure) cylinder cover is polished, a common feature of the early years of the last century. This, then, was the last years of the old Wilmslow. Soon, work would begin to rebuild the station, to enlarge and transform the place into the Wilmslow station that, give or take minor changes, is still with us today.

Wilmslow, June 4th 1960: Rebuilding of the station frontage has commenced, albeit slightly late in the day before September 12th approaches! In the main, the work consisted of the construction of an improved booking hall and lengthened entrance porch-all metal and timber-framed with a glass front. The whole ensemble connected with the existing frontage along the Styal line side. The embryo structure can be glimpsed above the Ford Prefect-EBY 488-a motorist far from home, this was a Croydon registration.. The contractor for the entrance work was Jones & Rawlinson Ltd., Salford. While the work was proceeding a temporary ticket office-more of a shed than anything else-stood on the right-hand side of the station entrance. It is good to see that much of the station's LNWR character was retained and, even today, Wilmslow station has something of a period feel to it. ***Graham Whitehead***

yards long, was sited alongside the Down Styal line running back just short of the junction with the two routes. The Down goods loop came much later. The previous footbridge was done away with and the new platforms were connected instead by means of a subway. Close by the goods yard, the LNW line plan shows an imposing-looking house-"Thornlee"-standing on the land between the yard and Land Lane. The landowner was one, J.Barlow, when the new yard was built in the early 1900s. In modern times, the house and gardens at "Thornlee"- variously "Thorn Lea" and "Thornley" on official documents, were sold under an agreement dated November 16th 1985. Part of the goods warehouse was leased from October 17th 1963 to A.Henshall & Son Ltd. The warehouse was then given over to North Cheshire Carpets under a seven-year lease from Christmas Day, 1981.

Wilmslow's Stationmaster at the time of the Styal line's opening in 1909 was Mr.T.H.Potter. He had started his railway service back in 1870 as a temporary porter, before becoming a parcels clerk at Stockport's Edgeley station. Becoming a guard, first at Chelford, then at Crewe, Mr.Potter returned to Stockport where he was a platform inspector. He retired from the railway in July,1913 and was duly presented with a "purse of gold" and gold watch, a present from a group of Wilmslow season ticket holders and townspeople. His successor was Mr.T.Grant who had moved to the post from the District Superintendent's office in Manchester. Remembered, also, in the post was Mr.Mason who was a churchwarden at St.Anne's, Fulshaw. Wilmslow's last Stationmaster, before such posts were abolished in the re-organisation of the mid-1960s, was Arthur Haynes who had held a similar post earlier on down the line at Chelford. Thereafter the job fell to Arthur Lamb, assisted by Bert Nicholson. Arthur's title-"Station Supervisor" had a far wider remit; his responsibilities entailed coverage of the whole of the Styal line and also the section south of Stockport from Cheadle Hulme as far as Chelford. For Bert Nicholson this was his second post at Wilmslow: he had previously worked at the station in the mid-1950s as a booking clerk.

A contemporary LNW line plan shows Station Road, oddly, as "Swan Street". When the new station opened, Station Road formed part of a T-junction with Manchester Road. Travellers from the Manchester and Macclesfield directions wishing to proceed south through the town continued down along Swan Street to Bank Square. From here progress could be made via either Grove Street

or Green Lane and thence on to Altrincham, Alderley Edge o Knutsford. The continuation of Manchester Road round in a gentl arc towards the town came much later; indeed, some locals still refe to this section of road as "the by-pass", though nowadays that term refers properly to the new A34 road which by-passes the town com pletely hard on the railway's eastern flank.

For the passenger, the importance of Wilmslow to the railway over the years has been reflected in the provision of stopping serv ices, both via Styal and via Stockport to Manchester and to Crew Equally, though, until recent years the place had been a port of ca for many express services. A random perusal of the summer 195 timetable shows six Up morning expresses calling to pick up pas sengers. These comprised two London trains, a Birmingha express, one for South Wales and two expresses for the West o England. And right up to its demise in the early 1960s, "Th Mancunian", non-stop to Euston, called at Wilmslow-and nowher else-on its homeward journey. A reflection of this practice continue into the "all-electric" era when the "Manchester Pullman" mac Wilmslow the first stop on its Down run in the evening.

But not quite so today. Changes in social habits, in particular th huge rise in car ownership and the fact that the "Wilmslow" con muter belt now extends as far out as Alderley Edge and Prestbur have meant a shift in travel patterns. Over the last few years trai services between Manchester and London have been in a more o less constant state of flux. This has been due to modernisatio work at Stockport station and to track and signalling upgrades o the Macclesfield ("Potteries Loop") and Wilmslow-Crewe line The phrase "Rail Replacement Service" has become a byword fo the myriad of bus services that have filled the breach in the mea time. Constrained by a lack of long-stay station car parkin today's Wilmslow traveller is far more likely to drive to Stockpo where a half-hourly service (at least on paper) exists to Londo But, although most Manchester-London expresses travel via Th Potteries, it is good to see in the latest timetable (July 2006) tha Wilmslow has regained some of its London services. Four morr ing and one afternoon express call in the Up direction and fou afternoon services stop on the Down side. And although there ar no longer any through trains to the West of England, this has to b accomplished today by a change at Birmingham, Arriva Train Wales do at least provide a good service to South Wales vi Shrewsbury and Hereford.

Wilmslow, August 1955: "Black 5" **No 45495** pauses at the south end (on bridge No 76) of the Up Stockport line platform with a southbound express. The Bollin Viaduct is just visible in the rear along with the Up Home signal that never did quite manage a full "off" position! All-in-all a scene so typical of a summer day's activity half a century ago. Loco enthusiasts might like to ponder on the engine, however. All through the 1950s, 45495 was a Warrington (8B) loco, but here it is plainly sporting a 5A shed plate. Looking spotless and gleaming, the engine may well be just ex-Crewe Works. Did someone put the wrong shed date on the door, or was 45495 on loan to Crewe North that summer? Perhaps someone out there knows? *R.Davenport*

(Centre) Wilmslow station, bridge No.76, October 17th 1957: A scene that must be familiar to every Wilmslow resident: one of two underline bridges required to carry the railway over Macclesfield Road and Station Road, this was the original stone-built structure, bridge No.76, 176 miles and 67½ chains to London. Clearly visible behind is its twin, brick-built bridge No.1-notice the much wider opening; the motor car was a long way off in 1842! To the right is the former Up side entrance to the station, the iron gates leading then to the bottom of the subway. Through the arch can be seen the walled steps on the Down Styal line side; these lead to the wooded footpath that meanders along past the cricket ground and comes to bridge 75A. The two bridges have lasted well; though today the Macclesfield Road side station entrance is boarded up, the trees have proliferated and a single-lane priority sign attempts to regulate the traffic. *British Railways*

Wilmslow, October 17th 1957: Two views (see also page 164) of the goods yard taken by the BR official photographer. **(Above)** Looking from the south end of the Down Stockport line, close by the end of the platform, this little panorama shows most of the station's goods facilities before the onset of modernisation. Bridge No.76 (Macclesfield Road) with its stone parapets and LNW number plates stands in the foreground. Behind, to the left, can be seen the brick base of the carriage landing. From here carriages and later, cars, could be loaded on or off; access being via a short incline and then into the goods yard approach some 60-odd yards down Macclesfield Road and still maintained by Network Rail today. The goods shed, an impressive brick structure, had its own office-the small, low building seen in front. Towering over all is the impressive signalbox, notice the extended lattice steelwork of the supporting gantry. A long line of goods wagons stretches away from the camera; most are wooden-bodied, with the odd 16T steel-bodied standard version dotted here and there. Fading into the mist, a goods train disappears towards Alderley Edge, while coming along the Styal line a three-car DMU makes its appearance en route to London Road via Styal. *British Railways*

Leaving Wilmslow, early 1950s: Longsight's Stanier 2-6-4 tank No.**42580** pulls away from the Styal line platform with a three-coach local. Strong shadows suggest an early afternoon time. The coaching stock is of special interest: first behind the bunker is an ex-LNWR 54ft. brake third to Diag.334. Built just before WWI, the coach is characterised by the "Toplights" in the van section and the truss rod underframe. Second is an LMS 57ft. composite to Diag.1736. This had four third and three first class compartments and a lavatory. Lastly, the train is made up with an LMS 57ft. five compartment brake third with lavatory to Diag.1737. The angle iron underframes of the LMS stock marking them out from the pre-Group vehicle. As no Styal line "stoppers" in this period reached Crewe (such services ran via Stockport) then the train may well be the 12.20 SO London Road to Sandbach calling at all stations over the Styal line. After Wilmslow, the service stopped at Alderley Edge, Chelford, Goostrey, Holmes Chapel and was due at Sandbach at 1.28 pm. This, remember, was a period when Saturday morning working was still a commonplace. *R.Davenport*

Wilmslow, c.1948/49: "Princess Royal" No **46208** *Princess Helena Victoria* pulls away from the Stockport line platform with a Manchester London Road to Crewe local on a running-in turn. The locomotive has the freshly-applied "BRITISH RAILWAYS", it received its BR number in May 1948. Clearly visible is the elevated signalbox-notice the toilet at the rear. Remembered from here are signalmen Stan Bradbury who transferred later to Adswood Road, Ted Plant, a former Midland man and Stan Hall who hailed from the North Staffordshire Railway. None appeared to have transferred to the new power box when the old Wilmslow cabin closed in 1959.
Gordon Coltas Photographic Trust

Wilmslow, July 1953: One of Longsight's five Caprotti-fitted "Black 5s", No.**44752** runs through on the Stockport line with an Up express. Clearly visible is the LNW-pattern overhead signalbox straddling the shunting neck at the north end of the goods yard. The box dated from the opening of the royal line in 1909 and would have ensured excellent visibility over the two Bollin viaducts and the entire station area.
R.Davenport

Wilmslow, August 1952: After "The Mancunian", by far the best-known Manchester-Euston express was "The Comet". Dating from September 1932, the train was invariably hauled by a "Royal Scot", something borne out here as Longsight's No.46131 *The Royal Warwickshire Regiment* runs through Wilmslow en route to Crewe, the train's next stop. Notice here the goods shed and the shunting neck which could be accessed from both the Styal and Stockport lines. In this era through coaches from the East Lancashire towns were still being attached at Stockport. (Q.V.46121 at London Road) "The Comet" had departed London Road at 5.50 pm and was due at Stockport at 6.03 pm. In the meantime the three through coaches had left Colne at 3.35; calling at Burnley, Blackburn and Bolton, they

were due in Manchester Victoria at 5.14. The engine, typically a Stanier 2-6-4 tank, would then have taken its short train out eastwards to travel vi￼ Droylsden Junction and Ashton Moss ("over the Snipe") arriving at Stockport Edgeley via Heaton Norris Junction. Tucked into the north bay the coach￼ es were attached to the rear of the train by the Edgeley north end station pilot. Described in the early 1950s timetables as "carrying Restaurant Car an￼ Through Coaches", the express was due in Crewe at 6.38; arrival at Euston was at 9.25.

R.Davenpor￼

(from page 162) The second picture looks to the station from a point just past the junction with the Styal and Stockport lines. Take a close look at t￼ wooden-bodied wagon standing at the end of the lay-by siding off the Styal line to the left. Just visible over the wagon top can be glimpsed a lady wi￼ her little boy. The object of their attention will no doubt be the activity in the goods yard, maybe part of the "Pilot"-the local pick-up goods that calle￼ daily. How many readers can identify with the situation depicted here? One wonders if the boy, now approaching probably his 60th birthday, became ￼ railway enthusiast. A touching moment. Good detail can be picked out from the wagons, three rows and a line of low-sided wagons in the centr￼ Straddling the running lines and the yard is the "Iron Bridge", No.75A leading from the local cricket ground and playing fields known as the "Cow Cro￼ over the railway and down towards Land Lane. The low building seen beyond the bridge on the far right of the yard was a small stable block. Notice t￼ loading gauge hanging down from the bridge-a novel use where confines were tight and it saved a structure! Two LNW gas lamps, the yard lamp, wat￼ tank and a platelayer's store hut complete the scene at the top of the yard. The signalbox, its functions taken over by the new power box, closed on Ju￼ 28th 1959. Wilmslow goods yard closed to traffic on May 4th 1970, and the sidings were subsequently removed- or "recovered"-in BR parlance. Thoug￼ the goods warehouse saw a new lease of life (Q.V.), the death knell for this part of the station came with the proposal for the new A34 trunk road in th￼ 1980s.. Eventually the land at the side of the railway was excavated for the new by-pass and, today, only the through lines remain under bridge 75￼ Where "Thornlee" once stood, the new road cuts a deep swathe alongside the town, changing the landscape here out of all recognition. *British Railwa￼*

Wilmslow, June 1950: The LMS Class '5X' 4-6-0's that began to appear from Derby towards the end of 1930 were known variously as 'baby scots' and 'Patriots'. Whichever name you chose, here is the first one, No **45500** *Patriot* leaving Wilmslow on an Up Birmingham express. The view looks across from the west side of the 'iron bridge giving an excellent view of the goods yard with the station on the horizon. These are still early BR days, only two of the ten coaches of the "Brummidgeham" have acquired the two-tone 'blood and custard' livery beloved of the decade. Notice the quite delightful goods shed, a more or less standard L&NWR product, with verandas on both rail and road sides, and the little weighbridge office tucked away at the back of the yard towards Land Lane. In typical contemporary fashion the goods yard is well stocked, even two ex-LMS coaches have found their way inside. With windows open, the signal box surveys all. Who was the mystery photographer seen by the buffer stop between the Styal and Stockport lines?   *Tom Lewis*

Wilmslow, June 1950: A splendid study of Longsight's "Royal Scot" No **46114** *Coldstream Guardsman* (still minus smoke deflectors) clearing Wilmslow with the 9.20 am express to Cardiff and the West of England. All of the coaches visible, there are seven in the train, still appear in the pre-1948 GWR "chocolate and cream" livery, notice the characteristic raised coach destination boards. After leaving London Road the train called at Stockport, departing at 9.39; Crewe was reached at 10.16. After Crewe, a stop was made at Shrewsbury to attach carriages from Birkenhead and Chester and to detach a portion for Cardiff. The West of England train then travelled to Plymouth (arr.6.40 pm) via Bristol, Exeter and Newton Abbot. From Shrewsbury the Cardiff train called at Hereford, (where engines were changed), Pontypool Road and Newport (Mon.) with arrival in Cardiff (General) at 2.15.   *Tom Lewis*

Wilmslow, March 2nd 1952: Our second look at the morning Manchester London Road to Cardiff express shows "Jubilee" Class No **45595** *Souther Rhodesia* storming past the goods yard on what looks like a cold winter day. The engine is paired with a Fowler 3,500 gallon tender still bearing th "LMS" lettering; these narrow-bodied tenders never really matched the "Jubilees" and, reportedly, they did not find favour with engine crews either. C particular interest are the two LMS-pattern bracket signals. Both have lattice post bases and tubular steel upper posts. Lattice posts had appeared on th LMS in the 1930s, at which time the use of wood was being abandoned. The idea was not a new one, however: both the Caledonian and the Highlan companies had used similar posts previously. To the left of the Down main line is the Down Goods loop (682 yards). Controlling the exit from this ar the two miniature signals (with 2ft.11in arms): Loop to Styal and to Stockport respectively. Next are the main line signals (with 4ft.9in.arms): Down mai to Styal or to Stockport.

Tom Lew

Wilmslow, c.1955: On towards Crewe with this photograph of Longsight's Caprotti "Black 5" No **44750** speeding south of the station with a seven-coach express, the easterly-lit shadows suggesting a late afternoon or early evening working. The photographer stands in between the Down Goods loop and the Down main line, in the distance can be seen the famous "iron bridge"-75A and the pair of bracket signals referred to previously. But how utterly the landscape here has changed today! Alongside the Up line here now runs the Wilmslow bypass (A34) with the Prestbury Link Road (A538) leaving eastwards. South of this point, though, the rural landscape resumes with views for the passenger over the fields towards Prestbury and Macclesfield. Thence onwards to Alderley Edge, Chelford, Goostrey and through Cheshire towards Crewe.

Author's collection

WILMSLOW
TRANSITION

Wilmslow, looking south, May 3rd 1958: The most striking feature of the modernised station-and certainly the most contentious-was the new signalbox. Wilmslow's residents were certainly not amused by the appearance of this gargantuan brick, steel and glass structure on their doorstep and a petition to have the box either scaled down or re-sited was led by local clergyman, Canon Reeman. Certainly of striking appearance, not least because of its very size, the four-storey structure sat in front of a much-lengthened platform between the Styal and Stockport lines. "Work proceeding" is probably the best title offered for this view as "Crab" No **42926** is crossed over from the Up to Down Stockport line. In immediate view, the new signalbox is taking shape. By bridge No.76 building materials, in the form of concrete slabs, await their place to form the newly-lengthened platform that will reach across the front of the new box. In the background, overhead line masts are springing up while the old LNW overhead box still surveys the scene.
E.R.Morten

Wilmslow,(new) signalbox, January 8th 1959: This winter view shows the old and the new Wilmslow sat cheek-by-jowl. The structure of the new box now complete, work must continue installing all the electronic apparatus required for the new signalling scheme. Peeping through the January haze can be seen the LNW goods shed and the old elevated signalbox with bridge 75A spanning the main lines and the goods yard. Facing the camera, a surviving semaphore works out its last few months; in front, its colour light successor-WW53.. Along with a second power box down the line at Sandbach, the two boxes controlled almost the whole of the southern end of the Manchester-Crewe railway. On the Styal line, Wilmslow took over control from a point beyond Heald Green and on the Stockport line from a point between Cheadle Hulme and Handforth Sidings. This then extended south to between Chelford and Goostrey, thereafter Sandbach was in charge as far as Alsop Goods Junction. Commissioned-Sandbach on June 8th and Wilmslow on June 29th 1959, the pair now controlled some 27 route miles on which there had

previously existed 14 separate signalboxes. Some subsidiary operations remained: at Goostrey, Chelford Goods and Holmes Chapel electrically-controlled shunting frames controlled sidings; while at Alderley Edge, Chelford Station, Sydney Bridge (near Crewe) and Handforth Sidings, sophisticated remotely controlled relay interlocking apparatus rooms were provided. At the time Wilmslow power box was considered "state of the art". Transistorised control of point and signal operations enabled up to 500 controls in a single second, the final operation being carried out by a relay. Both boxes had route-setting panels on the "one switch per route" system, with the usual illuminated diagrams behind the switch desks. Train descriptions, arriving as four-digit illuminated signs, indicated class and designation of train. Colour light signals had 12V 24W tri-pole lamps and were operated by 24v relays. Extreme care had been taken to immunise all point, track circuit and signal operations from interference from the overhead wire. All the signalling and remote control equipment was supplied by the Westinghouse Brake & Signal Co.Ltd. and the train describer system was the product of Standard Telephones & Cables Ltd. Wilmslow and Sandbach power boxes lasted until early 2006 before demolition took place; transfer to the Manchester Piccadilly signalling centre had been completed in the meantime. All the while the "Crewe blockade"-closure south of Wilmslow as far Crewe-was on-going. This was to enable a new signalling system of Italian design, coupled with bi-directional working, to be installed. Beginning in the autumn of 2005, the blockade has involved the longest single period of closure on this railway since its inception.
British Railways

WILMSLOW
MODERNISATION
AND BEYOND

Wilmslow, September 20th 1960: With the work completed on time, Wilmslow now has a frontage in keeping with the modernised railway along the platforms above, though one could hardly call the architecture "complementary" to that of the LNWR buildings immediately adjacent. Notice the station still had a parcels office over forty years ago. Due to the angle of photography, the ticket hall has the appearance of a car showroom; perhaps BR could not afford a polarising filter for their photographer's camera! Where are you now, 104 JMA and 5534 NA? ***British Railways***

(Centre) Wilmslow, Summer 1960: A scene that was repeated many dozens of times up to the onset of the electrification to Crewe. **E3036** is seen working "wrong line" alongside the Up Styal line platform with a training trip consisting of empty coal wagons and a brake van. E3036 was the first of ten locomotives to type "AL4". Built by GEC and the North British Locomotive Company at Hyde Park works, Glasgow, this series was the fourth generation of 25kV ac locos, this example leaving the works in March 1960. History does not seem to have favoured this small class. Early reported problems included burnt out transformer windings, failure of rectifiers, early wear in the motor spring drives and poor riding qualities, due, reputedly, to poor bogie design. Becoming Class 84 under the TOPS scheme, some of the problems were removed by rebuilding from the late 1960s onwards. All were withdrawn in the period 1977-80; this example, the latter-day 84 001, was preserved for the national collection by the NRM at York. AM1 EMU, No.009 looking spanking new waits in the Down platform. ***Author's collection***

(Right-lower) Wilmslow, 1975: A series of tests were carried out over the Styal line to investigate the feasibility of automatic train control (Q.V. Mauldeth Road). The signals for electric cables laid in the "four foot" being transmitted to the traction units. In platform 2 on the Styal line side of the station. Clayton Diesel D8598 and test coach Hermes rest between trips. ***Martin Welch***